Mississippi's Piney Woods

A Human Perspective

Courtesy the Forest History Society and the
University of Mississippi

Mississippi's Piney Woods

A Human Perspective

Edited by
Noel Polk

UNIVERSITY PRESS OF MISSISSIPPI
Jackson and London

This book has been sponsored by the
University of Southern Mississippi

Crosby Memorial Lectures
in Mississippi Culture, 1985

Library of Congress Cataloging-in-Publication Data
Main entry under title:

Mississippi's Piney Woods.

  Papers from a conference held at the University of
Southern Mississippi, Mar. 29–31, 1984.
  Includes bibliographies and index.
  1. Piney Woods (Miss. : Region)—Congresses.
I. Polk, Noel. II. University of Southern Mississippi.
F347.P63M57 1986   976.2'59   85-22680
ISBN 0-87805-288-7

Contents

Acknowledgments

The L. O. Crosby, Jr., Memorial Lectures in Mississippi Culture were established at the University of Southern Mississippi through a generous gift from the L. O. Crosby, Jr., Memorial Foundation, and through the cooperation and interest of Stewart and Lynn Crosby Gammill, whose wise counsel were an important part of every stage of planning the Crosby Lectures, from inception to fruition. Without them, the Crosby Lectures could not exist. Likewise, without the enthusiastic support of Dr. Aubrey K. Lucas, president of the University of Southern Mississippi, who made the resources of the university available to the organizers, the Crosby Lectures would not have come to be. To these three in particular the Crosby Lectures owes its existence, and I am grateful indeed for their support.

The Mississippi Committee for the Humanities also generously funded the conference and part of the publication costs of this volume. To that organization and its director, Dr. Cora Norman, I extend heartfelt thanks.

The USM Committee for the Crosby Lectures worked many hours: Dr. John D. W. Guice, Dr. Peggy W. Prenshaw, and Dr. Thomas J. Richardson. I am extremely grateful to them not just for their ideas, which helped identify topics, select speakers, and give shape and focus to the conference (indeed, made the idea of the Crosby Lectures a reality), but also for the many hours they spent working on the nuts and bolts of such a conference.

Introduction

NOEL POLK

In 1862 the historian J. F. H. Claiborne wrote this rapturous paragraph about the Mississippi Piney Woods:

> The soil is sandy and thin, producing small crops of rice, potatoes, and corn, a little cotton, indigo, and sugar-cane, for home consumption. But it sustains a magnificent pine forest, capable of supplying for centuries to come the navies of the world. The people are of primitive habits, and are chiefly lumbermen or herdsmen. Exempt from swamps and inundation, from the vegetable decomposition incidental to large agricultural districts, fanned by the sea-breeze and perfumed by the balsamic exhalations of the pine, it is one of the healthiest regions in the world. If the miraculous fountain, in search of which the brave old Ponce de Leon met his death in the lagoons of Florida in 1512, may be found any where, it will be in the district I am now wandering over. I have never seen so happy a people. Not afflicted with sickness or harassed by litigation; not demoralized by vice or tormented with the California fever; living in a state of equality, where none are rich and none in want; where the soil is too thin to accumulate wealth, and yet sufficiently productive to reward industry; manufacturing all that they wear; producing all they consume; and preserving, with primitive simplicity of manners, the domestic virtues of their sires. Early marriages are universal. Fathers yet infants in law, and happy grandams yet in the vigor of womanhood, may be found in every settlement; and numerous are the firesides around which cluster ten or a dozen children, with mothers still lovely and buoyant as in the days of their maiden bloom.[1]

Two major wars, a lumber boom, a depression, and three quarters of a century later, the *Mississippi Guide* of 1938 devotes only one paragraph to the Piney Woods:

> [Not very] sharply defined geographically, and gradually becoming less defined economically, are the Piney woods. . . . This is a rather haphazard and irregular triangle, whose scenery of stumps, "ghost" lumber towns, and hastily reforested areas tells its saga. Strong men and women have been reared here, but the earth

has been neither fecund enough to facilitate their getting away from it nor sterile enough to drive them away. Until lumbering built a few fair-sized towns out of the wilderness, it was a pioneer country; and now that the forests have been ravished, and the cheaply built mill houses are rotting, as the unused mill machinery rusts about them, it is pioneer country once more. Like all pioneers, the Piney Woods people are economically poor, politically unpredictable, and in a constant state of economic transition.[2]

With the sterling exception of Nollie Hickman's *Mississippi Harvest*,[3] these two passages constitute a very large portion of the entire body of literature about the Mississippi Piney Woods. To put it bluntly, the area has been simply ignored. In spite of its numerous contributions over the years to the state's economy, its politics—for good and for ill, of course— its literature, and its culture, it has somehow been forced off the historical map or, rather, has never really been allowed on it. A case in point: in a 1982 book entitled, comprehensively, *Mississippi*[4]—written and photographed by a prominent journalist couple from the Delta and sponsored by the Mississippi Department of Economic Development—there are dozens of pictures and pages devoted to the Delta, to Natchez and the Trace, to the Gulf Coast, and to Oxford and environs; but there is not one picture, not one single word in this best-selling coffee-table book, about the Piney Woods. It is as if Hattiesburg, one of the largest cities in the state, simply did not exist: I don't mind admitting that James Street is no William Faulkner and that Pearl Rivers is no Eudora Welty, but I do mind it when such a book, with such an all-encompassing title, looks me in the eye and, when asked about such a huge omission, shrugs its shoulders and says, after Steve Martin, "I forgot!"

Of course, I am somewhat chauvinistic about this sort of thing, being a Piney Woods native. But in the past few years I have come to understand, if not to appreciate, why we seem to have been historically treated like the idiot sibling of Mississippi's regions, and I think I understood it from novelist Walker Percy, our Piney Woods neighbor in Covington, Louisiana, who once explained why he lived in Covington, he who could live anywhere he chose—even in the Delta:

> The reason I live in Covington . . . is not that it is a pleasant place but rather that it is a pleasant nonplace. Covington is in the deep South, which is supposed to have a strong sense of place. It does, but Covington occupies a kind of interstice in the South. It falls between places. . . .
> The pleasantest things about Covington are its nearness to New Orleans— which is very much of a place, drenched in its identity, its history, and its rather self-conscious exotica—and its [Covington's] own attractive lack of identity, lack

of placeness, even lack of history. Nothing has ever happened here, no great triumph or tragedies. . . . [W]hen I first saw Covington, having driven over from New Orleans one day, I took one look around, sniffed the ozone, and exclaimed, unlike Brigham Young: "This is the nonplace for me!"[5]

I know whereof Percy speaks, and if the Piney Woods has an identity problem, it lies in its very *placelessness*, in the perception that nothing has really ever happened here; the Piney Woods has suffered by being located *between* such extraordinary places as New Orleans, Mobile, Natchez, Vicksburg, and the Delta, with their rich, colorful, dramatic histories: historians, like suitors, tend to court the flashier sisters first. My own little nonplace, Picayune, was not much of a town or community or even watering hole until just before the beginning of the twentieth century, so we had no statues of Civil War heroes adorning our courthouse square—we had no courthouse square, or even a courthouse, until well into the twentieth century, no bevy of fine colyummed antebellum homes sporting minié ball scars to show to visitors. I never, to my knowledge, talked to a Civil War veteran (or even to anybody who knew one); I never heard tales about *The War*. There were no Civil War battles that I know of in Pearl River County; Andrew Jackson and his men seem, like everybody else, to have gone *through* the area, looking for another place, but that was during another war, and so does not count.

Of course we know that plenty did happen in the Piney Woods, even if it was mostly less dramatic, less romantic, than the burning of Jackson, or the seige of Vicksburg, although I will leave it to others to decide whether the burning of Jackson was, finally, a greater tragedy than the disappearance of the great pine forests. But if it was in most ways less dramatic or flashy or outrageous, the history of the Piney Woods is nonetheless a worthy portion of the total portrait of Mississippi's—and the South's—history. Piney Woods history is remarkable for the sustained intensity of its people's sustained grappling with the normally undramatic realities of what remained essentially a frontier existence until well into the twentieth century.

One of the things that "happened" in the Piney Woods was the advent of the Crosby family and, in particular, of L. O. Crosby, Jr., whose memory is the occasion of this conference.

Lucius Osmond Crosby, Jr., was born in 1907 in Bogue Chitto. His father was a founder of the Goodyear Yellow Pine Co., which was established in Picayune in 1916 and became a parent company of many related wood product industries. Crosby first became involved in the family's business during the Great Depression, managing a rehabilitation effort to ease conditions of the unemployed associated with the lumber industry in the Picayune area. He developed experimental crops such as satsumas, peaches, strawberries and tung trees on cutover land, and began a program of truck farming. At the beginning of World War II, he took charge of his father's company, diversifying its holdings and rebuilding the business. He later became the president and general manager of Crosby Forest Products Co. of Picayune (formerly Goodyear Yellow Pine Co.). He was responsible for the construction in Picayune of plants making wirebound boxes, treating wood, extracting tung oil, and others. In addition to his business interests, Crosby was active in many local and national professional, religious, and civic endeavors. He was a generous supporter of the Boy Scouts of America, an organization which awarded him its highest honor, the Silver Buffalo, in 1963. He died in 1978.

But this brief sketch of his life hardly touches the essence of the man or of his legacy. Unlike so many lumbermen who raped the land and moved on, the Crosbys committed themselves to South Mississippi in ways that involved their recognition of their responsibility to the families of the men who worked for them, and to the public at large. When it became clear that the timber resources would no longer support the industry at the rate at which it had been operating, the Crosbys not only reforested the land, but searched for alternative crops congenial to the land and the climate—tung trees among them. They did not, in the industry's many lean times, abandon the people who worked for them: they helped them provide for their own welfare by making available to them, free of charge, tools, seed, and farming implements.

L. O. Crosby, Jr., inherited this tradition of generosity, a generosity first of mere money, which made him more than willing to reinvest his material goods in a world that had been generous to him—a library and a portion of a church testify to that form of generosity. There was also a generosity of spirit in Mr. Crosby. I am witness to it, as one who knew him—knew him, that is, as well as a child can know the father of a good friend. He spent many hours with several of us boys, almost as a crony, taking us to the Pontchartrain Beach amusement park himself because, he said, we needed a chaperon, but actually going, I always suspected, because he liked us and liked the beach; and he showed up regularly at Camp Tiak, a Boy Scout camp, while we were there, to take us out into the woods and talk about the forest. At the time, I suppose I thought he didn't have anything better to do, yet I knew he was also an author,

L. O. Crosby, Jr.

an outdoorsman, a politician, a businessman, a philanthropist: a man whose interests, to my own childhood's eye, seemed to range far and wide, in Picayune and out of it. Perhaps to the same degree that he loved the wilderness, he also represented, to me, a form of civilization: it is no small thing to me that I listened to my first opera in the Crosby house. I don't know whether Mr. Crosby ever articulated a philosophy of life, but the testimony of his example suggests a drive to use his money, his influence, in whatever amounts necessary, to make the resources of life available to all who came within his ken.

The L. O. Crosby, Jr., Memorial Lectures in Mississippi Culture have been established by Mr. Crosby's family as a memorial to him, and as a means of extending his passionate commitment to all aspects of Mississippi's life. The lectures will be held every second or third year. They have as their purpose to bring together the finest scholars available to focus on one aspect of Mississippi culture from as many different academic disciplines as possible; they are designed to be pioneer explorations of relatively untouched subjects in the study of Mississippi history and culture.

The papers collected in this volume are those delivered at the first of the Crosby Lectures, held at the University of Southern Mississippi 29–31 March 1984, and devoted, appropriately, to the Piney Woods, L. O. Crosby, Jr.'s, home. Among the twelve contributors are a former Mississippi governor, two forest historians, a botanist, two literary critics, two geographers, three historians and a musician, who deliver themselves of a fascinating variety of observations about the history and culture of the Piney Woods.

Harold K. Steen, executive director of the Forest History Society, opens the proceedings with "The Piney Woods: A National Perspective," which places the Piney Woods in the context of the larger scheme of the nation's forest economy. He is, he says, struck much more by the Piney Woods' "similarities with other places than by the differences" (ch. 1). John H. Napier III surveys Piney Woods history in his "Piney Woods Past: A Pastoral Elegy," which arises out of his lifelong affection for the people and land of his own native region. His survey begins with the recession of the "primordial ooze" into the Gulf, and ends with the "stumps and ghost towns" left in the wake of the lumber boom in the first years of the twentieth century (ch. 2).

Two other historians and a geographer are concerned to demonstrate how the character of the Piney Woods is a product of its roots in other, national and international, cultures, the degree to which it is an accumulation of deposits from migrant frontiersmen, fugitives, and adventurers, all of whom left their different marks upon the region. Thomas D. Clark's "The Piney Woods and the Cutting Edge of the Lingering Southern Frontier" points to the uniqueness of the development of the southern frontier in the first half of the nineteenth century, and contends that "no pioneer took on the precise characteristics of those who crowded into Alabama, Mississippi, northern Louisiana, and eastern Arkansas. These emigrants moved almost by a formula and proceeded to settle in their new homes within the general pattern of the established social and political order they had known earlier" (ch. 5). In what is probably the most controversial paper in the collection— "Antebellum Piney Woods Culture: Continuity over Time and Place"— Grady McWhiney argues that in order to understand Piney Woods culture, and that of the antebellum South, we must "recognize and discard" some pervading myths, the most important of which is "the widespread belief that southern ways were English ways." Through an analysis and comparison of names and of various cultural traditions, primarily the pastoral, McWhiney contends that the South was settled "mainly by Celts and culturally dominated by them. . . . [The] overwhelming majority of antebellum white Southerners were of Celtic, not English, ancestry" (ch. 4). For his part, however, geographer Terry Jordan, in "Evolution of American Backwoods Pioneer Culture: The Role of the Delaware Finns," argues rather that a comparison of names, architecture, methods of forestry, and the character of the people, shows Piney Woods culture to be significantly derivative from Finnish immigrants from the Delaware Valley and, through them, from Finland itself: "The Midland pioneer culture, including its Piney Woods offspring, derived in some substantial measure from New Sweden and, more particularly, from ethnic Finns who came to that colony" (ch. 3).

Three other papers provide closer examinations of the timber industry in the Piney Woods. Nollie Hickman, the dean of Piney Woods historians, in "Black Labor in Forest Industries of the Piney Woods, 1840–1933," documents the use of slave labor in the naval stores industry prior to 1865 and of free black labor after the war in an area of the state not traditionally associated with black labor: "Black workers . . . made important, significant contributions to the economic evolution of the Piney Woods. . . . Naval stores was, in fact, a black industry, and without the black man, could not have existed" (ch. 6). M. B. Newton, Jr., in "Water-Powered Sawmills and Related Structures in the Piney Woods," provides fascinating insight into the problems—and solutions—of nineteenth-century people who wanted to build water-powered sawmills in a landscape seldom hilly enough for simple gravity to provide the power. Warren Flick, in "The Wood Dealer System" (ch. 11), discusses the economic and social importance of the wood dealer, who operated as a middleman between lumberman and seller.

Former Mississippi governor William F. Winter, speaking about politics and politicians from the Piney Woods, notes that "it was in this geographically distinctive area of sand hills, pine forests, and clear streams that some of Mississippi's most fiercely contested political battles were fought; out of the Piney Woods emerged some of the state's most colorful and flamboyant political figures"—most notorious of whom was the irascible Theodore G. Bilbo (ch. 10). Two literary scholars, Thomas McHaney and W. Kenneth Holditch, discuss the Piney Woods' most important writers: James Street, who wrote epic novels based on the history of the Piney Woods, and Eliza Jane Poitevent ("Pearl Rivers"), a Piney Woods poet and pioneering newspaperwoman who, as the first female editor of a major newspaper, single-handedly made the New Orleans *Picayune* into a great daily newspaper (chs. 8, 9). Musicologist James Downey discusses shape-note hymnody and gospel quartet music, religious music phenomena which had their origins in the Piney Woods (ch. 7). Finally, to round out the proceedings, botanist Sidney McDaniel describes the unique flora of the Piney Woods (ch. 13).

If there is a central theme to all these papers, implicit or explicit, it is the central fact of Piney Woods life and history: the giant pine forest, the impact that the glorious dense forest of giant virgin pine trees had on the people who came to live here: on those who stayed, and on those who came, grabbed, and left. This relationship is one that has too often been overlooked in studies of the southern character. As Thomas Clark puts it:

> In the current rash of books and articles that attempt to define the "southerner," and to analyze his character and folk mores, his personal distinctiveness, and his place in American history, there is no material mention of the bearing of the great forest on the shaping of regional character and bent of mind. This is in sharp contrast to the historical interpretations of the historical backgrounds of the Great Lake states and the Northwest. The socially isolative grip of the backwoods in good measure accounted for the retention of a homogeneous population, black and white, over such a broad span of time, and for the shaping of enduring institutional patterns, and the formulation of narrow political attitudes [ch. 5].

The papers in this collection begin to correct this deficiency. They are offered, as proceedings of future Crosby Lectures will be, not as extensive answers to problems long discussed by historians, but rather as elaborate questions which have seldom been asked. The editor, the contributors, and the family of L. O. Crosby, Jr., hope that these papers will open doors into the Piney Woods through which future historians will, for the first time, be able to see the Piney Woods as they once were.

Notes

1. J. F. H. Claiborne, "Rough Riding Down South." *Harper's New Monthly Magazine*, June 1862, 437.

2. Federal Writers' Project of the Works Progress Administration, *Mississippi: A Guide to the Magnolia State.* New York: Hastings House, 1938, p. 6.

3. Nollie W. Hickman, *Mississippi Harvest: Lumbering in the Longleaf Pine Belt 1840–1915.* University, MS: The University of Mississippi, 1962.

4. Bern Keating and Franke Keating, *Mississippi.* Jackson: University Press of Mississippi, 1982.

5. Walker Percy, "Why I Live Where I Live," *Esquire,* April 1980, 35–36.

Mississippi's Piney Woods

A Human Perspective

The Piney Woods
A National Perspective

HAROLD K. STEEN

Maps tell us much about American history—and especially forest history. First, and most obviously, we note that America is a very large nation; an overlay with Europe would place the West Coast on top of England and the East Coast in interior Russia—the Lake States would cover Scandinavia and Texas would touch the Mediterranean. I was reminded of the relative distances last summer when a German scholar visited us. He remarked that it was an eight-hour drive to Rome from his home in Bavaria—I suspect that it takes about eight hours to drive from Nashville to Hattiesburg. To discuss American history, therefore, is an ambitious undertaking; the fact that we have regional variations should not be a surprise; it is probably more surprising to see that the variations are in many ways not particularly significant.

Figure 1 outlines the public lands survey system—six-mile squares of townships that stretch from the Appalachians west to the Pacific Ocean. Not all forest historians agree with me, but I strongly believe that we cannot understand forest history without knowing about the history of the land itself. In government, it has been the land and agricultural committees of Congress and also the land management agencies that have had the most important influence on the course of forest history. On the other side of the ledger, it has been the landowner who has worked with government, often as an influential—if unofficial—adviser, to assure that public land policies were rational. Until very recently, few citizens groups had much influence, unless they already supported the course of events. The American Forestry Association, for example, has worked effectively for over a century by serving as a catalyst to the governmental process.

As significant as the familiar story of how America acquired land in great clumps—'manifest destiny," some would say—is the way in which we dis-

3

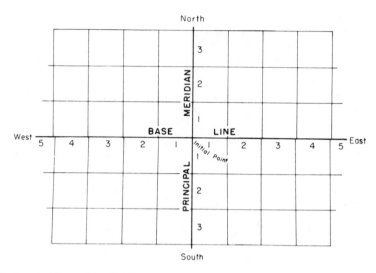

Figure 1. Township Grid

posed of the land—transferring it by myriad means from public to private ownership: over one-half of the U.S. landmass during the nineteenth century alone. These transfer laws form the centerpiece of nineteenth- and early twentieth-century forest history.

An important part of the transfer process was the unique township system that we developed to divide the land into manageable parcels—manageable at least by the government if not by the settler. Except for the original thirteen states and Kentucky and Tennessee, our land has been divided into one-mile squares, or sections, regardless of topography, soil type, or vegetation. Today we are faced with the extremely complex problem of trying to make ecological sense out of the geometrically uniform array of ownerships. From what is so generously referred to as my "national perspective," I see that since the highest point in Mississippi is 806 feet, the impact of geometric—as opposed to ecologic—land patterns on the Piney Woods is much less significant than in the mountainous West. The more rugged western terrain, interlaced with multiple ownerships wrought by railroad land grants, created management problems that the South has not had to deal with.

The process of converting public lands to private ownership had been completed in Mississippi by 1905, when the U.S. Forest Service was created by transferring responsibility for the forest reserves from the Department of the Interior to the Department of Agriculture. Thus and notwithstanding the later repurchases that created the Bienville, Delta, DeSoto, Holly Springs, Homochitto, and Tombigbee national forests, at the time that the federal government was beginning to flex its conservation muscles over the remaining public lands—approximately one-third of the nation—Mississippi, like most states in the eastern portion of the country, was little affected.

But I see many more similarities than differences in the history of the Piney Woods and that of other parts of the nation. Admittedly, I am not a southerner either by birth or residence. My interest in the South began while I was in graduate school; I initially wanted to write my dissertation on the navy department's live-oak plantations in western Florida during the 1820s. Although I eventually decided to work on another topic, my early investigations provided insights that I continue to use.

Many today would have us believe that government—or someone—should have done more, sooner, to protect the environment. I don't necessarily disagree with this point of view, but history reveals that until recently we have lacked the technical information necessary to proper conservation. To use the Florida experiments as an example, in 1828 President John Quincy Adams was a major advocate of live-oak cultivation to assure supplies of timber to our vital shipyards. His thoughts are recorded in a voluminous diary, where he described John Evelyn's *Sylva* as a primary forestry authority.[1] *Sylva* had been written nearly two centuries earlier, in 1664. It was the first book produced by the Royal Society of London and one of the earliest treatises about forestry in English. As you read *Sylva*, you quickly notice that the footnotes refer to classical scholars, such as Plato and his learned contemporaries.[2] Imagine: an American president in 1828 developing federal forest policy and using the "best" scientific information of the time—information that had been updated very little in over two thousand years! The current information explosion takes on new significance when contrasted with preceding millennia.

American universities initially focused on providing a classical education; it wasn't until the 1860s that land grant colleges appeared and legitimized the study of agronomy and related sciences. Since it is fairly well agreed that scientists were a moving force behind the conservation movement, the impact of public land policy—in this instance the creation of land grant colleges—on the course of conservation history is large for this reason as well.

Today, we hear the EPA administrator lament a lack of technical knowledge to implement environmental legislation. This sort of lament is not new; through history, we have had little enabling legislation and even less pertinent knowledge on which to base our resource decisions. One might wonder how and why the early conservation movement adopted such ambitious goals, when so little was known about how to achieve them. I suspect that the movement's leaders were little aware of how "unrealistic" their dreams were. Perhaps it's just as well.

An academic but still pertinent question is whether there is something called "local history." Depending upon the level of emotional security of the scholar, one hears that no event occurs completely in isolation; therefore, one cannot understand local history without understanding all concurrent global happenings. These days, a junior professor would hesitate to publish "local" history, lest the tenure committee decide that his devotion to scholarship was lacking. But local history has gained much credence; the Forest History Society book award a couple of years ago went to a study of the environmental history of Island County in Washington state, a very local area indeed.[3] The book won handily in competition with monographs that treated topics of national significance. The scholarly judges admitted by this action, at least, that local history had come into its own. Additionally, the society has completed studies of the lumber industry in Washington state and Aroostook County in northern Maine, and has just entered into a cooperative agreement to survey the industry in the South. So it seems that the legitimacy of local history has been fairly well established, where forestry is concerned.

As I have mentioned, in browsing through material on the history of the Piney Woods I became impressed much more by the similarities with other places than by the differences. For example, the lumber industry was one of the earliest industries and has remained important. The first sawmills were located on or near water—a fact demonstrating the lack of log-transport technology—and, probably as significantly, showing the native intelligence of the frontier businessman. Why, after all, build roads inland to cart logs to the mill, when there was ample timber standing at water's edge?

Another similarity is the purchase of timberland from the federal government during the nineteenth century. Congress had a peculiar vision of the western lands, and Mississippi used to be "out West." Congress believed that there were only two categories of land—agricultural and nonagricultural. Until the 1870s there was no official recognition that a lot of land had timber on it, or that timberland was not just a form of uncleared farmland. Thus, when the sawmill owner wanted to acquire standing timber to supply the mill, he had to operate within a land-sales program designed for farmers. But the frontiersman was usually a pragmatist who could exercise a brand of civil disobedience that would have made

Thoreau proud. With sincere belief that land laws enacted by a distant Congress were at the very least unrealistic, the timber was acquired by agreeing on the application that the lumberman was really a farmer at heart. Much has been made of these and similar so-called scandals, but within the context of the times, it doesn't seem all that serious; the lumberman was providing jobs, building materials, and in other ways benefiting the growing community, of which he was often the leading citizen. Much more could be said about the important roles lumbermen played in many communities, but historians have instead tended to focus on the evils of unregulated capitalism or the romance of the pioneer spirit.

To the ordinary citizen of these milltowns, however, large landowners did often seem to have an ominous aspect. It didn't matter whether the landowner was a major railroad, the government, or the local millman. The fear was that the control or ownership of blocks of land could be used in a monopolistic fashion—to control prices, restrict access to the market, and so forth. Therefore, it was common to see local opposition to the federal policies that allowed corporations to buy large blocks of land. Local people were also opposed to having the federal government "tie up" the public land, that is, restrict the use of those lands it retained; all seemed to agree that land was better settled and put to productive use.

What to do with cutover land was a question to be answered in many regions, including the Piney Woods. The issue was complicated and made more so by the perceptions one had: Was the lumberman the villain, or did cutover land reflect a failure in agricultural policy? After all, we were well into the nineteenth century before all logged-off land was not promptly converted to agricultural use. In fact, until midnineteenth century, much more land was cleared by farmers than by lumbermen. To those who thought about it at all, the early-day lumberman was providing a valuable service to the growing nation by clearing land ahead of the farmer. But, as we all know, the supply of cleared land exceeded the demand in many areas, and more and more we began to see logged-off land abandoned, as were the settlements that became ghost towns.

Much of the impulse behind the conservation movement stemmed from the spectre of these cutover lands. They became symbolic of the evils of a laissez-faire system that proclaimed that the marketplace needed no regulation. For some reason, in the South there was an added dimension. When some companies began reforesting their cutover lands in the 1920s instead of abandoning them, there were editorials that worried about the permanent "loss" of farmland to trees. It was surely a case of being damned whether you did or didn't. At the same time, the Mississippi Land and

Development Association was formed to bring northern farmers to settle on cutover land.

The interaction between forest and farm is fascinating to study. Initially we see forests cleared for farms—cotton perhaps. Then we see abandoned cotton fields reverting to forests. When we stand back a bit, we can see national agricultural policies out West affecting the Piney Woods of Mississippi. Cotton fields in Arizona are irrigated with ground water and other sources at costs far below the market value of water. This water subsidy provides cheap western cotton, causing out-migration of cotton farms from Mississippi, leaving abandoned fields in their wake. So now the land is once again available for forests, and the conservationists and lumbermen are happy. I don't know what the net impact of cotton versus timber on the local community has been, but one can be fairly certain that the federal decision makers did not apply a strict cost-benefit analysis to the situation or even consider the broader implications of their actions.

As the nation's commercial network expanded, it became necessary for local manufacturers to adopt marketplace standards. For an industry like lumbering, this requirement was especially significant; it took decades to reach agreement on standard dimensions for lumber, according to species and region. The formation of trade associations was in part a result of these efforts, with the added wrinkle that associations attempted to cope with the vagaries of the market itself. It has always struck me as ironic that the conservation movement is concerned with scarcity, as represented by cutover lands or whatever. To the lumberman, the problem was not scarcity but glut. There was too much lumber, and the market responded with prices that were often less than the cost of manufacture.

Many trade associations were formed primarily to deal with the problem of regulating supply—the notion of tinkering with demand through advertising came only years later. The Sherman Antitrust Act was passed in 1890, but the constitutions of associations formed after that date contained language that clearly proposed restraints on trade and price-fixing. It wasn't until after 1907, when Congress asked the Bureau of Corporations—later the Federal Trade Commission—to investigate the possibility of monopoly in the lumber industry, that these constitutions were purged of illegal language. During the 1920s, the Justice Department vigorously pursued allegations of price-fixing, and some associations in the South were required to modify their practices.[4]

Another issue with national scope but local importance is that of taxes on timberland. It may surprise newcomers to conservation history, but taxation has historically been a major concern, even in the nineteenth century. In the abstract, the issue is clear; no rational entrepreneur will elect long-term investments if uncertainty is a significant factor. Capital is very much afraid of uncertainty, and, given the fifty- to one-hundred-year period during which a local assessor can raise taxes on a particular stand of timber, forestland investments seem uncertain, indeed. Add to this tax uncertainty the possibility of future forest fires, hurricanes, or insect attacks, and one might ask whether anyone who owns timberland for the long term is rational.

The effect of property taxes on the timber and logging industries has been studied since 1909.[5] Based largely on questionnaires returned by forest landowners, the studies show that the rate of logging has rarely been influenced by property taxes. (It must be remembered that these are not recent studies.) Although in the abstract one can see that if taxes for standing timber are substantially greater than for cutover land, then many owners would decide to liquidate earlier rather than later and prevent having a larger tax bill.

Generally, however, this seems not to have been the case. Although taxes have been significant, other factors, such as rapid increases in stumpage and lumber prices, have contributed more to decisions about if and when to log. The data do show, however, that decisions to reforest or even to hold on to the logged-off land have been affected by tax policies.[6] Would prudent investors elect to tie up capital for a whole rotation and be taxed annually for their trouble? Not enough, obviously, and we see that state after state adopted some sort of forestland zoning plan in order to keep taxes at a long-term acceptable level for the landowner. Mississippi adopted the severance tax in 1940; the landowner paid taxes only at the time of logging, when the cash flow was good. Also, and significantly, there would be little incentive to log early or to abandon the land in order to reduce taxes.

There is one final comparison that I want to make. This concerns a situation that, although it has national interest, is historically southern. Fire, like taxes, is a topic that causes much posturing. Opinions run strong, even if the facts are not always clearly in support. A subtopic that is even more delicate is prescribed burning—deliberately ignited fires designed to benefit the forest.

While preparing this paper, I scanned a recent bibliography on prescribed burning in the South—8,122 citations on 131 pages. The earliest study was dated 1888; obviously this is a big topic. Certain aspects of fire appeal to me; during the 1960s I spent four years in fire research at the U.S. Forest Service's experiment station in Portland, Oregon. Much more recently, at the Forest History Society, we have been completing a film on the history of fire-fighting technology. The scripting stage provided an opportunity to review the full topic of fire. The use of fire as a forest management tool, especially in the South, was a significant aspect of our review.

The point is, a major piece of forestry drama has been acted out in the Piney Woods. Prescribed burning offers a superb example of administrative myopia, with the U.S. Forest Service insisting until the 1940s that all fires were bad. This policy necessitated the suppression of the research of its own scientists, who reported that under certain conditions, fire could be used beneficially. The pendulum swings, and in the West during the last couple of decades, some administrators—especially in the National Park Service—have espoused fire as the one certain route to environmental Nirvana. In the South, the Forest Service (less mystical than its western Park Service counterpart) has rejected its dogmatic opposition to fire in all forms and, along with state forestry agencies and forest companies, routinely uses fire under carefully controlled conditions to reduce hazardous debris following logging, to provide the optimal environment for forest growth, and to maintain favorable wildlife habitat.[7] If we do learn from history, and obviously I think that we do, we learn that at times the very institutions that are charged with taking the long view, in fact focus on the short run. And to defend their pursuit of the near term, the institutions are able to assemble "scientific" support of their aims.

From my "national perspective," I have seen more similarities than differences between the Piney Woods and other regions. This may be due to my unfamiliarity with your local history. Fortunately, the eminent and knowledgeable southern contributors will be able to fill many gaps and to correct—gently, one hopes—whatever errors I have committed.

Notes

1. Charles Francis Adams, ed., *Memoirs of John Quincy Adams Comprising Portions of His Diary from 1795 to 1848.* 12 vols. (Philadelphia: J. B. Lippincott & Co., 1876) VIII: 254.

2. John Evelyn, *Sylva, or a Discourse of Forest-Trees, and the Propagation of Timber in His Majesties Dominion* (London: Royal Society of London, 1664).

3. Richard White, *Land Use, Environment, and Social Change: The Shaping of Island County, Washington* (Seattle: University of Washington Press, 1980).

4. The annual reports of the Federal Trade Commission throughout the 1920s contain detailed reports of its investigations of illegal practices by forest industry trade associations. A good place to begin is: *Report of the Federal Trade Commission on Lumber Manufacturers' Trade Associations*, Part II *Southern Pine Association*. (Washington: GPO, 1922): 63-65.

5. Fred R. Fairchild, *Taxation of Timber Lands* in U.S. Senate, *Report of the National Conservation Commission*, 60 Cong. 2, Sen. Doc. No. 676, 3 Vols. (Washington: GPO, 1909) II: 606-08. Although Fairchild did not study Mississippi, he did include Alabama, Louisiana, and North Carolina in his survey of forest taxation laws and their effects.

6. Fred R. Fairchild, et al., *Forest Taxation in the United States*, USDA Misc. Pub. No. 218 (Washington: GPO, 1935), pp. 225-80; and R. Clifford Hall, "Forest Taxation Study, 1926-1935," OHI by Fern Ingersoll (Berkeley: Bancroft Library in association with Resources for the Future, 1967), pp. 64-85.

7. For historical context, see Ashley Schiff, *Fire and Water: Scientific Heresy in the Forest Service* (Cambridge: Harvard University Press, 1962). Good examples of recent scientific thought on fire is Gene W. Wood, ed., *Prescribed Fire and Wildlife in Southern Forests* (Georgetown, SC: Clemson University, 1981); and E. V. Komarek, *Economic and Environmental Evaluation of Prescribed Burning and Alternatives* (USDA Forest Service—Southern Region [1982]).

Piney Woods Past
A Pastoral Elegy

JOHN H. NAPIER III

I shall begin with two quotations. The first is from the Book of Genesis:

> And the Lord God planted a garden eastward in Eden; and there he put the man whom he had formed. And out of the ground made the Lord God to grow every tree that is pleasant to the sight, and good for food . . . And a river went out of Eden to water the garden.[1]

The second is from the 20 January 1700 entry in Pierre le Moyne, Sieur D'Iberville's *Journal:*

> I set out with my two feluccas and crossed Lake Pontchartrain . . . [which] is bordered by a prairie half a league to one league wide, after which one comes to the tall trees. This looks like a fine country to live in. . . . The islands here are covered with meadows; from among them issues a fresh water stream, flowing from the north. . . . They would make excellent pasture lands. The mainland north of these islands is a country of pine trees mixed with hardwood. The soil is sandy and many tracks of buffalo and deer can be seen.[2]

Well, it looks as though we blew it, didn't we? Not once, but twice.

When the primordial ooze receded into the Gulf, it left behind fingers of water passages from the higher lands, and a residue from which sprang life—cold- and warm-blooded, unseen and green life. Time brought to the land human life. All lived in harmony. And it was good.

When those first Europeans arrived here along the Mississippi Gulf Coast, the Indians shared the soil and its fruits as they did air and water, the idea of land as private property being unknown to them. The early French, British, and Spanish trappers taught them, however, that deerskins were a marketable commodity, and capitalism thus came to what we call the Piney Woods. These woods were not then overgrown thickets, but open parklike savannas, ideal both for hunting game and grazing livestock, some descended from De Soto's strayed hogs and cattle. Open woods were no accident of nature, for the Indians burned the woods regularly to check the forest understory. From the red men the early white settlers learned that practice, as they occupied Indian fields for tillage and herded their kine and swine on the open ranges. Stephen J. Pyne writes that "the herder with 40 acres and 400 head of cattle became a common figure in southern folklore, exploiting the open pine savannahs as his ancestors had the oak openings of England and the heathlands of Scotland."[3]

Along the southern frontier itinerant herdsmen organized themselves into "woods ranches," moving inland, as a seventeenth-century traveler observed, "in gangs . . . which move (like unto the ancient patriarchs or the modern Bedowins in Arabia) from forest to forest in a measure as the grass wears out or the planters approach them."[4] Indians and Europeans joined in a tremendous slaughter of deer for their skins. In 1748 Carolina's export of deer pelts peaked at 160,000, while at the same time the eastern forest bison was being hunted to extinction. As game dwindled, herding of horses, cattle, sheep, and hogs increased. The English practice of turning swine loose to forage in the woods continued on a greater scale on open southern ranges. Stockmen drove hundreds of thousands of animals to markets in the East or to Gulf Coast ports for shipment to the West Indies.

In 1763 Great Britain took from France that part of Louisiana lying east of the Mississippi River and made it the British Province of West Florida. British settlers from the Eastern Seaboard and the West Indies began to drift into the Gulf Coast plains, where they encountered the earlier French and Spanish colonists. The scarce population tripled between 1765 and 1775, when the American War for Independence brought Tory refugees in from the Carolinas and Georgia. At war's end, Spain gained West Florida from Great Britain, but encouraged American settlers to come into their province. William Faulkner well described

> the Anglo-Saxon, who would come to stay, to endure; the tall man roaring with Protestant scripture and boiled whiskey, Bible and jug in one hand and like as not an Indian tomahawk in the other, brawling, turbulent, uxorious and polygamous; a married invincible bachelor without destination but only motion, dragging his gravid wife . . . behind him into the trackless wilderness . . . without avarice or compassion or forethought either; felling a tree which took two hundred years to grow to extract from it a bear or a capful of wild honey.[5]

After the War of 1812 had ended and the United States had made its only territorial gain of that conflict by seizing West Florida from Spain, increasing numbers of American settlers came into the Piney Woods of the lower Pearl River, despite the continued, though declining, presence of the Indians, and despite the clouded land titles of the French, British, and

Spanish periods. Indeed, many settlers were veterans of that war and had served with Andrew Jackson at New Orleans on 8 January 1815. Since one could raise livestock on unclaimed government lands whether or not one owned land, herdsmen had little incentive before the Civil War to claim land other than their immediate homesteads. For instance, much of Pearl River County, Mississippi's land, that back from the old claims along the Pearl River bottoms, was not homesteaded until after the 1870s.

To be sure, there were among the settlers slave-owning planters who cultivated the fertile river bottoms for cotton. During and after the War of 1812 its price had shot up from 12.5 cents a pound in 1813 to 30 cents, briefly, in January 1819. Still, most settlers in this region sought the higher, healthier Piney Woods lands, where they could hunt, herd, and husband their subsistence crops without disturbance from the outside. By the 1820s the Pearl River district formed a back country to the aristocratic Natchez distirct, and it had a population of about ten thousand, of whom no more than two thousand were slaves. The two districts had little in common besides their mutual dislike (which may still persist!). After two successive Choctaw land cessions to the United States opened up central Mississippi to white settlement, many pioneer Pearl River planters moved north into those virgin lands. Some remained, but the prevailing culture remained that of the frontier, and it would continue to be so until later on, when trains and timber awakened the Piney Woods and thrust them into a modern industrial economy.

Mississippi's first historian, Colonel J. F. H. Claiborne, scion of "FFVs" and of Natchez aristocracy, son of a territorial governor and nephew of a hero of the Battle of New Orleans, rhapsodized over the idyllic life in the Piney Woods, not only in his 1860 *Harper's Magazine* essay, "Rough Riding Down South,"[7] but also in earlier newspaper articles of 1841–42 on which that essay was based, articles later collected as "A Trip through the Piney Woods."[8] Colonel Claiborne's praise must have been sincere: in 1853 he settled for his health's sake at his Laurel Wood Plantation on Mulatto Bayou near the mouth of the Pearl River in Hancock County.[9]

Colonel Claiborne praised the hospitality of the Piney Woods folks as "a prominent and cardinal virtue . . . handed down in its old-fashioned kindness and profusion, from father to son . . . ."[10] Coming as he did from the miasmic Mississippi River region, he was most favorably impressed by the excellent health that the people of the Piney Woods enjoyed—young, old, white, and black. He reported that "the men are robust, active and long-lived; the women beautiful, and the children lively as crickets and rud-dy as rosebuds," as he praised the bliss of their bucolic existence. Claiborne noted also the clarity and purity of the area's streams, "that flow to the south on the eastern side of Pearl and mingle their crystal floods with the chafing waters of the Gulf." He chastised the state legislature for failing to improve the Pearl River for navigation (even though it was his fellow Natchezians who were blocking improvement measures). He found the coun-try fit primarily for grazing; the grasses of the long-leaf pine forests were three feet high and the flora "rich beyond description," and he observed the "universal fondness for flowers that prevailed." Thousands of sheep and cattle grazed for the markets of Mobile and New Orleans, and the unbroken forests abounded with game—red deer, wild turkey, and partridges, or quail—all of which he said had multiplied since removal of the Indians a scant four or five years earlier.

Claiborne noted how thinly populated the Piney Woods were, how many deserted homesteads and plantations there were since former inhabitants had been lured to the newer lands available in central and north Mississip-pi during the "flush times." In the nine Piney Woods counties he visited, all but one of the seats of justice—old Williamsburg in fertile Covington County—were nearly deserted. Nonetheless, he cautioned readers of the *Natchez Free Trade Gazette* that they had an erroneous notion that east Mississippi was poor, barren, and destitute of resources. He pointed to the availability of cheap land, prophetically foretold the potential of lumber, and called for railroads to penetrate the interior from the coast. Claiborne praised "the comfort and ease that everywhere appears," and marveled that legal positions went unfilled, in Wayne County, at least, where "a more peaceful community does not exist in the world."[11]

A decade later, in 1851, my namesake ancestor John Staples Napier, a veteran of the War of 1812, wrote from Wayne County to his brother, living then in North Carolina, that "the land, poor in general, [is] well covered with pine. Well covered with summer ranges, to wit, grass, good water with milles [sic] and other conveniences and as great a portion of health as is attached to any part of the Southern States."[12] Although both extended families and entire neighborhoods had moved from the seaboard to the new states of the old Southwest, other contemporary letters reveal the pain caused by cutting old family ties by the dispersion of the great migration after 1812. In 1846 this same ancestor wrote nostalgically to a sister then living in North Carolina about their post–Revolutionary War childhood in old Virginia. He mentioned that the previous year he had visited another sister living a hundred miles away in Alabama's Black Belt, asked the whereabouts of one brother (by then in Arkansas), said he had not heard from another in North Carolina in seven or eight years, and went on to report that his first children "at the last account" were living in Illinois and Tennessee, but that his second family were living within thirty or forty miles of him in Mississippi.[13]

Today one comprehends such isolation and lack of communication with difficulty, unless one understands how terribly difficult overland travel was in this country before the coming of railroads. Navigable watercourses were the best means of travel, but, except for the Pearl River, there were but few in the Piney Woods. The majority of Piney Woods settlers came here from the Carolinas or Georgia, whence they were most likely to have journeyed via the Old Federal Road that ran from Milledgeville, Georgia, to Mobile and New Orleans. It was scarcely a road as we know it: the term "trace" is more descriptive, like that of Natchez. In 1806, Post Office Department specifications stated that the Federal Road should be from four to six feet wide, that causeways must be built across marshes, and that logs must be felled across streams so that the post rider could walk across, while his horse swam alongside. In 1818 a territorial official complained about "the tedious and unpleasant journey over almost impossible roads from Georgia," as did an army general about "the prairies so soft and fatiguing in the winter, and so dreadful to travellers and horses in the summer from numerous flies and scarcity of water."[14]

Nonetheless, immigrants and their wagons crowded such primitive thoroughfares with their families, wagons, stock, and chattels. Never mind that tree stumps and roots remained in the way, that boulders broke wheels and axles, overturning wagons and endangering lives and property, that often the way was too narrow for two wagons to pass each other, that ruts were often deep enough to stall empty wagons, or that the thick Black Belt clay sucked horseshoes off, and horses lost the hair on their legs, scraped off by the muck.[15]

After pioneer settlers had made their way with such hardships into their new homelands, they were unlikely to return to visit their old homes, or indeed, to go anywhere at all. They had sought land of the kind they were used to back east, whether or not it was particularly fertile. Typical was the pioneer who moved in 1785 from Emanuel County, Georgia; after four months of arduous travel, he arrived at the Leaf River in southeast Mississippi, and picked a spot surrounded by poor, barren pine woods. He justified his choice by saying "it was a good range for stock; but he had not an ox or cow on the face of the earth. The truth is, it looked like Emanuel County."[16]

Although some of the Pearl River settlers were prosperous planters, W. H. Sparks reminisced in 1872 that most who settled east of it were

> from the poorer districts of Georgia and the Carolinas . . . [and] were really refugees from a growing civilization. . . . They were not agriculturalists in a proper sense of the term. . . . They desired an open, poor pine country, which forbade a numerous population.
>
> Here they reared immense herds of cattle, which subsisted exclusively upon the coarse grass and reeds which grew abundantly among the tall, long-leafed pine and along the small creeks and branches numerous in this section. Through these almost interminable pine-forests the deer were abundant, and the canebrakes full of bears. They combined the pursuits of hunting and stockraising, and derived support and revenue almost exclusively from these."[17]

Sparks compared the Piney Woods folks unfavorably with those of the Natchez district: "in blissful ignorance [they] enjoyed life after the manner they loved. The country gave character to the people: both were wild and poor."[16] He also said that they were mostly illiterate, but a twentieth-century southern historian, Thomas P. Abernethy, has noted that a petition several hundred Mississippi territorial settlers from this area sent to Congress in 1803 "was expressed in excellent phraseology and couched in respectful language. Furthermore, among the numerous names attached, there was not one that was signed by the mark."[18]

Be that as it may, in 1952, Professor E. B. Ferris, an agronomist, recalled the Pearl River County to which he had been sent in 1902 to establish a Mississippi state agricultural experiment station at McNeill. It was

> located in the middle of a pine forest, among the crudest people it has ever been my good or bad fortune to know. . . . They often had their own standards, frequently had children out of wedlock and these suffered no stigma as a result thereof. . . . Human life at the time was quite cheap. . . .
>
> As an illustration of the types of our near neighbors, one was the son of an old lady said to be so high-tempered that when a nearby neighbor offended her, she rode her horse astride along the road running in front of his house cursing him for everything she could imagine, and when prosecuted for the offense, cursed out the justice of the peace and the prosecuting attorney, thus ending the affair.[19]

I have an uncomfortable feeling that I know exactly *who* she was, and if so, she was a daughter, comparatively privileged, of one of the more prosperous local planters who had been a leading slaveholder before the Civil War!

By the eve of that Civil War, in 1860, southern livestock was valued at a half billion dollars, more than twice the value of that year's southern cotton crop. Herding took much less effort than growing cotton. Since grazing was far from being labor intensive, stockmen did not need or want Negro slaves. Professor Grady McWhiney has written how, in antebellum times white southerners enjoyed leisure, whether they were slaveholding planters or nonslaveholding stock raisers.[20] Open-range grazing required practically no capital and little supervision, except at roundup and market times. Natural vegetation was so plentiful that in most of the Piney Woods animals could subsist year-round, needing little if any supplemental feeding. Although some southern stockraisers were affluent, their wealth did not show to the occasional Yankee reporter, such as Frederick Law Olmsted, because it consisted of livestock running unseen in the trackless forests, and because they lived simply and unostentatiously, unlike the so-called Natchez cotton snobs. Among these people there was little compulsion to earn money or to obtain material possessions. Leisure was more important to them than luxury.

In late antebellum times, however, arose a growing need for the timber under which our pastoral Piney Woodsman sheltered himself and his own. Then he had only his ax and his sweat with which to fell the virgin pine, and he had to do so on the banks of creeks of bayous, whence he could float his rafted timber down the Pascagoula, Leaf, Wolf, or Pearl rivers to the early lumber mills on the Gulf Coast. Alternatively, he could box and chip pine trees to make turpentine, or he could make charcoal, as he did at Kiln in Hancock County, for New Orleanians to use for fuel. In such ways as these, as well as driving his livestock to market, the Piney Woods settler earned the modest cash money he needed for such basics as coffee, salt, gunpowder, lead, cotton yard-goods, and gew-gaws for his wife and children, and the like. One thing he didn't have to buy was whiskey. That he made to his own satisfaction and standards, even though some of it was called "bust-head," or "forty-rod," which was supposedly how far an imbiber could walk before it felled him.

Gradually, however, the Piney Woods people's way of life came under threat. In the first place, population everywhere in the Western world was growing greatly in the nineteenth century. As it climbed in the Piney Woods, mostly through natural increase, pressure grew upon ranges of land hitherto unclaimed. Cane and reed for winter grazing began to disappear and game to dwindle. The old pioneer way of life was being undermined. Professor Nollie J. Hickman has pointed out that this was why the early Gulf Coast sawmill operations became important both economically and culturally to the Piney Woods pastorals: "The appearance of saws and steam engines on the banks of rivers and bayous near the Mississippi Sound heralded the approach of a new economic order. This new system would completely alter the economy of grass and game. It meant that volunteer refugees from civilization would be literally thrown into an environment from which they had tried to escape by retreat. . . . Their land of beauty, the fulfillment of all their simple requirements, would fade into a nostalgic remembrance."[21]

So, again there was irony in the fact that the very Piney Woods in which our rude settler had sought sanctuary from the outside world would betray him. Those magnificent, tall, cathedral-like, virgin yellow-pine forests, through which soft winds soughed in an otherwise silent world, would be a magnet to that outside world, its maw insatiable for more and yet more timber to help build the ships, railroads, and cities of the new Industrial Age. Timber companies, which had first desolated New England, and then the Great Lakes, would soon descend upon the primeval southern forests, and would render them a naked, howling wasteland in an all-too-short half-century.

But first worse would come—the American Civil War, the climactic clash between traditional agrarianism, whether the pastoral variety I have described, or the more exploitative plantation culture, on the one hand, and on the other, the onrushing, rapacious forces of industrialism and untrammeled capitalism. No reasonable scholar can doubt that the root cause of the conflict was slavery. But what had the Piney Woods to do with that, in a section where there were but few black bondsmen? "In the Pine Barrens the big planter was practically non-existent and the entire planter class was under ten percent in 1860."[22] Nonetheless, in 1861 Piney Woodsmen rushed to enlist under the banners of their local volunteer military companies, some of which bore such wild, woolly, and bellicose names as the Quitman Secessionists, Gainesville Volunteers, Jeff Davis Sharpshooters, Yankee Terrors, Tullahoma Hard Shells, and even the Ellisville Rosin Heels![23] But why? One answer was sheer prejudice, both against the Negro and the Yankee. They weren't about to have to compete with the Negro, who, if freed, would not only threaten their sense of racial superiority (which was about all some of them had), but with whom they would have to compete in the money economy that railroads and timber were introducing into their previously bucolic existence. As for the Yankee, he represented those forces of change that threatened them and the planter alike.

So, as Colonel John W. Thomason, Jr., wrote a couple of generations ago, such southern men marched out to try valiantly, but vainly, to stay the course of modernism, and, thus, of history. He wrote of an army composed not just of knightly-hearted zealots and great grandees, but also of solid middle-of-the-road men, of rascals, corpse-robbers, coffee-coolers, malingerers, deserters, of those Confederate soldiers who came from Texas and Arkansas and Mississippi, "the tall hunters who broke the cane and bridled

19

the western waters. . . . [T]hey were pastorals, and their economics were bounded by their fields and woodlots. . . . The point is, they all believed in something."[24]

They believed in something, even though in the pine barrens almost 63 percent of the farmers owned no slaves. On the other hand, only about 22 percent of them did not own land.[25] In the 1860 U.S. presidential election, both Marion and Hancock counties, on the lower Pearl River, returned large majorities for the Southern presidential nominee, John C. Breckenridge, and two months later overwhelmingly chose immediate secession.[26] Nearly 10 percent of the men of military age in those two Piney Woods counties rushed immediately to enlist in the first four volunteer military companies raised down there. By the war's end, 14 percent more men than had been of military age in those two counties in 1860 had seen military service. However, as the war wore on, and as the lower Piney Woods were effectively cut off from Confederate governmental authority, the desertion and AWOL rates were also high—24.7%, compared with Mississippi's average of 14%. Nonetheless, by the surrender in April 1865, 43.7% of Marion's and Hancock's men were still with their units, compared with a statewide average of but 24.7%.[27]

There was also outright disloyalty to the Confederacy, ranging from the patrician Colonel Claiborne's passing intelligence to the Union Army commander in New Orleans,[28] through bands of jayhawkers preying upon an isolated citizenry, to "Captain" Newt Knight's so-called Free State of Jones.[29] In the spring of 1864, Confederate authorities were forced to send Colonel Robert Lowry with parts of five regiments to sweep the lower Pearl River district and Honey Island Swamp, and he rounded up and returned to duty a thousand men.[30] Nonetheless, one out of seven men from the lower Pearl River district who served in the war died in it.

The shattered South's young timber industry revived quickly, as lumber was needed to build what war had destroyed. As lumber near rafting streams was cut and disappeared, railroads were built into the interior to exploit the virgin pine forests of the Piney Woods; the simple life was ending for the Piney Woods people. There were inventions to increase the timber yield—in the mill the continuous circular saw, in the woods the two-man cross-cut saw, the caralog, the pole-road locomotive, and the dry kiln. Such technological developments required greater specialization of labor and entailed monumental social consequences. The rafting of logs would pass, as once-clear navigable streams silted up, and railroads carried more and more of the Piney Woods' lumber.

Business boomed in the Piney Woods. Settlers went to work as section hands, helping first to build and then to maintain the new railways. Farmers sold livestock and produce to feed the construction crews. Canny landowners extracted as much money as they could for railroad rights of way, and crossroads merchants prospered and became bankers. Population increased, as new towns sprang up overnight along the railroads, while older river towns began to die on the vine. Along the Pearl River Valley, life shifted from Monticello, Columbia, Gainesville, Logtown, and Pearlington inland to Laurel, Hattiesburg, Lumberton, Poplarville, and Picayune. As people moved from farms and hamlets to sawmill villages and towns, their new lives gave them better living conditions and more economic opportunities. They also surrendered their old free life for the discipline of the machine culture, regimented by steam whistle or time clock.[31] Although most of the settlers became bound to the Industrial Age as underpaid wage hands, those who were not ardent agriculturists as their country filled up would have had to farm their poor soil more intensively, or else migrate west to yet-vacant lands.

Down in my neck of the Piney Woods, in south Pearl River County, such population shifts brought those of Anglo-Saxon or Celtic ancestry into closer contact with those of Latin origins, the Cajuns, as well as with freed Negros, the labor force of the turpentine camps. From Picayune south is an ethnic borderland, where "peckerwood" Baptists and "coon-ass" Catholics live alongside each other, and where their customs and cuisines have tended to overlap. Whether they are named Stockstill, Dubuisson, or Cuffey, most folks enjoy eating both fried chicken, barbecue, catfish, sweet potatoes, okra, and cornbread, on the one hand, and shrimp, crawfish, rice, and "po-boys," on the other. Many people still prefer their coffee strong with chicory, à la New Orleans, and, despite puritanical fundamentalist strictures, many have been known to take a drink of bourbon and branch.

Out in the county, there has been less moving around than in the towns, and surnames dating back to those of War of 1812 veterans are seen alike on rural mailboxes and on gravestones in country churchyards. These traditionally Piney Woods folks can be some of the most hospitable people this side of the Sahara and Gobi deserts, but also some of the orneriest ones God ever made. They can be sin-haunted or sanctimonious, or both, yet capable of rather spectacular transgressions against the Decalogue, transgressions sometimes accompanied by a "damn your eyes" attitude. Since the Civil War, they have continued to send their sons—out of proportion to their numbers—to fight America's wars against Spain, Germany, Japan, North Korea, and Viet Nam.

It was World War I that hastened the lumber boom in south Mississippi, which along with the rest of the South received, as George B. Tindall has written, "a taste of affluence such as it had never before experienced and lifted economic expectations to levels from which they would never again completely recede. Industry expanded, farm prices rose, and workers, even sharecroppers, became acquainted with the feel of folding money. . . . Higher wages created a taste for new clothes, picture shows, tin lizzies. The taste of prosperity was sweet and it lingered into the lean years that followed."[32] Alas, the lean years would soon come upon the Piney Woods. Huge lumber companies raced each other and local governments greedy for taxes to cut out the vast virgin forests. By 1908 U.S. foresters estimated that more than half of Mississippi's longleaf-pine lands had already become barren stump-dotted wastelands, and that the rest would be exhausted in twenty-five years. Their estimate was right on target. Most lumbermen then did nothing about reforestation. Some large lumber companies "cut and ran," moving to the Pacific Northwest to repeat what they had done earlier in Maine, Michigan, and Mississippi. After "the Piney Woods entered a period in lumbering that is equalled in Mississippi only by the early flush times of cotton speculation," the boom ended, and "the Piney Woods inhabitant whose grandfather was a small cattle raiser, and whose father had been a small time sheepman, was no longer a sawmill hand."[33]

The scenery of stumps and ghost towns told the saga. What had earlier been pioneer country became pioneer country once more, but shorn of its forests, grazing lands, and game. South Mississippi's James Street wrote how railroad engineer Jimmie Jackson saluted what had been:

> "De voodoo lan's" railroading hero was Jimmie Jackson. He used to bring "Old 42" out of New Orleans for Meridian. He left the Louisiana station exactly at 8 p.m., crossed the seven-mile bridge over Lake Pontchartrain and started the ghost run through Mississippi.
>
> He passed a chain of dead towns, wholly deserted villages, which once were bustling little places in the "voodoo lan' " until men stole the cypress from the swamp and the pine from the ridges and left the people with only mud and mortgages.
>
> Red Top, Wilco, Nortac, Pytonah, Orvisburg, Hillsdale, and Richburg, all were thriving mill centers a few years ago. Now they are stark and bare, their buildings still intact, their plants cold and forlorn, their streets a wallow for hogs.
>
> But Jimmie, remembering in his old age the days of his youth when he picked up hundreds of cars of lumber along the route, always blew a salute to the towns' memories as he made the ghost run through the "voodoo lan'."[34]

So, that's the way it was in the ruined lumber towns of the Mississippi Piney Woods. Most of them never recovered. Where they did, their leaders and their citizens made heroic efforts to find other uses for their stump-dotted wastelands. They tried row crops, such as cotton, corn, and sugar cane, but the sterile acid soil gave poor yields. They tried growing truck, such as strawberries. They tried tree crops, such as satsuma oranges, peaches, and pecans. Finally, there was the tung-oil tree economy. Ultimately, all these failed. Meanwhile, large landholders, mainly the remaining lumber companies, had begun reforesting the raped Piney Woods. Then, other landowners once more began to raise cattle. Both succeeded. So, one sees irony in that the land has returned to producing timber and livestock, the two products our land yielded so generously to our pioneer ancestors.

Notes

1. Gen. 1:8-10.
2. R. G. Williams, ed., *Iberville's Gulf Journals* (University: University of Alabama Press, 1981), pp. 112-13.
3. Stephen J. Pyne, *Fire in America: A Cultural History of Wildland and Rural Fire* (Princeton, N.J.: Princeton University Press, 1982), 147.
4. Quoted in Ray Allan Billington, *Westward Expansion*, 4th ed. (New York: MacMillan, 1974), 60.
5. William Faulkner, "Mississippi," in *Essays Speeches and Public Letters of William Faulkner*, ed. James B. Meriwether (New York: Random House, 1965) p. 14.
6. Thomas Perkins Abernethy, *The South in the New National 1789-1818*, vol. 4 of *A History of the South* (Baton Rouge: Louisiana State University Press, 1961), 473.
7. J. F. H. Claiborne, "Rough Riding Down South," *Harper's New Monthly Magazine*, 25 (June 1862):29-37.
8. _____, "A Trip through the Piney Woods," *Publications of the Mississippi Historical Society* 9 (1909):487-538 (hereafter, "A Trip").
9. Herbert H. Lang, "J. F. H. Claiborne at 'Laurel Wood' Plantation, 1853-1870," *Journal of Mississippi History* 18 (January 1956):1-17.
10. "A Trip."
11. Ibid.
12. John S. Napier to Davis S. Napier, 2 April 1851. Copy in author's possession.
13. John S. Napier to Mrs. Frances Godsey, 5 August 1846. Copy in author's possession.
14. Clarence E. Carter, ed., *Territorial Papers of the United States* (Washington, D.C.: Government Printing Office, 1937 and later), 5:459-61, 478; 18:402.
15. Author's lecture notes from contemporary accounts.
16. W. H. Sparks, *The Memories of Fifty Years* (Philadelphia: Claxton, Remsen & Haffelfinger, 1872), 331-32.
17. Ibid.
18. Abernethy, *South in the New Nation*, 453.
19. Reminiscences of Dr. Eugene B. Ferris, 18 Aug. 1852, Ferris Papers, Center for the Study of Southern Culture, University of Mississippi.
20. Grady McWhiney, "The Revolution in Nineteenth-Century Alabama Agriculture," *Alabama Review* 31 (January 1978):3-32. However, McWhiney's thesis that Celtic people

predominated among southern herdsmen is not borne out by an examination of the surnames of early settlers on the lower Pearl River. In 1814, of claimants to land there, 44 bore Anglo-Saxon surnames, 7 Celtic, 4 French or Spanish, and 1 German. In the first U.S. census after Mississippi attained statehood, that of 1820, in Hancock County there were 91 "Latin" cognomens among family heads, 75 English, 19 Celtic, and 1 Germanic. Farther inland and upriver, in Marion County, the corresponding numbers were 4, 221, 32, and 2. Walter Lowrie, ed., *The American State Papers, Public Lands* (Washington, D.C.: Gales & Seaton, 1834), 3:7-38; McElhinney and Thomas, [U.S.] *1820 Census of Mississippi* (Tuscaloosa: Willo, 1964), 72-76, 114-20.

21. Nollie J. Hickman, *Mississippi Harvest* (University, Ms.: University of Mississippi, 1962), 14, 42.

22. Herbert Weaver, *Mississippi Farmers 1850-1860* (Nashville: Vanderbilt University Press, 1945), 42.

23. Dunbar Rowland, *Military History of Mississippi* (Nashville: M.D.A.H., 1908; Spartanburg, S.C.: Reprint Co., 1978), 68, 181, 190-91, 264.

24. John W. Thomason, Jr., *Lone Star Preacher* (New York: Scribners, 1945), ix-xi.

25. Weaver, *Mississippi Farmers*, 100.

26. Percy Lee Rainwater, *Mississippi: Storm Center of Secession 1856-1861* (Baton Rouge: Otto Claitor, 1938; New York: Da Capo Press, 1969), 15, 78, 198, 206. 210.

27. John H. Napier III, "Lower Pearl's Civil War Losses," *Journal of Mississippi History* 23 (April 1961):94-103.

28. Lang. "Claiborne at 'Laurel Wood' Plantation," 1-17.

29. Ethel Knight, *The Echo of the Black Horn* ([Nashville]: Parthenon Press, 1951), 89-90 (Knight's company's muster roll).

30. U.S. Government, *Official Records of the War of the Rebellion* (Washington, D.C.: Government Printing Office, 1880-1901), 1st series, vol. 32, pt. 3, pp. 819-21.

31. Hickman, *Mississippi Harvest*, 253.

32. George B. Tindall, *The Emergence of the New South*, vol. 10 of *The History of the South* (Baton Rouge: Louisiana State University Press, 1967), 55-59.

33. Federal Writers Project, *Mississippi: A Guide to the Magnolia State* (New York: Hastings House, 1949), 61, 109.

34. James Street, *Look Away! A Dixie Notebook* (New York: Viking, 1936), 114-15.

Evolution of American Backwoods Pioneer Culture
The Role of the Delaware Finns

TERRY G. JORDAN

The evolution of distinctive regional cultures in the colonial eastern seaboard of the United States and their subsequent spread westward has long fascinated historians, cultural geographers, folklorists, and other students of American culture. To what degree were various contemporary European cultures implanted, modified, simplified, or hybridized? How great a role did the African and Amerindian play? How potent a shaping force was the frontier experience?[1]

In light of these questions, perhaps no traditional American way of life seems more intriguing than that of the frontier backwoodsmen, those highly successful woodland pioneers whose cultural and genealogical roots lay in the Middle Atlantic colonies, particularly Pennsylvania. By the time of the Revolution, their prowess as settlers permitted the Delaware Valley colonies to place a cultural imprint on a huge interior domain extending from upstate New York to Kentucky and the Carolina back country, a domain I will refer to as the Midland culture area. Our frontier at independence literally bulged westward in the center because of these backwoodsmen, and in the succeeding seventy years their children and grandchildren claimed most of the American heartland, even reaching the Pacific shore.[2]

By contrast, bearers of the other two principal colonial cultures—the Puritan New Englanders and the southern planters—had scarcely ventured a day's journey from the sea by 1776. Vermont, a scant ninety miles from the Atlantic breakers, remained largely unoccupied at American independence, and plantation southerners awarded much of their back country by default to the Pennsylvanians. In the light of such comparisons, the success of the Midland "leatherstocking" seems all the more remarkable.

The questions I wish to raise concern the origin and evolution of this backwoods culture. Why did successful woodland pioneering arise only in the Delaware Valley? What explains the preeminence of the Pennsylvanian pioneer? These are questions relevant to the Piney Woods and to Mississippi, both because the Midland pioneer, in the decades following the Revolution, penetrated the forests of the Gulf South and, perhaps more important, because his frontier way of life found a refuge in these forests that permitted survival well into modern times. Indeed, vestiges remain to the present day. The very environs of Hattiesburg display some of these traces. Mississippians should begin to think of themselves as displaced Yankees, as bearers of a partially Pennsylvanian culture. Mississippi's Confederate dead buried at Gettysburg constitute but one of several links to the Keystone State.

At the outset, a description of the Midland backwoods culture is in order. Its major traits included (1) log construction; (2) woodcraft, especially ax-manship; (3) the importance of the nuclear family; (4) dispersed farmsteads, as opposed to farm villages or hamlets; (5) locational instability of the people, amounting to an almost compulsive mobility; (6) a lack of concern for conservation; (7) an absence of social classes; (8) unspecialized, subsistence agriculture based in small fields; (9) a slash-and-burn system of clearing; (10) open-range livestock, particularly hogs; (11) considerable dependence upon hunting, fishing, and the gathering of wild plants; (12) accommodation of Amerindians, with adoption of their crops and techniques, accompanied by occasional intermarriage; and (13) disrespect for central authority. The list might be enlarged, but I believe these traits adequately describe the backwoodsman.[3]

According to the generally accepted view, the Midland pioneer culture was syncretic. That is, it grew out of a blending of several major ethnic groups present in the colonial Delaware Valley, in particular the English, Scotch-Irish, and Germans. For example, Germans supposedly contributed the covered wagon, log cabin, and long rifle; the British introduced informal, low-church varieties of Protestantism and the county form of government, both of which were well suited to the frontier; and the Scotch-Irish lent subsistence hill-farming.[4]

Most of the same scholars who propose diverse European bases for Midland American culture deny any input by the first ethnic groups who effectively settled the Delaware Valley—the Swedes and Finns of the New Sweden colony. Beginning in 1638, these northern Europeans created a chain of settlements from Delaware Bay to the site of Philadelphia, a string of farms and forts that endured after Swedish rule was extinguished in 1655.

Cultural geographer Wilbur Zelinsky and folklorist Henry Glassie, among others, have expressed the prevailing belief that the Delaware Valley Swedes and Finns were too few in number to have made any imprint on the regional culture, that they quickly succumbed to the numerically dominant British and Germans.[5]

As the title of my paper implies, I do not accept this view. The thesis I wish to propose is that the Midland pioneer culture, including its Piney Woods offspring, derived in some substantial measure from New Sweden and, more particularly, from ethnic Finns who came to that colony. I will attempt to lend credence to this thesis by establishing (1) that Finns formed a major constituent group in New Sweden; (2) that they possessed, before coming to the New World, a successful woodland pioneering culture containing most elements subsequently typical of the American frontier; (3) that northern Europeans remained proportionally important in the Delaware Valley population during a crucial period of contact with other immigrant groups; (4) that they mixed early and readily with foreign elements in the Delaware Valley; and (5) that their descendants spread widely on the expanding Midland frontier.

At the time of its American colony, Sweden ruled a multiethnic Baltic empire that included Finland as well as parts of the present Soviet Union, Poland, and the two Germanys. New Sweden's population reflected the human diversity of the parent empire; Swedes, Finns, and Germans, particularly Holsteiners, all came to the colony. That Finns formed a sizable proportion of New Sweden's inhabitants is generally accepted, and the distinct possibility exists that the colony had a Finnish majority.[6] Because Finns were obligated to accept Swedish surnames, the actual ethnic makeup became clouded, given the fragmentary nature of biographical data on the colonists. My own feeling is that the proportion of Finns in the population steadily increased during the 1640s and early 1650s. Perhaps a Finnish majority came about even after Swedish rule in the Delaware Valley was extinguished in 1655, for many ethnic Swedish officials and soldiers returned to Europe at that time, while the Finns stayed and others continued arriving even as late as 1664.[7] For example, in March 1656 the ship *Mercurius* delivered 92 Finns and only 13 Swedes to the Delaware, while the arrivals in 1664, numbering 140, were exclusively Finns.[8]

Within the Swedish Baltic empire, even as early as the sixteenth century, the prowess of Finns as forest pioneers was recognized and esteemed. Particularly after 1590, but earlier as well, the crown introduced Finnish settlers into unoccupied northern and central areas of Sweden proper, mainly into the western interior provinces of Dalsland, Värmland, Närke,

Västmanland, and Dalarna.[9] A sizable tract of Värmland and adjacent Norwegian Hedmark still bears the name Finnskogen, or "Finn's Woods," and many traces of the distinctive Finnish culture persist there, though not the language.

By the 1630s, the backcountry Finns had made such drastic inroads on the forests and wildlife of interior Sweden that the monarch became distressed. In part, the king's change of heart resulted from the rise of the Swedish copper and iron industries, both of which lay in Finnish-settled areas and demanded large amounts of timber. The previously worthless woods opened to the Finns had acquired monetary value. A campaign began in the 1630s to rid certain provinces of the "forest-destroying Finns," many of whom were arrested and transported to the Delaware Valley.[10] Perhaps the first of these, consisting of four families, departed Sund parish in Dalsland in 1640. Within a decade, word filtered back to the Finns in Sweden that the American colony offered splendid forests to settle, and from that time emigration became voluntary. For example, a petition on behalf of two hundred Värmland Finns who wished to go to America reached officials in 1649.[11]

Which, then, of the thirteen previously enumerated traits of Midland backwoods culture might have Finnish antecedents? The most compelling material evidence, well-nigh irrefutable, is provided by pioneer American log carpentry and architecture. Midland log construction has previously been interpreted as German in origin and attributed, insofar as carpentry is concerned, to the Pennsylvania Dutch.[12] My own research, carried out during four field excursions into various parts of northern and central Europe, leaves little doubt that, in particular, the primitive "cabin" stage of American log construction, as opposed to the more refined "house" stage, is essentially backcountry Finnish in origin.[13] Among the major features seemingly of Fenno-Scandian origin are (1) four common types of log corner joint—the "diamond," "V," "saddle," and "square" notches; (2) the board-covered, "ridgepole-and-purlin" roof, in which beams running the length of the structure and notched into gable logs, rather than rafters, provide the weight-bearing support; (3) the "dogtrot" or "double-house" plan, distinguished by an open-air, roofed passageway between the two log rooms; and (4) the log corncrib, a small front-gable granary with a board hatchdoor. All of these formal elements, and others as well, find their most precise prototypes in northern Europe. In both the Baltic lands and America, for example, the dogtrot plan is recognized as a pioneer type, and its earliest vernacular name on the Midland frontier, "double house," is likely derived from the Swedish cognate *dubbelhus*.[14]

Log construction, in turn, implies an array of woodsman skills involving the long-handled ax. In the sixteenth century, Finns often bore the title *kirvesmen* (axmen) in Swedish tax registers, and this skill led them to be introduced into the forests of Sweden.[15] The Delaware Finns obviously possessed these same skills, and one should recognize that the English, Welsh, Scotch-Irish, and Rhenish Germans did not. One Englishman, in 1683, impressed by the huge Pennsylvania oaks, "many of them about two foot through, and some bigger," was even more awed that "a Swead will fell twelve of the bigger in a day."[16] Alone among the Europeans arriving in colonial America, the Finns were consummate axmen, and the reason was simple. Great Britain, Ireland, and the Rhine Plain retained few forests by 1650, and the islandlike remnant woods had come under royal protection.

Adding to the Finns' ability to decimate woodland was their use of fire in a practice called *svedjebruket* or burn-beating. In this primitive and wasteful technique, trees were felled in autumn, the useful trunks removed, and the remaining wood, after drying, set afire the following year. In the spring the Finns, after using a small wooden plow, sowed seed in the ashes amid the charred stumps, thereby offsetting the acid infertility of the coniferous forest soil. Two or three harvests could be obtained from such fields, and the Finns, rather than apply manure, then made new clearings, abandoning the old.[17] This shifting cultivation system, involving a highly extensive use of resources, made it necessary for the Finnish farmer to move, periodically, to a new settlement site, a seminomadism suggested by the terms *drift-finnar* (roaming Finns) and *ostadige finnar* (unsettled Finns) often employed by seventeenth-century Swedish authorities.[18] It was particularly these seminomadic burn-beaters, these "forest-destroying" or "vagrant" Finns, who were rounded up and sent to America. Their fellow Finns, who chose to establish permanent settlements and fields, by use of manure, fared better with the authorities.

In these roaming Finns, I suggest, we find a perfect prototype for the American backwoods pioneer. The same locational instability, the same wasteful use of resources and lack of concern for conservation, even the same clearing techniques occur on the American frontier.[19] In fact, shifting cultivation persisted into modern times in parts of the South. To be sure, certain eastern Indian tribes cleared forest and farmed in a manner similar to the Finns, but the Midland pioneer method displayed greater affinity to the northern European type, in such details as chopping rather than girdling trees and the use of steel axes.

The resultant farming system, both in Sweden and America, was subsistent in nature, with little concern for marketing surplus produce. The fired clearing supplied grain for the farm family, though livelihood for the backwoods Finn, as for his American counterpart, depended more on hunting, gathering, and fishing than on tillage. Pathfinding skills enabled the Finns in northern Europe to wander far from their clearings in spring and autumn as huntsmen, and apparently most possessed firearms. Deer, elk, and fur-bearing animals constituted their favorite game, to the extent that laws, even as early as 1608, forbade them to hunt some of these animals.[20] The Finns were among the last European commoners to hunt freely, in an era when remnant fauna came under royal protection. At a time when German peasants had only the folk legends of Hubertus to remind them of the former hunting skills of their people and the English had only the tales of Robin Hood, backcountry Finns still lived the life of the chase.

Their methods, as in forest clearing, were wasteful, and Swedish authorities particularly objected to their custom of shooting elk only for the hides, leaving carcasses to rot.[21] One cannot but be reminded of the American bison experience. Swedish laws did little to prevent poaching by the Finns, and among the emigrants forcibly sent to America were criminals convicted of shooting elk. In America, the Finns and Swedes perpetuated their traditional hunting methods. An Englishman commented in 1698 that, along one marshy stream in southern New Jersey, "the Sweeds used to kill the Geese in great numbers, for their Feathers only, leaving their Carcasses behind them."[22]

The devastating impact of Finns upon Sweden's flora and fauna was heightened by their tendency to disperse through the forest in nuclear family units, settling in isolated homesteads rather than clustering in villages, as did most Swedes and the large majority of other Europeans in that era. The Swedish toponymic suffic -torp (croft) occurs frequently in Sweden's Finnmarks, while the suffix -by (village) is less common. A suggestive placename, *Finntorp* (Finn's croft) survives to the present day in six different Swedish provinces.[23] This same atomistic settlement pattern also characterized the Midland frontier and persisted to become the dominant rural American type. One looks in vain among the other early colonists from Europe for an equally satisfactory prototype, for they, by and large, had inhabited villages or clan hamlets in the Old World.

Nor does doubt exist that the settlers of New Sweden established dispersed farmsteads. The Dutch, during their brief periods of rule in the Delaware Valley after 1655, tried in vain to make the rural folk move from scattered homesteads to villages, and a 1697 traveler noted that "the people live much apart and scattered."[24] Peter Kalm found the same pattern prevalent a half-century later on the New Jersey side of the river. "The farms are most of them single," he reported, "and you seldom meet with even two together." His observation that "now and then you see a single farm, and a little grain field round it," could just as well have been made in one of Sweden's back-country Finnmarks.[25] In this context, one should remember that farm villages prevailed in early colonial New England and in the Dutch patroon-ships along the Hudson. The plantation South, too, developed a clustered rural settlement form, as the quarters of indentured servants or slaves formed hamlets or villages adjacent to the owners' houses.[26]

The American frontiersman displayed an ability to interact with the Indians. While the popular image remains that of bloody hostility between natives and settlers, in fact a great deal of cultural exchange and even intermarriage occurred in the frontier contact zone. Indeed, little difference existed between backwoodsmen and the adjacent "civilized" tribes, and a quite remarkable number of Americans claim partial Indian blood. In this manner, many useful features of Amerindian culture passed to the whites, perhaps most notably corn. The major Indian-European cultural exchanges occurred in the Middle Atlantic colonies, beginning in the Delaware Valley. New Englanders, despite sharing a first Thanksgiving feast, and southern planters, Pocahontas aside, borrowed little and chose to exterminate the natives by military means. Even the tobacco raised by Chesapeake planters came from elsewhere in the Americas. True, the early Delaware Valley was not without conflict, and Indians killed some Finns, but the prevailing pattern was that of peaceful contact and trade.[27]

I suggest that the Midland model of Indian-white contact owed a partial formative debt to the Finns. They arrived in America with the background of a millenium of frontier contact with the Lapps and other northern tribes. Indeed, some aspects of the backcountry Finnish life-style may have been acquired originally from the Lapps. The ancestral experience of dealing with, borrowing from, absorbing, exploiting, and displacing these tribes prepared the Finns exceedingly well for coping with Indians.[28]

Too, the peaceful contact between Finn and Indian rested in part on their similarity to each other. Both engaged in shifting cultivation and relied heavily upon hunting and gathering. Both were at home in the woods and close to nature. One Indian group in the Delaware Valley, recognizing this similarity, called the people of New Sweden *netappi* (our race) in contrast to the British and Dutch, whom they regarded as alien.[29] Interestingly, Indians in the north woods of the upper Midwest made a similar judgment when confronted with Finnish immigrants in a much later era, around 1900.[30]

Kalm reported, perhaps with some exaggeration, that the people of New Sweden "were already half Indians" when the Quakers arrived in 1682, and Penn used them as interpreters in his dealings with the local natives. By then the Finns cultivated Indian corn and tobacco, used Indian words for certain wild plants and herbs, and had adopted the canoe.[31]

Contempt for central authority and disrespect for the law, occasionally laced with a dose of criminality, characterized the American backwoodsman. The frontier remained a place to escape legal jurisdiction. Now, there has never been a shortage of criminals among immigrants to America, from Virginia's transported felons to the Marielitos, but the Delaware Finns may have set the pattern on the Midland frontier. Indeed, they exhibited a disregard of and contempt for Swedish authority long before coming to America by ignoring game and forest laws specifically directed at them. Some had fled into Norway to escape Swedish prosecution. Among the Finns arriving on the Delaware were convicted elk poachers, tree and orchard destroyers, army deserters, and adulterers.[32] In America this behavior persisted and even intensified. While still under the rule of Sweden, one Delaware Valley colonist admitted that "there has been a disorderly and riotous life here," and some Finns fled to Maryland to escape Swedish authority.[33] Succeeding rulers also encountered problems with the Finns. They ignored edicts of the Dutch government, and a man known as the "Long Finn" led a rebellion that terrorized local British authorities.[34] Perhaps the disrespect for central authority exhibited by some of the Delaware Finns contributed to a similar attitude in the Midland pioneer of later generations.

By no means do these traits provide an exhaustive list of possible Finnish influence in the Midland culture. Northern European roots may lie beneath such items of material culture and practice as the split rail fence and tar boiling.[35] The crude wooden "Finnish plow" may be related to the one used by backwoodsmen in the United States, and the keelboat common on eastern rivers could be derived from the Delaware Valley "church boat."[36] Nor should we overlook the fact that only the Finns and their Swedish companions among the European colonists along the Delaware had previous experience with winters as cold as those encountered in Pennsylvania.

In sum, the Finns possessed well in advance of reaching colonial America a viable, proven woodland pioneering culture, one bearing a startling resemblance to the subsequent Middle Atlantic backwoods way of life. In almost every respect, they were ideally prepared to succeed as New World forest colonizers and to provide a pioneer prototype. Indeed, the Finns could be described as culturally preadapted to success. When the English, Dutch, Scotch-Irish, and Germans began arriving in force, they encountered an established, successful northern European, essentially Finnish, population of log-cabin-dwelling axmen dispersed as burn-beaters through the woods along the river, each in his private clearing. They encountered folk who displayed an ability to accommodate the Indian and a contempt for conservation and central authority. The latecomers encountered, in short, the American frontiersman.

If this be true, then how might the Finnish backwoods culture have been transferred to the pioneer population at large? How could this way of life preadapted to success in the American wilderness have diffused to the other, less-prepared immigrants? The answer, I feel, is multifaceted, resting upon the Finns' time of arrival, their situation, their proportional importance, their willingness to mix, their ethnic tolerance, and their propensity to disperse.

Not the least of the factors at work involved timing. Wilbur Zelinsky, in an attempt to explain the processes at work in the creation of distinctive colonial subcultures, proposed a "doctrine of first effective settlement," holding that "the first group able to establish a viable, self-perpetuating society in an empty land [is] . . . of crucial significance for the later social and cultural geography of the area, no matter how tiny the initial band of settlers may have been."[37] Further, the first effective colonists are of crucial importance in the shaping of "derivative frontier zones."[38] In other words, we should look to the early colonial period if we wish to understand American sectionalism. The Finns and Swedes accomplished the first effective settlement of the Delaware Valley, an area that subsequently served as the nucleus of the Midland culture. We should not be surprised that the northern Europeans helped shape the local and derivative life-style.

A second factor contributing to the diffusion of Finnish techniques was location. In part because of their settlement pattern of dispersed farmsteads, the settlers of New Sweden, though few in number, already occupied the banks of the Delaware from its mouth to above the site of Philadelphia before Penn's arrival and the beginning of large-scale British and German immigration.[39] The newcomers had to run a gauntlet of Finnish and Swedish farms as they journeyed by river or road to Philadelphia. In this manner, the successful Finnish pioneer culture achieved maximum display on the "main street" of the middle colonies.

In addition, the Finns and Swedes, while not numerous, formed a significant proportion of the Delaware Valley population throughout the seventeeth century and, in some locales, as late as the Revolution. That is, during the crucial early period of contact with British and German immigrants, Finns constituted a high enough percentage of the inhabitants to have made a major impact on the resultant syncretic culture. In 1655, at the close of Swedish rule, the northern Europeans numbered about 300 and made up three-quarters of the Delaware Valley white population.[40] An early census of the New Castle area of Delaware, dated 1677, suggests that Finns and Swedes accounted for about 23 percent of the inhabitants, a proportion that still held true a century later.[41] William Penn, in 1685, estimated that the English in his colony were as numerous as all other groups combined, and by implication the Finns and Swedes may have formed a third or more of the total population, not an unreasonable assumption, since they numbered at least 939 in the Valley by 1693.[42]

During the same early period, the Finns and Swedes proved willing to mix, both by neighborhood and through marriage, with the British, Germans, Hollanders, and others who came to the Delaware Valley.[43] The Scandinavians "live scattered among the English and Quakers," wrote an observer in 1697, and "around and between them live English people, whose language together with Welsh and Dutch, they know perfectly."[44] Very early in the development of the Delaware Valley, an atmosphere of tolerance developed among the diverse European ethnic groups present, a tolerance that encouraged cultural exchange and intermarriage. While the Quakers promoted this atmosphere, particularly in religious matters, it predated Penn's arrival. Perhaps the roots lay in the multiethnic character of the Swedish Empire, and the first fruit borne in America may have been the blending of Finn, Swede, and Holsteiner German into a composite colonial culture, whose members were content to call themselves "Swedes," to speak a Gothic dialect, to bear Swedish surnames, but to practice a backcountry Finnish life-style, even to the use of *saunas*.[45] That Swedish rather than Finnish prevailed as the language probably was owing to the Lutheran clergy, who even into the eighteenth century came from Sweden.

Wider mixing followed. A list of 139 "Swedish" families compiled in the early 1690s included Dutch, British, and German surnames such as Koenig, Talley, Dennis, and Van der Weer.[46] This merging, though dooming long-term Finnish-Swedish ethnic survival, enhanced the ability of the northern Europeans to transfer certain elements of their culture to the population at large and increased the potential number of their genetic descendants.

The mixing process continued until perhaps about 1750, accommodating the masses of Scotch-Irish and Rhenish-Swiss Germans who arrived after 1710. The scene of interaction shifted away from the valley, where a post-pioneer culture displaying few Finnish traits prevailed by 1700, to the interior frontier. Many Scandinavians, rather than cling to the dying, riddled ethnic enclave along the river, where their backwoods life-style was no longer possible, moved west. By the end of the seventeenth century, in possession of land grants from Penn, Finns and Swedes had led the way to the interior, settling above the falls of the Schuylkill.[47] This path, in another generation, led them down that jugular of Pennsylvanian migration, the Great Valley of the Appalachians. Distinctive Delaware Valley Swedish surnames such as Rambo, Yoakum, Justice, Olson, Paulson, Holston, Lykens, and Swanson (see Table 1) became identified with the outer edge of the exploding Midland frontier through the remainder of the colonial period.

TABLE 1

Some Colonial American Surnames Derived
Exclusively from New Sweden

Major American Forms	Swedish-Finnish Forms
Bankson, Bankston	Bengtsson
Bartleson	Bertilsson
Clemson	Clementsson, Klemelsson
Dalbow	Dahlbo
Ericson	Ericksson
Holston	Hollsten, Holstein
Justice, Justis	Göstasson, Juustinen?
Longacre	Långåker
Likens, Lykens	Laican, Laikkonen, Leikkonen
Mecum	?
Mollika	Mulikka
Olson	Olsson, Olofsson
Paulson, Pawson	Påfvelson, Påwelson, Påvelsson
Rambo	Rambo
Senecker, Senecca	Senecksen, Sinikka
Stallcup	Stalcop, Stålkofta
Swanson	Swensson, Svenson
Walraven	Wallrawen
Yoakum, Yokum	Jochim, Jochimson

Sources: S. Ilmonen, *Amerikan Ensimäiset Soumalaiset eli Delawaren Siirtokunnam Historia* (Hancock, Michigan: Suomalais-Luteerilaisen Kustannusliikkeen Kirjapaino, 1916), pp. 100–101; E. A. Louhi, *The Delaware Finns* (New York: Humanity Press, 1925), pp. 301, 320; Amandus Johnson, *The Swedish Settlements on the Delaware, 1638–1664* (New York: D. Appleton, 1911), 2:673–726.

For example, Rambos, Yoakums, Olsons, and others appeared in the Shenandoah Valley of Virginia well before 1750.[48] Swain Paulson, still bearing a corrupted Swedish given name, crossed Cumberland Gap with Kentucky's first Salt River settlers.[49] The Holston River settlement in earliest northeastern Tennessee bore the name of a Delaware Scandinavian family, as did colonial frontier outposts such as Yoakum Station in Lee County, southwestern Virginia.[50] Edward Swanson was among a band of nine forming the initial expedition, in 1779, to Middle Tennessee, where he became the first settler of Williamson County.[51]

Perhaps the most remarkable Midland pioneer of proven Scandinavian origin was Stephen Holston. In the manner of a *drift-finn*, he moved from Pennsylvania to western Virginia, then, even before 1750, into northeastern Tennessee, well ahead of the currents of migration. By midcentury, Holston and a few companions journeyed down the Tennessee, Ohio, and Mississippi rivers as far as Natchez, providing the first human link between the Delaware Valley and the Piney Woods. Though Holston returned to the Appalachians, his descendants, remembering his stories of the lower Mississippi, came to settle in the Natchez area before 1800. Back east, Stephen Holston continued to drift, moving to the Saluda country of western South Carolina, again well ahead of the crowd, then back to Virginia and, finally, to Grainger County in East Tennessee, where death finally slowed him down.[52]

These examples could be enlarged a hundredfold, but the point is clear. The genetic offspring of New Sweden's families dispersed to the interior, often at the forefront of the frontier. Certainly, by the end of the colonial period few of the far-flung pioneers bearing Swedish surnames remained purely of northern European ancestry. English, Scotch-Irish, German, Dutch, and Welsh blood also flowed in their veins. By the same token, many persons whose family names derived from these other groups had some Finnish ancestry as well. By 1775 few if any pioneers, regardless of surname, could accurately be described as ethnic Finns or Swedes, but that is precisely the point. The price they paid for mixing and dispersing was their vestigial, even mongrelized ethnic identity. Their reward, perhaps unconscious, lay in the incidental transfer of some substantial part of Finnish pioneer culture to the population at large, completing a diffusion begun well before 1700 in the Delaware Valley nucleus.

The northern Europeans in colonial America, then, possessed an Old World woodland pioneer life-style preadapted environmentally and culturally to success on the Midland frontier, accomplished the first effective settlement of the Delaware Valley, occupied the major portal of later British and

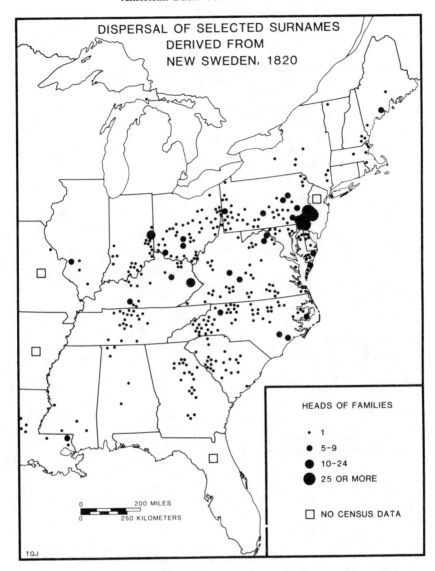

German immigration, remained proportionately important in the Midland
nucleus during an early period of contact with other European groups,
displayed a propensity to mix and marry with those not of their kind, and
subsequently scattered to the interior frontier. Through these attributes,
achievements, attitudes, and tendencies, they attained the ability to dif-
fuse parts of their backwoods culture to a far larger population and area.
If much of America bears the mark of Pennsylvania and the Midland
culture, considerable credit is due the forest-destroying Finns.

Notes

1. See, for example, Thomas J. Wertenbaker, *The Founding of American Civilization: The Middle Colonies* (New York: Charles Scribner's Sons, 1938); Robert D. Mitchell, "The Formation of Early American Cultural Regions: An Interpretation," in *European Settlement and Development in North America* ed. James R. Gibson (Toronto: University of Toronto Press, 1978), 66–90; Henry Glassie, *Pattern in the Material Folk Culture of the Eastern United States* (Philadelphia: University of Pennsylvania Press, 1968); Frederick J. Turner, *The Frontier in American History*, 3d ed. (New York: Henry Holt, 1958).
2. Milton B. Newton, "Cultural Preadaptation and the Upland South," *Geoscience and Man* 5 (1974):143–54; John S. Otto and Nain E. Anderson, "The Diffusion of Upland South Folk Culture, 1790–1840," *Southeastern Geographer* 22 (1982):89–98.
3. Newton, "Cultural Preadaptation," 152.
4. Fred B. Kniffen and Henry Glassie, "Building in Wood in the Eastern United States: A Time-Place Perspective," *Geographical Review* 56 (1966):58, 59, 63; Wilbur Zelinsky, *The Cultural Geography of the United States* (Englewood Cliffs, N.J.: Prentice-Hall, 1973), 20–21; Mitchell, "Formation of Early American Cultural Regions," 69.
5. Henry Glassie, "Eighteenth-Century Cultural Process in Delaware Valley Folk Building," *Winterthur Portfolio* 7 (1972):49; Zelinsky, *Cultural Geography of the United States*, 20.
6. John H. Wuorinen, *The Finns on the Delaware 1638–1655: An Essay in American Colonial History* (New York: Columbia University Press, 1938); Amandus Johnson, *The Swedish Settlements on the Delaware, 1638–1664* (New York: D. Appleton, 1911), 2:693–726.
7. Wuorinen, *Finns on the Delaware*, 79.
8. Carolus Davis Arfwedson, *A Brief History of the Colony of New Sweden* (Lancaster, Pa.: New Era Printing, 1909), 25; Adolph B. Benson and Naboth Hedin, *Swedes in America, 1638–1938* (New Haven, Conn.: Yale University Press, 1938), 27.
9. Ivan Bill, "Om finnkolonisationen i Värmland," *Folkets Historia* 10 (January 1982):18–23; Johnson, *Swedish Settlements on the Delaware*, 1:147–48.
10. C. T. Odhner, "The Founding of New Sweden," *Pennsylvania Magazine of History and Biography* 3 (1879):406; Johnson, *Swedish Settlements on the Delaware*, 1:149.
11. Johnson, *Swedish Settlements on the Delaware*, 1:149, 267.
12. Terry G. Jordan, "Alpine, Alemannic, and American Log Architecture," *Annals of the Association of American Geographers* 70 (1980):154–55.
13. Terry G. Jordan, "A Reappraisal of Fenno-Scandian Antecedents for Midland American Log Construction," *Geographical Review* 73 (1983):58–94.
14. Martin Wright, "The Antecedents of the Double-Pen House Type," *Annals of the Association of American Geographers* 48 (1958):109–17; Richard H. Hulan, "The Dogtrot House and its Pennsylvania Associations," *Pennsylvania Folklife* 26 (Summer 1977):25–32.
15. Axel Sömme, *A Geography of Norden* (Oslo: J. W. Cappelens Forlag, 1960), 150.
16. Thomas Paschall, "Letter of Thomas Paschall, 1683," in *Narrative of Early Pennsylvania, West New Jersey and Delaware, 1630–1707* ed. Albert C. Myers (New York: Charles Scribner's Sons, 1912), 254.
17. Gösta Grotenfelt, *Det primitiva jordbrukets metoder i Finland under den historiska tiden* (Helsinki; Simelii Arfvingars Boktryckeri, 1899), 27–30, 36–39, 147–50; Johnson, *Swedish Settlements on the Delaware*, 1:147–48.
18. Odhner, "Founding of New Sweden," 405, 406.
19. John R. Stilgoe, *Common Landscapes of America, 1580 to 1845* (New Haven, Conn.: Yale University Press, 1982), 172–76; Otto and Anderson, "Diffusion of Upland South," 92.
20. Eino Jutikkala and Kauko Pirinen, *A History of Finland* (New York and Washington: Praeger, 1974), 11, 15; Johnson, *Swedish Settlements on the Delaware*, 1:147–48.
21. Christopher Ward, *The Dutch and Swedes on the Delaware, 1609–64* (Philadelphia: University of Pennsylvania Press, 1930), 103.
22. Gabriel Thomas, "An Historical and Geographical Account of Pensilvania and of West-New-Jersey," in *Narratives of Early Pennsylvania, West New Jersey and Delaware, 1630–707* ed. Albert C. Myers (New York: Charles Scribner's Sons, 1912), 349.

23. Sweden: Official Standard Names Approved by the United States Board on Geographic Names, Gazetteer No. 72 (Washington, D.C.: Office of Geography, Dept. of the Interior, 1963), 198-99.

24. E. A. Louhi, The Delaware Finns (New York: Humanity Press, 1925), 108-111.

25. Peter Kalm, Travels into North America (Barre, Mass.: Imprint Society, 1972), 210, 214.

26. Glenn T. Trewartha, "Types of Rural Settlement in Colonial America," Geographical Review 36 (1946):568-96.

27. Glenn J. Jessee, "Culture Contact and Acculturation in New Sweden, 1638-1655" (M.A. thesis, College of William and Mary, 1983), 33-38, 42-44; Johnson, Swedish Settlement on the Delaware, 2:708.

28. Jutikkala and Pirinen, History of Finland, 13-14.

29. Benson and Hedin, Swedes in America, 28.

30. Frances Karttunen, interview with author, 7 Oct. 1983.

31. Kalm, Travels into North America, 39-40, 88, 178, 217, 248-49, 255.

32. Johnson, Swedish Settlements on the Delaware, 1:126, 147-48, 239, 243; Ward, Dutch and Swedes on the Delaware, 103.

33. Peter Lindeström, Geographia Americae, with An Account of the Delaware Indians, tr. and ed. Amandus Johnson (Philadelphia: Swedish Colonial Society, 1925), 125-26.

34. Louhi, Delaware Finns, 108-11, 134-38.

35. Richard H. Hulan, "Whatever Happened to Baby Swain? Diffusion of New Sweden's Folk Culture to the Interior." Paper presented at the meeting of the American Folklore Society, Pittsburgh, October 1980, pp. 6-7. I am grateful to Dr. Hulan for providing me a typescript of his presentation.

36. Jutikkala and Pirinen, History of Finland, 11; Bill, "Om finnkolonisationen," 20-21; Hulen, "Whatever Happened to Baby Swain?" 7.

37. Zelinsky, Cultural Geography of the United States, 13.

38. Ibid., 34.

39. Paschall, "Letter, 1683," 250.

40. Sally Schwartz, "Society and Culture in the Seventeenth Century Delaware Valley," Delaware History 20 (1982):103.

41. "Taxables Living within the Jurisdiction of New Castle Court in November, 1677," Pennsylvania Magazine of History and Biography 3 (1879): 352-54; American Council of Learned Societies, "Report of the Committee on Linguistic and National Stocks in the Population of the United States," Annual Report of the American Historical Association for the Year 1931 (Washington, D.C.: Government Printing Office, 1932), 1:393.

42. William Penn, "A Further Account of the Province of Pennsylvania, by William Penn, 1685," in Narratives of Early Pennsylvania, West New Jersey and Delaware, ed. Albert C. Myers (New York: Charles Scribner's Sons, 1912), 260; Jehu C. Clay, Annals of the Swedes on the Delaware (Philadelphia: F. Foster, 1858), 167-68.

43. Schwartz, "Society and Culture in Delaware Valley," 115.

44. Arfwedson, Brief History of the Colony, 25; Roy W. Swanson, "The Swedes and the New History," Swedish-American Historical Bulletin 3 (September 1930):11-12.

45. Thomas M. Horner, "Sauna Baths along the Delaware, 1638-1682," American Swedish Historical Foundation Yearbook (1971):23-28.

46. Clay, Annals of the Swedes, 167-68.

47. Edward J. Gibbons, "The Swedes' Tract in Upper Merion Township, Montgomery County, Pennsylvania: Land Transaction and Settlement, 1684-1710," American Swedish Historical Foundation Yearbook, (1968):1-10.

48. F. B. Kegley, Kegley's Virginia Frontier (Roanoke, Va.: Southwest Virginia Historical Society, 1938), 96, 145.

49. Lewis Collins, History of Kentucky (Covington, Ky: Collins & Co., 1874), 2:606.

50. Samuel C. Williams, "Stephen Holston and Holston River," East Tennessee Historical Society's Publications, no. 8 (1936):26-34.

51. William H. McRaven, Life and Times of Edward Swanson (Nashville and Kingsport, Tenn.: Kingsport Press, 1937), 17-19.

52. This paragraph is based upon Williams, "Stephen Holston," 26-31.

Antebellum Piney Woods Culture
Continuity over Time and Place

GRADY MCWHINEY

People who visited the Piney Woods of southern Mississippi, southwestern Alabama, southeastern Louisiana, and western Florida before the Civil War reported that the inhabitants of this region possessed large herds of livestock, principally cattle and hogs. That observation is basic to any understanding of antebellum Piney Woods culture, but my focus here is not on the livestock industry itself, since such writers as John D. W. Guice, Terry G. Jordan, and Kenneth D. Israel have covered that subject admirably.[1] My emphasis instead is on how the antebellum Piney Woods folk lived—their habits, traditions, and values—and how they maintained to a remarkable degree over time and distance the ways and manners of their forebears from the British Isles.

To understand Piney Woods culture—indeed, to understand the antebelleum South—one must put aside some myths. The most important myth to recognize and to discard is the widespread belief that southern ways were English ways. To insist, as most authorities do, that the white people in all regions of the United States during the antebellum period were overwhelmingly of British extraction is true but quite misleading.

Deep cultural divisions had shaped the history of Great Britain. When Roman invaders arrived in the British Isles in A.D. 43, they encountered Celtic people who had been there for about seven centuries and who had conquered and acculturized the natives. The ancestors of these British Celts, once dominant throughout much of southern Europe from Spain to the Balkans, had gradually retreated westward, pressed by both Romans and Teutonic peoples. Those Celts who survived the Roman conquest of England and Wales were either absorbed into Roman Britannia or pushed northward and westward. There, in Scotland and Ireland, Celts maintained their culture and power not only during the Roman occupation of the remainder of the British Isles but also during the subsequent Anglo-Saxon invasion, and by A.D. 650 the Celts had retaken Wales, Cornwall, the Isle of Man, and the northwestern areas of Cumberland, Westmoreland, and Lancashire. Later Norman and Scandinavian invaders influenced both Celtic and Anglo-Saxon culture, but by medieval times a clear cultural and geographical division of the British Isles had been fixed—Celtic in the north and west, English in the south and east.[2]

Conflict, cultural and often physical, between the English and their Celtic neighbors has continued to the present. The English eventually managed to dominate the whole of what became the United Kingdom through persistence, orderly habits, an internalized sense of propriety, a unique system of common law, the habit of obedience to that law, literacy, a capacity for devising flexible but stable political institutions, and other cultural traits. The Celtic peoples who occupied Cornwall, Wales, Scotland, Ireland, and the Hebrides, and strongly influenced the culture of the "Celtic fringe" of England—those areas contiguous to Cornwall, Wales, and Scotland—resisted successive English attempts over the centuries not just to rule them but to obliterate their culture.

For several years Professor Forrest McDonald and I have insisted that the people who settled in the American South and in the American North were significantly different—in their ways and in their values—because their cultural heritages were different. More specifically, we contend that the North was settled mainly by Englishmen and culturally dominated by them and that the South was settled mainly by Celts and culturally dominated by them.[3]

One of our major discoveries about this prevailing cultural sectionalism in antebellum America resulted from analyzing family names. We used various systems of name analysis to determine migration and settlement patterns in the United States from the eighteenth century to the Civil War, and all of these methods of analysis indicate that the overwhelming majority of antebellum white southerners were of Celtic, not English, ancestry.[4] No special effort has been made to analyze the names of Piney Woods folk, but even a cursory examination of the sources reveals that the region was, and still is, full of people with Celtic surnames.

An excellent example is the man honored by these lectures. The name "Crosby," sometimes spelled "Crosbie" or "Crosseby," is indigenous to both Scotland and Ireland. Members of the Crosby family were among the "knights of Annandale" who supported Scotland's national hero Robert Bruce in his struggles against the English. Scottish records indicate that in 1298 John de Crosseby was minister of a church in Selkirk; in 1440

Thomas de Crosby lived in Glasgow; and in 1546 Sir James Crosby, a cleric, was called as a witness. Moreover, the Crosby name is prominent in the Celtic fringe region that borders Scotland and Wales—in Cumberland, Westmoreland, and Lancashire; it also appears, spelled "Crosbie," on gravestones in Bangor Abbey graveyard, Ulster, Northern Ireland, that date back to the eighteenth century.[5]

Most antebellum Piney Woods folk were as Celtic as the Crosbys. John F. H. Claiborne, whose account of his trip through the Piney Woods in the 1840s is perhaps the most comprehensive antebellum treatment of the area, makes four references to the Celtic background of the settlers in the space of few pages. "Spent the night with our old friend, Esquire Hathorn, of Covington County—a type of old Ireland, generous, ardent, enthusiastic, hospitable and a true-blue Republican," recalled Claiborne, who noted that the Piney Woods were full of "the Old Scotch [Scottish] families that originally settled this country," and remarked that "there are yet living in Greene [County] some of the original immigrants who speak nothing but the Gallic." A few pages later, Claiborne referred to the descendants of what he called "an ancient and honored race of Scotch [Scots] Presbyterians," and then mentioned, in discussing the "numerous herds of cattle" found in the region, a "worthy friend of ours, for many years a Senator in the Legislature, and universally known as *Long Johnny McLeod*, [who] owns, we were told, some two thousand head [of cattle]."[6]

Other sources confirm the prominence of Celtic names in the Piney Woods. "Tom Sullivan and a goodly number of the other piney woods settlers termed themselves Scotch-Irish," noted the historian of Sullivan's Hollow.[7] When the Walton Guards, of West Florida, organized to fight for the Confederacy in 1861, three of their four elected company officers bore the obviously Celtic names of McPherson, McKinnon, and McLeod.[8] And the names of cattlemen found in *Florida Cowman: A History of Florida Cattle Raising* could have been taken from the Belfast telephone directory.[9]

A comparison of the cultural characteristics of the premodern British Celts with those of the antebellum Piney Woods folk suggests that not only did the Celtic settlers of the Piney Woods bring with them and continue to practice their traditional ways and values; they appear to have imposed their life-style so successfully upon whatever ethnic minorities settled among them that a list of the Piney Woods traits most observed by contemporaries reads like an inventory of traditional Scottish, Irish, and Welsh cultural characteristics.

In making such comparisons it is important to recognize that only those cultural traits associated with British Celts up to the late eighteenth century are relevant. There are two reasons for this: first, all significant migration from Scotland, Ireland, and Wales to the American South ended before 1800; and second, English efforts to acculturize the Celts, which had been ongoing for centuries, forced a number of important changes in Celtic ways during the latter part of the eighteenth century.

Rather than give up their traditional customs, a significant number of Celts managed to preserve their old ways and values by migrating to such accommodating environments as the relatively unsettled wilderness of the American South. Had they stayed at home, they would have been compelled to change—to become more Anglicized—but by migrating to such isolated places as the southern Piney Woods, Celts could remain pretty much what they and their ancestors had always been.[10] As the distinguished cultural geographer Milton Newton points out, Celts were preadapted to the prevailing southern environment.[11] Celts had been pastoralists since antiquity, and they continued to be pastoralists in the American South.

In no place during the antebellum period was this more evident than in the Piney Woods, which was an ideal place for Celts to practice their pastoral traditions. "[T]he vast number of wild cattle which range about this quarter of North America, are almost incredible," wrote one Piney Woods visitor.[12] Another traveler referred to the region as being "peculiarly adapted to the rearing of hogs and cattle; . . . no where in the United States are they raised in greater number."[13] Other observers noted that the pine forests provided "excellent and abundant range for cattle";[14] that the region contained "immense herds of cattle";[15] that "the horned cattle and horses bred [there were] . . . large, sleek, sprightly, and fat";[16] and that the "high grass, which grows everywhere among the pine trees, opens an immense range for cattle."[17] In the 1840s John Claiborne defined both the region's economy and culture in a sentence: "The people are for the most part pastoral, their herds furnishing their chief revenue."[18] But it remained for another Mississippian to estimate the extent and the success of this grazing culture. In 1850 Ebenezer Ford of Marion County informed the U.S. Commissioner of Patents that for the past twenty years or more "a square [area] of about 200 miles," consisting of "about eight counties of [southern] Mississippi, two parishes in Louisiana, and two counties of Alabama bordering upon Mississippi" had raised "one million head of cattle yearly. The beef is sold," said Ford, "at 3 to 4 years old, from $10 to $12 per head."[19]

Besides cattle, the Piney Woods folk also produced large numbers of hogs. "Hogs are easily raised," noted one man, who saw herds of "from 500 to 1000."[20] Other observers mentioned vast quantities "or horses, hogs, and horned cattle";[21] how "hogs . . . pay largely, not only giving us all we can

43

consume but something to sell";[22] the significant amount of pork sent from the Piney Woods to Mobile and Pensacola;[23] and speculated that the "pine country . . . will probably forever remain an excellent range for hogs, cattle and horses."[24]

Data from the federal censuses confirm the observations of contemporaries that herding was the basic activity throughout the Piney Woods. In 1840 no fewer than twenty-five of the thirty-two counties of southern Mississippi (those south of the thirty-third parallel) contained more than four times as many beef cattle and hogs as people. Greene and Perry counties had thirteen times as many cows and pigs as people; Jones and Smith counties nearly eleven times as many. In 1850, although more people had moved into the Piney Woods, twenty-three of the thirty-two counties of southern Mississippi still contained more than four times as many beef cattle and hogs as people.[25]

The herding of cows and hogs on the same range was typically southern; indeed, it is one of the seventeen traits that Professor Terry Jordan shows, in his excellent study of the southern roots of western cattle ranching, to have been characteristic of herding practices throughout the antebellum South. Also included in Jordan's list of southern herding traits are such Piney Woods practices as "the use of open range, unrestricted by fences or natural barriers"; "the accumulation by individual owners of very large herds, amounting to hundreds or even thousands of cattle"; "the neglect of livestock"; "the marking and branding of cattle"; "overland cattle drives to feeder areas or markets along regularly used trails"; "the periodic burning of the range"; "and the raising of some field and garden crops, though livestock were the principal products of the system."[26]

In an article in the *Journal of Southern History*, which Forrest McDonald and I see as an extension rather than a criticism of Jordan's fine work, we show that the traits which Jordan says characterized southern herding were traditional in Scotland, Ireland, and Wales long before they were practiced in the American South.[27]

Unlike the English, who loved to plow and basically were tillage farmers,[28] the Celtic peoples of the British Isles objected to hard work. They disdained tillage agriculture, preferred instead to let their livestock make their living, and worked little except to mark or to drive their animals to market. In these and other ways their herding practices were almost exactly those that prevailed throughout the Old South, including open-range herding, overland-trail drives, and the neglect of their animals.[29] Scottish highlanders "trusted for winter provender solely to pasture grass," recalled a native. "Having little straw, and no hay, many cattle, in severe winters, perished for want."[30] An eighteenth-century visitor to the Western Isles of Scotland found no barns and reported that "common Work-Horses are expos'd . . . during the Winter and . . . have neither Corn, Hay, or but seldom Straw. . . . The Cows are likewise expos'd to the Rigour of the coldest Seasons, and become mere Skeletons in the Spring, many of them not being able to rise from the ground without help; but they recover as the Season becomes more favourable, and the Grass grows up."[31]

Livestock was no better cared for in Ireland or Wales. Barns were rare items in Ireland, where livestock "wintered on withered grass left ungrazed and uncut during the summer. The mild Irish winters made this possible," explained a scholar, "though on farms where no hay was available during periods of hard frost or snow, many cattle, especially in the north, actually perished from starvation, and all normally lost condition to such an extent that it took until the month of June each year before they began to thrive again." Even today, admits an authority, "Irish farmers . . . tend to be rather haphazard in their arrangements for stock wintering." In Wales the native cattle grew tough from neglect.[32]

The foremost characteristic of antebellum Piney Woods culture was its orientation toward leisure. "The men are generally idle, devoted to hunting, and the attention of their numerous herds," wrote a northerner who lived for a time in Mississippi.[33] There was no pressing need for the Piney Woods folk, at least the menfolk, to do much work, since most of them made their living from their livestock. They had ample free time, for they neither built barns nor grew special feed for their animals, which foraged and cared for themselves in the woods, and were only rounded up a couple of times a year to be branded or driven to market.[34] "One great advantage this country has over the northern states," a contemporary observed, "is that the men are not obliged to work for the beasts, the winter being so mild, that the cattle are fat in the woods all the year; this prevents a great deal of hard labour, which must be done in the hottest season, in the northern states."[35]

Neither the Piney Woods people nor their Celtic forebears devoted much time to tillage agriculture. Unlike Englishmen and Yankees, who were compulsive plowers and often obsessed with agricultural improvements,[36] Celts and most southerners cultivated crops reluctantly and haphazardly. They rarely used manure or other fertilizers, and their primitive techniques appalled outsiders.[37] "You will perceive that little improvement is made at the South in agricultural pursuits generally," a Mississippian admitted in 1850. Corn production in the Piney Woods averaged only "15 to 20 bushels per acre," compared to fifty to sixty bushels per acre in New York, thirty-five to forty in Ohio and Indiana, and thirty to forty in Maine and Massachusetts. In 1849 near Augusta, Maine, where corn was heavily manured and carefully cultivated, one man raised "95 bushels of shelled corn, to the acre"; another "72 bushels"; and a third "71 bushels, at an estimated cost of $17." It cost the Piney Woods folk, using their lackadaisical methods, only fifty cents to produce a bushel of corn. Besides their carelessly grown corn, they frequently raised sweet potatoes; indeed, John Claiborne reported that in some counties "the main crop is the *sweet potato.*" It would grow "with little culture" on soils that were "too thin to produce corn." Claiborne claimed that a single acre would "yield from three to five hundred bushels," but another Mississippian considered 150 bushels of sweet potatoes per acre, at a production cost of twenty cents per bushel, an average yield.[38]

It was traditional among the Scots, Irish, and Welsh to devote no more of their energy to tillage than did the Piney Woods people. At the end of the eighteenth century one Highland minister estimated that the average farm in his parish consisted of 27 acres devoted to tillage and 34,973 acres devoted to open range; another minister confessed that most of his parishioners preferred fishing to working, and that "their mode of farming required little of their attention."[39]

A scholar noted that "Ireland is a country of grass and pasturage," and that it has depended "less upon tillage than any other European land." "Tillage, though ample to supply the limited needs of the country, was not extensive," observed an authority on seventeenth-century Ireland. "Tillage does not thrive in this country," bemoaned an eighteenth-century visitor to Ireland; another traveler stated: "agriculture is at a very low ebb in this country; . . . you may ride for miles, in the most fertile part of it, without seeing an acre of ploughed ground." Critics claimed that the Irish would plant only cabbages and potatoes, which grew appropriately enough in "lazy beds."[40]

Nor were the Welsh different. "From very early times the rearing of cattle rather than crops has been the chief occupation of Welsh Farmers," noted an authority. Another scholar concluded that the Welsh clung to their old agricultural ways well into the nineteenth century. "Agriculture remained medieval in simplicity until about 1760," insisted still another authority, who stated that as "late as 1812, 1,700,000 acres, out of the entire area of Wales [approximately 8,000 square miles], were left uncultivated, though nearly half of this was capable of development."[41]

Observers of traditional British Celts and observers of antebellum Piney Woods folk, apparently without any awareness of each other's observations, found the two cultures to be remarkably similar, even in the habits and customs these observers deplored. Some of the failings they attributed to Celts and Piney Woods people alike were indolence, drinking, swearing, smoking, gambling, and fighting. Scottish Celts, the Welsh, and the Irish, observers claimed, were generally "indolent," noted "for their remarkable Laziness"; "averse to industry, never working but from necessity"; "holding that bodily labour of all sorts was mean and disgraceful," they were devoted to "sloth," and were cursed with "nastyness and laziness, wherefore having enough before hand to furnish them with potatoes, milk & tobacco . . . sitting upon their hams, like greyhounds in the sun, near their cabbin, they'l work not one jott." Moreover, insisted observers, these British Celts were "a drunken kind of people," whose "propensity for intoxication has been remarkable from the earliest times." They gambled, sometimes recklessly, used great quantities of tobacco "in all its forms," and were much addicted to swearing and fighting (often their duels were bloody).[42]

According to observers, the Piney Woods folk possessed these same characteristics. "The people . . . are indolent, devoted to raising cattle, hunting, and drinking whiskey," complained a Yankee. "They are a wild race, with but little order or morals among them."[43] The laziness of a Piney Woodsman, who "owned more than a thousand cattle," surprised one visitor. In response to his request for a cup of milk, the cattleman replied that his family never used milk "because the cows were always ranging through the woods, [and] he had found it too troublesome to hunt them up and milk them."[44]

Another observer stated that Piney Woods folk rarely worked, and were much too "fond of drinking, gambling, and horse racing. From these sports," he explained, "quarrels often arise, which are sometimes ended by the dirk (the most common mode of fighting is gouging and dirking) or [by the] pistol."[45] Other visitors complained about the "deplorable" state of Piney Woods society,[46] the roughness and "wickedness" of the people,[47] and their addiction to tobacco and spitting.[48] Moreover, exclaimed a Yankee, "They are profane, and excessively addicted to gambling. This horrible vice . . . prevails like an epidemic. Money gotten easily, and without labour, is easily lost. Betting and horse-racing are amusements eagerly pursued, and often times to the ruin of the parties."[49] Not only did the Piney Woods folk gamble, they drank—wine, whiskey, sweet potato liquor—whatever came to hand. One visitor saw a town full of people "playing *seven up, old sledge*, or some such game, on the head of a whisky barrel, and others were discussing the preliminaries of a quarter [horse] race."[50] Another traveler watched a native drink "between supper and bed time . . . nearly a whole decanter of bad whiskey."[51]

Drinking often led to violence. John Claiborne noted that several "affairs of honor" at a resort in Marion County had shut the place down. He also mentioned that the violent ways of one man had won him "the title of 'Bloody-shoe.' "[52] "The men [of this region]," insisted another visitor, "are 'sudden and quick in quarrel.' The dirk or the pistol is always at hand. Fatal duels frequently occur."[53] Anyone who doubts the violent nature of Piney Woods society should peruse Chester Sullivan's little book on Sullivan Hollow.[54]

The informal and rural ways of Piney Woods culture seemed primitive to most observers. John Claiborne noted that the houses, "built of logs, partly left unchinked at all seasons of the year," often "stand from ten to twenty miles apart."[55] Charles Lanman, who traveled from Mobile to Augusta in the 1850s, spent the first night of his journey "in a cabin on Dog river. Our . . . bed-room was ventilated on an entirely new principle; that is to say, by wide cracks in the floor, broad spaces between the logs that composed the walls, huge openings in the roof, and a window with a shutter that could not be closed."[56] Roads and bridges—where there were any—were poorly constructed and maintained.[57] This was typical, one man claimed, because of the people's "extraordinary indifference to practical internal improvements."[58]

Towns in the Piney Woods were few and dilapidated. "There is nothing in the town [of Winchester, in Wayne County] to cheer up the spirits of the traveler," wrote one man. "The town is literally tumbling to pieces."[59] A visitor to Augusta, in Perry County, wrote: "I must not attempt to describe [it], except as one of the worst specimens of a Mississippi village."[60] John Claiborne claimed that Augusta consisted of

> some eight or ten miserable tenements. . . . Scarce a tree stood in the gaping square for the eye to rest upon; the grass was all withered up. . . . Even of these dilapidated dwellings several were unoccupied, and we rode round half the town before we could find a living thing to direct us to the tavern. We finally reached it and found it "alone in its glory," a small log cabin with one room and a shed! Stable there was none, nor bar, nor landlord, nor barkeeper.[61]

What observers said about houses, inns, towns, and internal improvements in the Piney Woods was precisely what observers said about those things in pre–nineteenth-century Scotland, Ireland, and Wales. Critics agreed that the British Celts usually lived in "badly built," "miserably dirty, smoky, and meanly furnished" cabins that were often as full of gaps and cracks as any Piney Woods structure. Observers also emphasized that in Scotland, Ireland, and Wales inns and towns were few and unimpressive. Some men claimed that there were no decent inns in all of Celtic Britain;

others simply referred to the inns and towns they visited as "wretched" or "loathsome." Moreover, all agreed that in general roads were bad, bridges were few and rickety, and travel through the wilds of Ireland, Scotland, and Wales was difficult and uncomfortable.[62]

The furnishings in both Celtic and Piney Woods homes were as simple and as unpretentious as the manners of the homeowners. Charles Lanman described staying overnight at a "cabin in the pine woods, belonging to an . . . obliging man [whose] estate numbered a thousand acres. . . . It was evident that this family was well enough off to live in comfort," observed Lanman, "but, true to habits which prevail among a large class in the South," they lived quite modestly. Slaves of all ages, with a market value that Lanman estimated at "not less than ten thousand dollars," roamed about the dwelling,

> yet . . . wooden benches were used in the place of chairs, one iron spoon answered for the whole family, and the mother added the sugar . . . to the coffee with her fingers, and tasted each cup before sending it round to ascertain if it was right. Such things as andirons, tongs, and wash-basins were considered useless; and the bedstead upon which we slept was a mere board. . . . All [twenty members of] the family, excepting the parents and two sons, were barefooted, and yet the girls sported large finger rings in abundance, and wore basque dresses of calico.[63]

Despite the informal style of Celts and Piney Woods folk, few people anywhere could match their hospitality. Even some of the most critical travelers mentioned the warmth with which these plain people received them. It was customary in both the Celtic areas of the British Isles and the Piney Woods to overwhelm people with food and to encourage them to eat all they could; it also was traditional in both places, as an eighteenth-century Scottish lady explained, "to please your company." Travelers could hardly say enough in praise of the kindness of Piney Woods folk, who were, in the words of John Claiborne, "ever ready to welcome the wayfarer to their hospitable firesides"; "if you are disposed to be convivial, you may dine with some one . . . every day." "They welcomed us to everything and we set off with our pockets filled with biscuits, jerked venison and *potato chips*. . . . Few persons quenched their thirst [even in the most ramshackled towns] . . . without inviting the strangers to join them."[64]

Both Celts and Piney Woods people tried to be self-sufficient, supplementing their rude tillage with fish and game. Expert marksmen, they hunted regularly and with delight. Fast horses and packs of dogs were as much a part of their lives as hogs and cattle.[65] "Among their ancient amusements, which are still unchanged, is hunting," wrote a Piney Woods visitor. "They keep fine horses, and have their trained packs of hounds."[66] "The woods abound with game; the streams with fish; many persons keep hounds," and even small boys were experts at hunting and fishing, observed one traveler, who dined on delicious venison and trout brought in by "two little fellows that looked almost too small to shoulder a gun."[67] In a log cabin that another traveler called "one of the worst of its kind," he counted thirteen "guns . . . *hung* up along the rafters or stacked up in the only two rooms of the house."[68]

This observation about guns revealed much about values. Celts, antebellum southerners, and Piney Woods people were less materialistic—less oriented toward the making of money—than most Western cultures. Pre–nineteenth-century Celts boasted that they coveted no wealth; as pastoralists and warriors, they "despised" trade and what they called "mercenary Employments." To show her contempt for money, an eighteenth-century Scottish woman, in the words of her debtor, "lighted her pipe with the note I gave her for the money I owed her."[69] A Yankee who visited the Piney Woods of southwestern Alabama said that " 'Take no thought of the morrow' appears to be the motto of very many of the southern population."[70] Another Yankee observed that southerners, including Piney Woods folk, "are more reckless of the value of money, than any people that I have seen." He also noted that southerners were less impressed by wealth than most other people.[71] Still another visitor insisted that there was "no part of the world where great wealth confers so little rank, or is attended with so few advantages [as in the South]."[72] Indeed, a man who traveled through the Piney Woods contended that southerners coveted dogs more than money.[73]

Celts and Piney Woods people were alike in numerous other ways. They married early, had lots of children, enjoyed their sensual pleasures, and usually lived long and healthy lives.[74] "Marriages take place when the parties are very young, and mothers of fifteen are not uncommon," remarked a Piney Woods visitor, who also claimed the natives were so remarkably healthy that doctors either moved away or starved.[75] Other visitors observed farmhouses "literally swarming with children," families with from ten to fifteen children, and one family that "consisted of . . . *eighteen* children, three of whom were girls, whose average weight we estimated at two hundred pounds."[76]

Neither Celts nor Piney Woods people were "bookish"; formal education meant less to them than learning to master their natural environment.[77] "Only two of [one Piney Woods family's] . . . eighteen children . . . knew how to read," observed a sojourner,[78] and another traveler stated that throughout the South "there is not attached sufficient importance to that part of education which fits for rational conversation and usefulness."[79]

Southerners and Celts were oral and aural people, who delighted in oratory—from the stump or the pulpit; they also were clannish, superstitious, and more emotional than rational in their personal, political, and religious beliefs and actions. Nothing delighted them more than parties and music.[80] The fiddle, which became the favorite instrument in Scotland and Ireland after the English government outlawed harps and bagpipes,[81] was always the favorite in the Piney Woods. Whole families played the fiddle by ear, as did their Celtic ancestors, and the tunes they played most often—the ones the people of the Piney Woods most loved to hear and dance to—were Scottish reels and Irish jigs.[82] Also in keeping with their Celtic cultural tradition, Piney Woods folk—young and old—"were so fond of dancing," exclaimed one visitor, "that . . . they would 'dance all night till broad daylight.' "[83]

There is no indication that either the Celts or their Piney Woods descendants regarded their ways as unusual or reprehensible. Laziness and a lack of ambition—which good Englishmen and Yankees considered deplorable—were viewed differently by traditional Celts and antebellum southerners. They delighted in their livestock culture and their comfortable customs. Being lazy did not mean to them being indolent, shiftless, slothful, and worthless; it meant being free from work, having spare time to do as they pleased, being at liberty, and enjoying their leisure. They saw no point in working when their livestock would make their living; they thought anyone who worked when he did not have to was crazy. Nor did they see any reason to have more than they could eat, or drink, or wear, or ride. Unlike a conscientious Englishman or northerner, when a Celt or southerner said that he was being lazy, he was not reproaching himself but merely describing his state of comfort. He suffered no guilt when he spent his time pleasantly—hunting, fishing, dancing, drinking, gambling, fighting, or just loafing and talking.

Notes

1. John D. W. Guice, "Cattle Raisers of the Old Southwest: A Reinterpretation," *Western Historical Quarterly* 8 (1977):167–87; Terry G. Jordan, *Trails to Texas: Southern Roots of*

Western Cattle Ranching (Lincoln and London: University of Nebraska Press, 1981), 25–58; Kenneth D. Israel, "A Geographical Analysis of the Cattle Industry in Southeastern Mississippi from Its Beginnings to 1860" (Ph.D. diss., University of Southern Mississippi, 1970). See also Joe A. Akerman, Jr., *Florida Cowman: A History of Florida Cattle Raising* (Kissimmee, Fla.: Florida Cattlemen's Association, 1976).

2. Anne Ross, *Everyday Life of the Pagan Celts* (London: B. T. Batsford, 1970); T. G. E. Powell, *The Celts* (New York: Frederick A. Praeger, 1958); Gerhard Herm, *The Celts: The People Who Came out of the Darkness* (New York: St. Martin's Press, 1977); Goldwin Smith, *A History of England*, 4th ed. (New York: Charles Scribner's Sons, 1974), 1–164; Archibald A. M. Duncan, *Scotland: The Making of the Kingdom* (New York: Barnes & Noble, 1975), 1–132; Eoin MacNeill, *Celtic Ireland* (1921; reprint, Dublin: Academic Press, 1981); L. M. Cullen, *Life in Ireland* (London: B. T. Batsford, 1979), 1–49; Lloyd Laing, *Celtic Britain* (New York: Charles Scribner's Sons, 1979), 1–171.

3. See, for example, Forrest McDonald and Grady McWhiney, "The Antebellum Southern Herdsman: A Reinterpretation," *Journal of Southern History* 41 (1975): 147–166; Forrest McDonald and Grady McWhiney, "The South from Self-Sufficiency to Peonage: An Interpretation," *American Historical Review* 85 (1980): 1095–1118; Forrest McDonald and Grady McWhiney, "The Celtic South," *History Today* 30 (1980): 11–15; Forrest McDonald and Ellen Shapiro McDonald, "The Ethnic Origins of the American People, 1790," *William and Mary Quarterly* 37 (1980): 179–99; Forrest McDonald, "The Ethnic Factor in Alabama History: A Neglected Dimension," *Alabama Review* 31 (1978): 256–65; Grady McWhiney, "The Revolution in Nineteenth-Century Alabama Agriculture," *Alabama Review* 31 (1978): 3–32; Grady McWhiney, "Continuity in Celtic Warfare," *Continuity: A Journal of History* 2 (1981): 1–18; Grady McWhiney, "Saving the Best from the Past," *Alabama Review* 32 ((1979): 243–72; Grady McWhiney and Perry D. Jamieson, *Attack and Die: Civil War Military Tactics and the Southern Heritage* (University: University of Alabama Press, 1982); Grady McWhiney and Forrest McDonald, "Celtic Names in the Antebellum Southern United States," *Names: Journal of the American Name Society:* 31 (1983): 89–102; Grady McWhiney and Gary B. Mills, "Jimmie Davis and His Music: An Interpretation," *Journal of American Culture* 6 (1983): 54–57; Grady McWhiney, "Education in the Old South: A Reexamination," in *The Southern Enigma: Essays on Race, Class, and Folk Culture*, ed. Walter J. Fraser, Jr., and Winfred B. Moore, Jr. (Westport, Conn.: Greenwood, 1983), 169–88.

4. McWhiney and McDonald, "Celtic Names in the Antebellum Southern United States," 93–102; McDonald and McDonald, "The Ethnic Origins of the American People, 1790," 179–99.

5. G.W.S. Barrow, *Robert Bruce and the Community of the Realm of Scotland*, 2d ed. (Edinburgh: Edinburgh University Press, 1976), 30; George F. Black, *The Surnames of Scotland: Their Origin, Meaning, and History* (1946; reprint, New York: New York Public Library, 1979), 187–88; Edward MacLysaght, *The Surnames of Ireland* (1964; reprint, Dublin: Irish Academic Press, 1980), 66; Robert E. Matheson, *Varieties and Synonymes of Surnames and Christian Names in Ireland . . .* (Dublin: His Majesty's Stationery Office, 1901), 37; Henry Barber, *British Family Names: Their Origin and Meaning . . .* (1903; reprint, Baltimore: Genealogical Pub. Co., 1968), 123; Charles W. Bardsley, *A Dictionary of English and Welsh Surnames . . .* , rev. ed. (Baltimore: Genealogical Pub. Co., 1980), 219; A.C.W. Merrick, comp., *Barony of Ards*, vol. 17 of *Gravestone Inscriptions: County Down* (Belfast: Ulster Historical Foundation, 1978), 48. None of the standard sources lists Crosby as an English name, but only as a Scottish, Irish, or border country name. Barber, *British Family Names*; Bardsley, *Dictionary of English and Welsh Surnames*; Henry Brougham Guppy, *Homes of Family Names in Great Britain* (1890; reprint, Baltimore: Genealogical Pub. Co., 1968); Sir William Addison, *Understanding English Surnames* (London: B. T. Batsford, 1978).

6. John F. H. Claiborne, "A Trip through the Piney Woods," *Publications of the Mississippi Historical Society* 9 (1906): 515, 521, 527, 530.

7. Chester Sullivan, *Sullivan's Hollow* (Jackson: University Press of Mississippi, 1978), 13.

8. William James Wells, *Pioneering in the Panhandle: A Look at Selected Events and Families as Part of the History of South Santa Rosa County, Florida* (Fort Walton Beach, Fla.: Melvin Business Services, 1976), 43.

9. Akerman, *Florida Cowman*, 281–87.

10. McWhiney and McDonald, "Celtic Names in the Antebellum South," 93-102; McDonald and McWhiney, "The South from Self-Sufficiency to Peonage," 1107-1111; McDonald and McWhiney, "The Celtic South," 11-15; Sir John Sinclair, ed., *The Statistical Account of Scotland, 1791-1799*, 20 vols. (1791-99; reprint, East Ardsley, England: EP Publishing, 1981), 17: 20-21, 523.

11. Milton Newton, "Cultural Preadaptation and the Upland South," *Geoscience and Man* 5 (1974): 143-54.

12. James Sharan, *The Adventures of James Sharan: Compiled from the Journal Written during His Voyages and Travels . . .* (Baltimore: G. Dobbins & Murphey, 1808), 99.

13. Samuel R. Brown, *The Western Gazetteer; or, Emigrant's Directory, Containing a Geographical Description of the Western States and Territories . . .* (Auburn, N.Y.: H. C. Southwick, 1817), 126, 230.

14. William Darby, *The Emigrant's Guide to the Western and Southwestern States and Territories . . .* (New York: Kirk & Mercein, 1818), 35.

15. Claiborne, "A Trip through the Piney Woods," 523.

16. [Daniel Blowe], *A Geographical, Historical, Commercial, and Agricultural View of the United States of America; Forming a Complete Emigrant's Directory through Every Part of the Republic . . .* (London: Edwards & Knibb, 1820), 714.

17. Timothy Flint, *Recollections of the Last Ten Years*, ed. C. Hartley Grattan (1826; reprint, New York: Alfred A. Knopf, 1932), 306-7.

18. Claiborne, "A Trip through the Piney Woods," 515.

19. Eben'r Ford to Thomas Ewbank, 6 Nov. 1850, *Report of the Commissioner of Patents, for the Year 1850. Part II. Agriculture* (Washington, D.C.: Office of Printers to House of Reps., 1851), 260-61.

20. H[arry] Toulmin, "A Geographical and Statistical Sketch of the District of Mobile," *American Register* 6 (1810):332-33.

21. John Pope, *A Tour through the Southern and Western Territories of the United States of North America . . .* (Richmond, Va., 1792), 43.

22. Edward G. Stewart [of Tangipahoa Parish, Louisiana] to John W. Gurley, 27 Jan. 1859, John W. Gurley Papers, Louisiana State University.

23. David B. Warden, *A Statistical, Political, and Historical Account of the United States of North America* (Philadelphia: T. Wardle, 1819), 18.

24. Brown, *Western Gazetteer*, 230.

25. *Compendium of the . . . Inhabitants and Statistics of the United States, . . . from the Returns of the Sixth Census . . .* (Washington: Thomas Allen, 1841), 56-57, 226-27; *Statistical View of the United States, . . . Being a Compendium of the Seventh Census . . .* (Washington: A. O. P. Nicholson, 1854), 261-63.

26. Jordan, *Trails to Texas*, 25-26.

27. Grady McWhiney and Forrest McDonald, "Celtic Origins of Southern Herding Practices," *Journal of Southern History* 51 (1985):165-82.

28. Warren O. Ault, *Open-Field Farming in Medieval England: A Study of Village By-Laws* (London: George Allen & Unwin, 1972), 46-52, 90, 102-51; Joan Thirsk, ed., *The Agrarian History of England and Wales, 1500-1640* (Cambridge: Cambridge University Press, 1967), 2-6.

29. Duncan, *Scotland*, 357; E. Estyn Evans, *Irish Heritage: The Landscape, the People and Their Work* (Dundalk: Dundalgan Press, 1977), 48-49, 51-52, 55; Mary Corbett Harris, "Drovers and Hill Farms," *Crafts, Customs and Legends of Wales* (Newton Abbot, England: David & Charles, 1980), 10-11, 19-20; Eugene O'Curry, *On the Manners and Customs of the Ancient Irish*, ed. W. K. Sullivan, 3 vols. (1873; reprint, New York: Lemma Pub. Corp., 1971), 1:ccclxx; Ian Whyte, *Agriculture and Society in Seventeenth-Century Scotland* (Edinburgh: John Donald Pubs., 1979), 85; Henry Boswell, *Historical Description of New and Elegant Picturesque Views of the Antiquities of England and Wales . . . and Other Curiosities in Scotland and Ireland . . .* (London: Alexander Hogg, [1786]); Raymond D. Crotty, *Irish Agricultural Production: Its Volume and Structure* (Cork: Cork University Press, 1966), 2-6; Bruce Lenman, *An Economic History of Modern Scotland, 1660-1976* (Hamden, Conn.: Archon Books, 1977), 23-24, 39, 57, 63, 67-68, 70-71, 87-89; R. Ian Jack, *Medieval Wales* (Ithaca, N.Y.: Cornell University Press, 1972), 196-97; Sir Leonard Twiston Davies and Averyl

Edwards, *Welsh Life in the Eighteenth Century* (London: Country Life, 1939), 1–2, 6, 8–9, 10, 20, 225; C. A. J. Skeel, "The Cattle Trade between Wales and England from the Fifteenth to the Nineteenth Centuries," *Transactions of the Royal Historical Society*, 4th ser., 9 (1926):135–58; C. Lowther, *Our Journey into Scotland Anno Domini 1629, 5th of November from Lowther*, ed. W. D. (Edinburgh: David Douglas, 1894), 13–14; Robert Forbes, *Journals of the Episcopal Visitations of the Right Rev. Robert Forbes, M.A., of the Dioceses of Ross and Caithness, . . . 1762 & 1770 . . .*, ed. J. B. Craven (London: Skeffington & Son, 1886), 144; John Loveday, *Diary of a Tour in 1732 through Parts of England, Wales, Ireland and Scotland* (Edinburgh, 1890), 111, 162; William Gilpin, *Observations, Relative Chiefly to Picturesque Beauty, Made in the Year 1776, on Several Parts of Great Britain; Particularly the High-Lands of Scotland*, 2 vols. (London: R. Blamire, 1789), 2:135–36; Edward Burt, *Burt's Letters from the North of Scotland*, ed. R. Jamieson, 2 vols. (1754; reprint, Edinburgh: John Donald Pubs., 1974), 2:132–33, 151–54; Martin Martin, *A Description of the Western Islands of Scotland*, 2d ed. (1716; reprint, Edinburgh: James Thin, 1981), 85–86, 205–6; David W. Howell, "The Economy of the Landed Estates of Rembrokeshire, c. 1680–1830," *Welsh History Review* 3 (1966):165–83; Sinclair, ed., *Statistical Account of Scotland*, 17:19–20, 27, 234, 287, 408, 672; J. G. Fyfe, ed., *Scottish Diaries and Memoirs, 1746–1843* (Stirling: Eneas MacKay, 1942), 260–61; P. Hume Brown, ed., *Scotland before 1700 from Contemporary Documents* (Edinburgh: David Douglas, 1893), 7, 10; W. R. Kermack, *Historical Geography of Scotland* (Edinburgh: W. & A. K. Johnston, 1926), 67, 71–72; Daniel Defoe, *A Tour through the Whole Island of Great Britain*, ed. Pat Rogers (1724–26; reprint, New York: Penguin, 1971), 377, 599, 664; Arthur Young, *Arthur Young's Tour in Ireland (1776–1779)*, ed. Arthur Wollaston Hutton, 2 vols. (London: George Bell & Sons, 1892), 1:150–51, 345; Edward MacLysaght, *Irish Life in the Seventeenth Century* (1939; reprint, Dublin: Irish Academic Press, 1979), 167–68, 171–72, 181, 243–44; E. Estyn Evans, *Irish Folk Ways* (London: Routledge & Kegan Paul, 1957), 20, 33; Maire de Paor and Liam de Paor, *Early Christian Ireland* (London: Thames & Hudson, 1978), 77, 79, 88, 92.

30. Sinclair, ed., *Statistical Account of Scotland*, 17:547.

31. Martin, *Description of the Western Islands*, 154–55.

32. MacLysaght, *Irish Life in the Seventeenth Century*, 170; Young, *Arthur Young's Tour in Ireland*, 2:107–8; Michael Dillon, "Farmers and Fishermen," *Ireland by the Irish*, ed. Michael Gorman (London: Galley, 1963), 42; Thirsk, *Agrarian History of England and Wales*, 116–17; Harris, "Drovers and Hill Farms," 16; Davies and Edwards, *Welsh Life in the Eighteenth Century*, 3.

33. James Pearse, *A Narrative of the Life of James Pearse . . .* (Rutland, Vt.: William Fay, 1825), 52.

34. Claiborne, "A Trip through the Piney Woods," 515, 521, 522, 530; Flint, *Recollections*, 305, 306–7; Brown, *Western Gazetteer*, 126; Walter Prichard, ed., "A Tourist's Description of Louisiana in 1860," *Louisiana Historical Quarterly* 21 (1938):1160; Wells, *Pioneering in the Panhandle*, 264.

35. John Budd, quoted in Eugene L. Schwaab, ed., *Travels in the Old South: Selected from Periodicals of the Times*, 2 vols. (Lexington: University Press of Kentucky, 1973), 1:21.

36. John Yeoman, *The Diary of the Visits of John Yeoman to London in the Years 1774 and 1777*, ed. MacLeod Yearsley (London: Watts, 1934), 20; Henri Misson, *M. Misson's Memoirs and Observations in His Travels over England . . .*, trans. Mr. Ozell (London: D. Brown, 1719), 43; Frederika Bremer, *England in 1851; or, Sketches of a Tour in England*, trans. by L. A. H. (Boulogne: Merridew, 1853), 124; Thirsk, *Agrarian History of England and Wales*, 2–15; Eric Kerridge, *The Agricultural Revolution* (New York: Augustus M. Kelley Pubs., 1968), 161–64; William Faux, *Memorable Days in America: Being a Journal of a Tour in the United States . . .* (London: W. Simpkin & R. Marshall, 1823), 409–11; Felix de Beaujour, *Sketch of the United States of North America . . .*, trans. William Walton (London: J. Booth, 1814), 84; William Cobbett, *A Years Residence in the United States of America* (1818–19; reprint, New York: Augustus M. Kelley, 1969), 12, 79, 163, 183; Timothy Dwight, *Travels in New England and New York*, ed. Barbara Miller Solomon with the assistance of Patricia M. King, 4 vols. (Cambridge: Harvard University Press, 1969), 1:75–77, 272–73; 2:165; 3:100, 212–13; 4:216–17; *Report of the Commissioner of Patents, . . . 1850*, 276, 282–83, 303, 312–15.

37. Sir William Brereton, *Travels in Holland the United Provinces, England, Scotland, and Ireland, 1634–1635*, ed. Edward Hawkins (Manchester: Chetham Society, 1844), 132; John Knox, *A Tour through the Highlands of Scotland and the Hebrides Isles in 1786* (1787; reprint, Edinburgh: James Thin, 1975), 122; Sinclair, *Statistical Account of Scotland*, 17:231, 305, 414, 562; Defoe, *Tour*, 660; Burt, *Burt's Letters*, 2:145–48; Young, *Arthur Young's Tour in Ireland*, 1:211, 237, 249; 2:21–22; Evans, *Irish Heritage*, 87–88; MacLysaght, *Irish Life in the Seventeenth Century*, 173–74; Robert Everest, *A Journey through the United States and Part of Canada* (London: J. Chapman, 1855), 84–85, 100; Charles F. Hoffman, *A Winter in the West*, 2 vols. (New York: Harper & Bros., 1835), 2:248–49; Henry B. Whipple, *Bishop Whipple's Southern Diary, 1843–1844*, ed. Lester B. Shippee (Minneapolis: University of Minnesota Press, 1937), 80, 189; Charles G. Parsons, *Inside View of Slavery; or, a Tour among the Planters* (Boston: J. P. Jewett, 1855), 53–66; Schwaab, ed., *Travels in the Old South*, 1:142; *Farmers' Register* 1 (1833):167; *Tennessee Farmer* 2 (1837):41, 115; Sullivan, *Sullivan's Hollow*, 9; J. F. H. Claiborne, *Rough Riding Down South* (1862; reprint, Hattiesburg: University of Southern Mississippi, 1984), 29. It is significant that seventeen of some twenty-four antebellum southern agricultural journals devoted to the improvement of farming techniques failed before they had published for five years. These statistics were compiled from Albert L. Demaree, *The American Agricultural Press, 1819–1860* (New York: Columbia University Press, 1940), 367, 373–74, 393–98.

38. Ford to Ewbank, 6 Nov. 1850, *Report of the Commissioner of Patents, . . . 1850*, 259–60; Flint, *Recollections*, 316; *Report of the Commissioner of Patents, . . . 1850*, 251, 269, 296, 374, 396, 434; Claiborne, "Trip through the Piney Woods," 533.

39. Brown, ed., *Scotland before 1700*, 45; R. W. Chapman, ed., *Johnson's Journey to the Western Islands of Scotland and Boswell's Journal of a Tour to the Hebrides with Samuel Johnson, LL.D.* (Oxford: Oxford University Press, 1970), 144; Sinclair, ed., *Statistical Account of Scotland*, 17:198–99, 177, 133, 547.

40. Conrad M. Arensberg, *The Irish Countryman: An Anthropological Study* (1937; reprint, Glouchester, Mass.: Peter Smith, 1959), 38; Young, *Arthur Young's Tour in Ireland*, 1:400; Thomas Campbell, *A Philosophical Survey of the South of Ireland, in a Series of Letters to John Walkinson, M.D.* (London: W. Strahan, 1777), 151; MacLysaght, *Irish Life in the Seventeenth Century*, 171, 110; Taylor Downing, ed., *The Troubles* (London: Thames/Mcdonald Futura Publishers, 1980), 38.

41. Leslie Alcock, "Some Reflections on Early Welsh Society and Economy," *Welsh History Review* 2 (1964):3; Harris, "Drovers and Hill Farms," 15; Davies and Edwards, *Welsh Life in the Eighteenth Century*, 1.

42. Burt, *Burt's Letters*, 1:110, 113; Defoe, *Tour*, 590; Sinclair, ed., *Statistical Account of Scotland*, 17:4, 33, 64, 133–36, 193, 300, 323, 334, 370, 441, 473–74, 493, 518, 681–82; Charles Rogers, *Social Life in Scotland: From Early to Recent Times*, 2 vols. (1884; reprint, Port Washington, N.Y.: Kennikat, 1971), 2:256, 340; Davies and Edwards, *Welsh Life in the Eighteenth Century*, 3, 46, 139–40; Fynes Moryson, *Shakespeare's Europe: Unpublished Chapters of Fynes Moryson's Itinerary; Being a Survey of the Conditions of Europe at the End of the 16th Century*, ed. Charles Hughes (London: Sherratt & Hughes, 1903), 483; Philip Luckombe, *A Tour through Ireland* (Dublin: J. & R. Byrn, 1780), 40; Young, *Arthur Young's Tour in Ireland*, 1:249, 144–45; Thomas Dineley, *Observations in a Voyage through the Kingdom of Ireland . . . in the Year 1681* (Dublin: University Press, 1870), 17–19; James Erksine, *Extracts from the Diary of a Senator of the College of Justice, 1717–1718*, ed. James Maidment (Edinburgh: Thomas G. Stevenson, 1843), 28–31; Lowther, *Our Journal*, 16–17; *Journal of a Tour through the Northern Counties of Scotland and the Orkney Isles, in Autumn 1797* (Edinburgh: J. Ritchie, 1798), 87; John Mill, *The Diary of the Reverend John Mill, Minister of the Parishes of Dunrossness, Sandwick and Cunninghsburgh in Shetland, 1740–1803 . . .* , ed. Gilbert Goudie (Edinburgh: Scottish Historical Society, 1889), 24, 47; Joseph Taylor, *Journey to Edenborough in Scotland*, ed. William Cowan (Edinburgh: William Brown, 1903), 136–37; Fyfe, ed., *Scottish Diaries and Memoirs*, 79, 106–7, 133, 180–82, 190–91, 228, 320, 330–331, 491, 496–97, 552; John Edward Walsh, *Sketches of Ireland Sixty Years Ago* (Dublin: James McGlashan, 1847), 18, 60, 62–63, 66; Edward D. Clarke, *A Tour through the South of England, Wales, and Part of Ireland, Made During the Summer of 1791* (London: R. Edwards, 1793), 326–27; *Letters from an Armenian in Ireland, to his Friends*

at Trebisond, &c., trans. Edmond S. Pery, Viscount Pery (London: W. Owen, 1757), 147–48; James Logan, *The Scottish Gael; or, Celtic Manners, as Preserved among the Highlanders . . .* , 2 vols. (1876; reprint, Edinburgh: John Donald, 1976), 2:316; Loveday, *Diary of a Tour in 1732*, 164–65; Gilpin, *Observations*, 1:211; De Latocnaye, *A Frenchman's Walk through Ireland, 1796–97*, trans. and ed. John Stevenson (Belfast: McCaw, Stevenson & Orr, 1917).

43. Flint, *Recollections*, 307.

44. Lanman, *Adventures*, 2:168.

45. Pearse, *Narrative*, 52.

46. John Freeman Schermerhorn and Samuel J. Mills, *A Correct View of That Part of the United States Which Lies West of the Allegany Mountains, with Regard to Religion and Morals* (Hartford, Conn.: P. B. Gleason, 1814), 30.

47. Jacob Young, *Autobiography of a Pioneer; or, the Nativity, Experience, Travels, and Ministerial Labors of Rev. Jacob Young; with Incidents, Observations, and Reflections* (Cincinnati: Cranston & Curts, 1857), 222–23.

48. David W. Mitchell, *Ten Years in the United States; Being an Englishman's View of Men and Things in the North and South* (London: Smith, Elder, 1862), 47.

49. Flint, *Recollections*, 324.

50. Claiborne, "Trip through the Piney Woods," 519–20. See also Joseph G. Baldwin, *The Flush Times of Alabama and Mississippi* (New York: D. Appleton, 1853), 43; Flint, *Recollections*, 323.

51. Lanman, *Adventures*, 2:192.

52. Claiborne, "Trip through the Piney Woods," 512, 510–11.

53. Flint, *Recollections*, 324.

54. Sullivan, *Sullivan's Hollow*, 13, 17, 32–50, 63–64, 70, 78–81.

55. Claiborne, "Trip through the Piney Woods," 515.

56. Lanman, *Adventures*, 2:191.

57. [Rev. George Rogers], *Memoranda of the Experience, Labors, and Travels of a Universalist Preacher* (Cincinnati: J. A. Gurley, 1845), 265; Young, *Autobiography*, 223; Claiborne, *Rough Riding Down South*, 34, 36; Claiborne, "Trip through the Piney Woods," 518.

58. Claiborne, "Trip through the Piney Woods," 510.

59. Ibid., 529.

60. Lanman, *Adventures*, 2:194.

61. Claiborne, "Trip through the Piney Woods," 518.

62. Fynes Moryson, *An Itinerary: Containing His Ten Yeerss Travell . . .* , 4 vols. (Glasgow: James MacLehose and Sons, 1617-18), 3:482–83; John Bush, *Hibernia Curiosa: A Letter from a Gentleman in Dublin, to His Friend at Dover in Kent, Giving a General View of the Manners, Customs, Dispositions, &c. of the Inhabitants of Ireland* (London: W. Flexney, 1769), 19, 44–45; R. L. Willis, *Journal of a Tour from London to Elgin made about 1790 . . .* (Edinburgh: Thomson Bros., 1897), 61, 63; Forbes, *Journals of the Episcopal Visitations*, 143; Charles Cordiner, *Antiquities & Scenery of the North of Scotland, in a Series of Letters to Thomas Pennant, Esq.* (London, 1780), 89, 97, 102, 114; Barnaby Rich, *A New Description of Ireland: Wherein Is Described the Disposition of the Irish . . .* (London: Thomas Adams, 1610), 24–25; Latocnaye, *Frenchman's Walk*, 74, 115; Taylor, *Journey*, 145; Clarke, *Tour*, 256; Gilpin, *Observations*, 2:141–42; Fyfe, ed., *Scottish Diaries and Memoirs*, 234, 259; Burt, *Burt's Letters*, 2:59, 61, 63–64, 65, 80; Young, *Arthur Young's Tour in Ireland*, 1:35, 105, 177, 249, 462; Defoe, *Tour*, 600; *The Comical Pilgrim; or, Travels of a Cynick Philosopher, Thro' the Most Wicked Parts of the World, Namely England, Wales, Scotland, Ireland, and Holland* (London: S. Briscoe, 1723), 47, 83; Sinclair, ed., *Statistical Account of Scotland*, 17:81, 154, 202, 323–24, 366, 410–11, 521–22.

63. Loveday, *Diary*, 163; Taylor, *Journey*, 134; Burt, *Burt's Letters*, 2:136; Faye, ed., *Scottish Diaries and Memoirs*, 228–29, 274; Davies and Edwards, *Welsh Life in the Eighteenth Century*, 3, 6, 16–17; MacLysaght, *Irish Life in the Seventeenth Century*, 106–8; Claiborne, "Trip through the Piney Woods," 527, 533–34; Lanman, *Adventures*, 2:196, 192–93.

64. Cordiner, *Antiquities*, 92; Burt, *Burt's Letters*, 1:148; Forbes, *Journals*, 169; Willis, *Journal*, 57-58; Sinclair, ed., *Statistical Account of Scotland*, 17:80, 157–58, 371, 401-2, 666; Fyfe, *Scottish Diaries and Memoirs*, 26–27, 31-32, 65, 75, 180–81, 193, 239–40, 455–57, 481-83;

Campbell, *Philosophical Survey of the South of Ireland*, 39, 293–94; Dineley, *Observations*, 19; George Holmes, *Sketches of Some of the Southern Counties of Ireland, Collected during a Tour in the Autumn, 1797* (London: Longman & Rees, 1801), 73–74; *Letters from an Armenian*, 247; Bush, *Hibernia Curiosa*, 26; Richard Pococke, *Pococke's Tour in Ireland in 1752*, ed. George T. Stokes (Dublin: Hodges, Figgis, 1891), 92; Latocnaye, *Frenchman's Walk*, 36, 68–70; Davies and Edwards, *Welsh Life in the Eighteenth Century*, 25; Darby, *Emigrant's Guide*, 62; Lanman, *Adventures*, 2:192–93; Claiborne, "Trip through the Piney Woods," 509, 520, 529, 532–35.

65. Fyfe, ed., *Scottish Diaries and Memoirs*, 490–91, 559; Brown, ed., *Early Travellers in Scotland*, 8, 27, 41, 61; Defoe, *Tour*, 666; Giraldus Cambrensis, *The First Version of the Topography of Ireland*, trans. John J. O'Meara (Dundalk: Dundalgan Press, 1951), 29; Sinclair, ed., *Statistical Account of Scotland*, 17:507; MacLysaght, *Irish Life in the Seventeenth Century*, 38, 132, 137, 143–45, 169, 173, 198, 208, 214, 228, 241; de Paor and de Paor, *Early Christian Ireland*, 97, 99, 106; Davies and Edwards, *Welsh Life in the Eighteenth Century*, 11, 24; Claiborne, "Trip through the Piney Woods," 509, 514–16, 522, 529; Lanman, *Adventures*, 2:191, 195–96; Flint, *Recollections*, 325–26; Edouard de Montule, *Travels in America, 1816–1817*, trans. Edward D. Seeber (1821; reprint, Bloomington: Indiana University Press, 1951), 96; George A. McCall, *Letters from the Frontiers* (Philadelphia: J. B. Lippincott, 1868), 277; Darby, *Emigrant's Guide*, 61; Sullivan, *Sullivan's Hollow*, 9–10; Claiborne, *Rough Riding Down South*, 29.

66. Flint, *Recollections*, 325.

67. Claiborne, "Trip through the Piney Woods," 509, 522.

68. Lanman, *Adventures*, 2:195.

69. Martin, *Description of the Western Islands*, 22; Defoe, *Tour*, 596; Burt, *Burt's Letters*, 1:50–51; Twiss, *Tour in Ireland*, 31; Dineley, *Observations*, 35–36; Latocnaye, *Frenchman's Walk*, 20; Claud Jaunice, *A Genuine Letter from a French Officer Late Prisoner of War in Ireland, to His Friend at Plymouth, Describing the Customs and Manners of the Inhabitants of Dublin . . .* (Dublin: Peter Wilson, 1760), 23–25; Fyfe, ed., *Scottish Diaries and Memoirs*, 346, 119.

70. Whipple, *Bishop Whipple's Southern Diary*, 60.

71. Flint, *Recollections*, 323, 327.

72. John Dix, *Transatlantic Tracings; or, Sketches of Persons and Scenes in America* (London: W. Tweedie, 1853), 230.

73. Lanman, *Adventures*, 1:400.

74. Campbell, *Philosophical Survey*, 147; Fyfe, ed., *Scottish Diaries and Memoirs*, 68–69, 75–76; Sinclair, ed., *Statistical Account of Scotland*, 17:5, 37, 64, 73–74, 84, 156, 177–78, 230, 241, 263, 324–25, 338, 359, 436, 450, 468, 572, 643–44; Logan, *Scottish Gael*, 1:104–5; 2:182–83; J. Howlett, *A Essay on the Population of Ireland* (London: W. Richardson, 1786), 22–23; William Shaw Mason, *Survey, Valuation, and Census of the Barony of Portnekinch* (Dublin, 1821), 14; Thomas Newenham, *A Statistical and Historical Inquiry into the Progress and Magnitude of the Population of Ireland* (London: C. & R. Baldwin, 1805), 10–15, 18–19; T. Crofton Croker, *Researches in the South of Ireland . . .* (1824; reprint, New York: Barnes & Noble, 1969), 235; MacLysaght, *Irish Life in the Seventeenth Century*, 46; Maire O'Brien and Conor Cruise O'Brien, *A Concise History of Ireland* (New York: Beekman House, 1972), 106; Flint, *Recollections*, 316–17, 325; Darby, *Emigrant's Guide*, 35; Claiborne, "Trip through the Piney Woods," 513, 515–16, 520, 524–25, 530, 534–35; Lanman, *Adventures*, 2:192.

75. Flint, *Recollections*, 325, 316–17. See also Claiborne, *Rough Riding Down South*, 29, 31.

76. Claiborne, "Trip through the Piney Woods," 524–25, 515; Lanman, *Adventures*, 2:192.

77. Burt, *Burt's Letters*, 2:63, 135–36; Sinclair, ed., *Statistical Account of Scotland*, 17:136, 142, 157, 158, 188, 200, 204, 364, 402; Boswell, *Historical Descriptions*; Fyfe, ed., *Scottish Diaries and Memoirs*, 66–67, 253–54, 291, 553, 556; Croker, *Researches*, 325, 328–29; *Journal of a Tour through the Northern Counties of Scotland and the Orkney Isles*, 52; Davies and Edwards, *Welsh Life in the Eighteenth Century*, 119–20; Flint, *Recollections*, 311, 3; Lanman, *Adventures*, 2:193.

78. Lanman, *Adventures*, 2:193.

79. Flint, *Recollections*, 311, 325. See also McWhiney, "Education in the Old South: A Reexamination," 169–88.

80. Burt, *Burt's Letters*, 2:63; Sinclair, ed., *Statistical Account of Scotland*, 17:296; Fyfe, ed., *Scottish Diaries and Memoirs*, 57, 71–72, 237, 281, 284, 294–96; Martin, *Description of the Western Islands*, 612; Alwyn Rees and Brinley Rees, *Celtic Heritage: Ancient Tradition in Ireland and Wales* (London: Thames & Hudson, 1961), 83–84; Croker, *Researches*, 220–37; de Paor and de Paor, *Early Christian Ireland*, 106–9; Rogers, *Social Life in Scotland*, 1:43–134, 231–83; 2:256–54; David Steward, *Sketches of the Character, Manners, and Present State of the Highlanders of Scotland . . .* , 2 vols. (1822; reprint, Edinburgh: John Donald, 1977), 1:93–120; MacLysaght, *Irish Life in the Seventeenth Century*, 13–80; 128–82; Campbell, *Philosophical Survey*, 44–46, 141; Dineley, *Observations*, 19; Willis, *Journal*, 54; Sinclair, ed., *Statistical Account of Scotland*, 17:324, 531; Young, *Arthur Young's Tour in Ireland*, 1:366, 446; Holmes, *Sketches of Some of the Southern Counties of Ireland*, 36; Davies and Edwards, *Welsh Life in the Eighteenth Century*, v, 7, 46, 117, 139–40; Sullivan, *Sullivan's Hollow*, 15–17, 32–33, 35, 59, 79; Flint, *Recollections*, 323–25; Claiborne, "Trip through the Piney Woods," 535, 537; Lanman, *Adventures*, 2:192; Everest, *A Journey through the United States and Part of Canada*, 111.

81. The harp was proscribed in Ireland in the seventeenth century; harpers could be sentenced to death, and anyone harboring a harper was liable to severe penalties. Allen Feldman and Eamonn O'Doherty, *The Northern Fiddler* (Belfast: Blackstaff Press, 1980), 5; MacLysaght, *Irish Life in the Seventeenth Century*, 35–36. Although technically not proscribed along with the clan system and many other elements of Celtic culture after the English defeated the Highland Scots at Culloden in 1746, the bagpipe nevertheless fell into disfavor for a time, along with most other Highland ways. Dr. Samuel Johnson wrote, after visiting the Highlands in 1773, "among other changes, which the last Revolution introduced, the use of the bagpipe begins to be forgotten." Chapman, ed., *Johnson's Journey*, 93.

82. Claiborne, "Trip through the Piney Woods," 537; Sullivan, *Sullivan's Hollow*, 17; Claiborne, *Rough Riding Down South*, 31, 32.

83. Lanman, *Adventures*, 2:192. On the dancing habits of the pre-nineteenth-century Scots and Irish, see especially Holmes, *Sketches*, 36; Willis, *Journal*, 54; Sinclair, ed., *Statistical Account of Scotland*, 17:324; Young, *Arthur Young's Tour in Ireland*, 1:366, 446.

The Piney Woods
and the Cutting Edge
of the Lingering Southern Frontier

THOMAS D. CLARK

The history of frontier expansion across the North American continent is segmented by wide varieties of folk experiences, most of them conditioned by geography and environment. Emigrants were drawn westward by attractions of plentiful resources, temporary escape from past follies, and seductive pursuit of fresh excitement and adventure. The great crescent of the old Southwest sounded its own siren calls of seduction. The human horde that penetrated the seemingly endless web of pine and hardwood forests of the Atlantic and gulf coastal South were immediately entrapped in a region of what appeared to be almost inexhaustible resources. The land and its virgin timber cover were golden treasures. A single heartland area seemed to substantiate this fact. As late as 1880 a pioneer timber cruiser estimated that the region between the Pascagoula and Pearl rivers would yield six thousand board feet of prime lumber per acre. The surrounding hardwood-shortleaf pine belt promised an equally bountiful harvest of virgin timber.[1]

The historian must assume that in the face of such plentiful natural riches, the early Anglo-American settlers penetrating the great southern forest crescent brought with them a strong portent of tragedy in their wanton destruction of the central resource. When settlers first penetrated this part of the old Southwest no individual or corporate body possessed knowledge of forest management or silviculture, of transportation, lumber production, or the availability of a profitable market for so rich a natural bounty.

The folk approach to the vast southern littoral was shaped in large measure by migrating subsistence yeoman farmers who had turned their backs on the scenes of their sins against land and nature in the older settled states of the South. There were within the straggling emigrant bands who entered the southern frontier many of the habitual wasters whom Edmund Ruffin called "land killers."[2] Behind them they left farmlands gutted and eroded into a state of soil exhaustion by their slovenly management. On the face of the formal record the claimants of the fresh frontier lands in the old Southwest appeared to be simple and long-suffering cotters who came in search of tranquillity and fortune in a sylvan Eden.[3]

Writing in the *Literary Magazine and Register* in 1807, New Orleans merchant and congressional delegate Daniel Clark gave an idyllic profile of a prospective southern frontier yeoman settler. He said that for the modest sum of $1,306 a man, his wife, and four children could create a prospering two-hundred-acre homestead within a very short time. "He will see himself," said Clark, "instead of being a poor forlorn creature on the extreme border of population, a respectable and opulent planter in the midst of a rich and populous settlement. Such [undoubtedly were the hopes and] beginnings of ninety in a hundred of all wealthy inhabitants of the Mississippi territory of Bayou Sarah, and of the western territory of Orleans."[4] This was the sweet siren song of a shrewd Irish mercantile-political land promoter. Clark comprehended the gleam in the eyes of the pioneers to his region. Yeoman emigrants perhaps had little realistic sense of the true arduousness involved in subduing the dense southern woods, of clearing homesites, hacking out corn and cotton fields and pastures, and fallowing the land.[5]

Pioneers who moved west of the Ocmulgee River in central Georgia came not as woodsmen but as pastoral folk in pursuit of Daniel Clark's fleeting promise that they could quickly advance themselves from being "poor forlorn creatures on the extreme borders of civilization" to becoming squires of estates set admist a prosperous settled countryside.[6]

A sound historical assumption seems to be that settlers moving onto the southwestern frontier after 1810 were people largely in conflict with the land and nature in their places of origin. They approached the western country with the same ingrained emotional conflicts and practiced the same wasteful exploitations with which they had raped their earlier landholds. They brought with them the eternal flame of woods fires, the ravaging range hog, and the irrepressible folk belief that many of man's physical ills sprang from the floor of the virgin woods.[7] No statistician before 1875–80 came even close to guessing the extent of monetary loss to the South from the chronic annual woods burnings. In the latter year census enumerators said that in Mississippi alone 222,800 acres of woods were burned at an estimated cash loss of $78,500. These acres were lost because farmers and hunters set wild fires. If this annual loss were multiplied by almost three quarters of a century for the entire South, it is easy to see that the cost was astronomical.[8]

One might well contend that many social and economic setbacks in the region from the James to the Sabine in the nineteenth century were due to the fact that much of the old Southwest was settled fully three quarters of a century before people were able to take proper advantage of its resources: southern frontiersmen, like their counterparts all across expanding America, were both physically and intellectually unready and incapable of exploiting such a rich but wild forest empire intelligently. As late as 1852, J. S. Springer wrote in *DeBow's Review*, "Yes, the southerner will stand by with folded hands, or strut about with the vain pomposity of Mr. Wilson McCawber, and wait for 'something to turn up,' while others, possessed of more energy, lay hold of the prize, and appropriate the treasure to their own advantage."[9] This prophecy was realized in full measure before the century's end.

The impact of land and forest on the settlement and establishment of sustainable land claims was tremendous everywhere there were open lands on the American frontier. In every area of the westward movement in-rushing settlers displayed reckless disregard for the conservation or replenishment of natural resources. Ever-present were the rapacious squatters and wasters who grabbed from the land the most readily accessible bounties and moved on to wreak fresh havoc in other new lands.[10] The southwestern border had a generous infestation of such folk, who, devoid of sanction of legitimate property title, preempted sizable areas of forest lands for cattle and hog ranges, and stole stands of virgin cypress and pine spar timbers adjacent to streams. Subsequently they defied federal government efforts to halt their vandalism.[11] Again, squatters on the earlier southwestern frontier were far from being singular Americans.[12]

A prevalent attitude on the southwestern frontier was that Anglo-American destiny rested with the white settlers from the older southern states, who felt that they had a God-given right to take the land away from Indian and Spanish occupants. Repeatedly this predestinarian note crept into the self-pitying petitions of "suffering squatter settlers."[13] Such a plaint was that of those settlers who had invaded Chickasaw lands in 1807 and were driven back. They petitioned president and congress alike, saying that such harsh treatment by border officials had brought "many women and children to a state of starvation, all of this merely to gratify a heathan [sic] nation who have by estimation nearly 100,000 acres of land to each of their nation and of no more use to government and society than to saunter upon like so many wolves and bares."[14] The petitioners said they were denied access to a spot on which to raise their families and were forced to rent poor stony ground while so much fertile land remained unoccupied. The plaintive note running through this early petition became a continuing theme of settler dissatisfaction throughout the isolated pockets of settlement in the old Southwest.

Administration and distribution of public lands throughout the broad national domain was a bitter and nagging problem, and still is.[15] Historically every wave of emigrant movement intensified the problem. Nearly always land was a disrupting influence in harmonious local and national human relationships, if not of morals and respect for the law. Far removed from the central source of federal power in Washington, and with governmental controls virtually invisible except for widely dispersed land offices and weakling district courts, there existed no effective barrier against land squatter and timber thief. Eloquently reflected in both private and public records is the salient fact of increasing regional lawlessness and border violence in the South.[16]

There are perhaps no dependable standards by which historian and regional sociologist can assess accurately the influence of the dramatically lawless southern frontiersman upon the persistent image of the South as a violent region. However, numerous pockets of rowdiness and lawlessness, which have surfaced so often in southern history, have persisted even into this century. True, there were few sensational and persistent blood fueds such as those which occurred in the mountain-bound fastness of Appalachia, but the swampy and forested areas of the South were to know outbreaks of socially disturbing bloodshed and disorder.[17]

The location and stage of development of any particular segment of the frontier in the South at any given date are nearly as hard to describe as that mythical creature, the "true southerner." No two localities of the broader national frontier advance fell under precisely the same geographical and environmental influences, and of course human responses and experiences differed from place to place. This was eloquently true on the southern frontier. There was no unified and cohesive population advance into the southwest in the sense that there was an even spread of regional civilization. There were in earlier years natural and peculiar domestic and international political influences, which bore directly upon this area and which were not comparable to those in most of the other frontier regions. Few places in expanding America in the eighteenth and early nineteenth centuries fell under such a wide divergency of natural forces and political intrigues and cross-currents as did the gulf coastal and lower river South. This was especially true of the territory generally designated the Piney Woods.[18]

Fundamentally the process of population movement always involved exploitation of land and natural resources, the transfer of cultures, and the transplanting of social and political institutions. Perhaps in no place were these made in greater variety or implanted more indelibly than in the southern forests. Old folk ways and institutions were often recast in the harsh crucible of raw contacts with an uncompromising nature. From the outset of Euro-American penetration of most of the arboreal borderland there was forced upon men the necessity of blending the aboriginal and international with national cultures, of engaging in economic and political conflicts, and of being sealed into an isolative vacuum of great and difficult land barriers, within a virtually seamless forest. Of the three open conduits into the Southwest at the beginning of the major population advance onto the frontier (the Atlantic and gulf coastal waters, the overland routes, and the central river systems), the Mississippi, including its laterals from the Ohio southward, was the largest and most important. Down these streams drifted traders, flatboatmen, farmers, and settlers from the older western areas, who had already undergone rugged pioneering experiences. These folk were well suited to take up border life again in the pinelands of the lower valley South.[19]

Geographically and sociologically it was significant that no inland river system, possibly excepting the Ocmulgee and Tombigbee, flowed through or even near older and populous communities. Travelers and emigrants alike found it extremely difficult to make their way through monotonous pine forests, across boggy swamps, and over gulf-coastal streams. Thus few or no foreign travelers included this part of the South in their itineraries. Except for some commercial and official travelers along the Tombigbee and Mobile rivers, and a few in the eastern Georgia and upper Florida pinelands, almost no visitors visited this frontier and went away to write and publish journals of their observations and experiences.[20]

The pine forests of the maritime belt, much like the landlocked coves of Appalachia, sucked emigrants into their fastness and kept them prisoners to geographical and cultural isolation. Repeatedly this fact was revealed in personal letters and the stream of petitions for federal and state concessions. No observer in the region, however, was more aware of conditions than that English-born universal man of the Kentucky and Alabama frontiers, Harry Toulmin. In 1810 he wrote,

> The people are considerably dispersed and have enjoyed but few opportunities for mental improvement. We have no colleges—no permanent schools, no regular places of worship—no literary institutions—no towns—no good houses, and but few comfortable ones. Not many of our plantations exhibit any appearance of neatness, and the greater part of our cotton, and a large proportion of our corn, is raised in open fields in the river swamps, without even a fence to protect it.

There are no manufactures carried on, except some small ones of cotton in the household way. There are but few mechanics, and scarcely any professional men but lawyers. This disheartening prospect originated partly, perhaps, in the negligence of the inhabitants, but still more probably in other causes. The country long languished under Spanish government—After the Americans obtained possession of it, the titles to land were for some years unsettled—But what has more than retarded prosperity of the district is its insulated situation and its peculiar political connection with the Mississippi territory. Our neighbors on every side are Indians or Spaniards—We naturally catch their spirit and manners. . . . The rivers of this country, not extending, as the Mississippi does, through populous settlements of civilized men, bring no visitors to our district, and the attention of emigrants by land, who have no money to spend, is naturally fixed on the part of the southern country which has some political consideration which is more likely than ours to engross the care and the power of the local government and to enjoy a representation in the national legislature—Hence this country from its first settlement has received but a small accession of agricultural or domestic improvement, of learning and taste.[21]

Running through official communications and settler petitions prior to the War of 1812 was the coarse thread of conventional border discontent over feelings of sectional, regional, and general political neglect. Initially sparse population movement into so vast and rugged a territory as the old Southwest created a sense of almost intolerable social and political detachment from the nation itself. At stake were such critical matters as establishing and registering defensible land titles, curbing border lawlessness, and the dealing with everyday administrative and judicial affairs. Remedies for this condition lay in several areas, but the opening of transportation and communication routes across the southern forests and swamps could only be accomplished effectively by the rise of national emergencies and major population pressures. Prior to the War of 1812 population expansion in the region was sporadic and spotted in nature.[22]

The war and the changes it wrought after 1815 saw the dawning of a new era in southern frontier expansion. Movement of militia across the backcountry from Georgia on the east and from Kentucky and Tennessee on the north brought a widening of old bridle paths and Indian trails, and the opening of new roads. These became parts of a future regional highway system, which fed hundreds of thousands into the old Southwest and formed the commercial routes over which to transport goods and farm products.[23]

Three main roads channeled settlers into the region to mold new states and to create a new southern personality. These were (1) the old Federal Road, opened in 1811 from Georgia to Mobile; (2) the traditional entryway through the Holston country to Knoxville and southward down the Tennessee to the big bend of the river and Madison County; and (3) the Cotton Ginport lateral, which branched off the Natchez Trace to connect with Mobile.[24] From these main roads future laterals connected with the rising new settlements.

The Atlantic Ocean and the Gulf of Mexico formed an outer rim transportation route for both emigrants and goods. Coastal vessels delivered settlers to a half dozen or so entrepots, and hauled timber and farm products to outside markets. Low-lying and sandy coastal lands, however, were seldom conducive to the opening of main roads. Fortunately the Mobile and Tombigbee rivers formed entryways for populations traveling far inland.[25]

Coincidental with the opening of major routes onto the southern frontier, two dramatic incidents were to hasten profoundly the rise of population. Removal of the British-Spanish-Creek barriers in the gulf-coastal region coincided propitiously with the introduction and refinement of at least three important mechanical advances. On 6 May 1815, a thirty-five-ton stern-wheel steamboat, built in Brownsville, Pennsylvania, pushed its way upstream from New Orleans. It ascended the Mississippi and Ohio to reach Louisville in twenty-eight days; three days later it was in Cincinnati.[26] This historic incident placed the southern frontier within a reasonably efficient transportation connection of the heartland of a rising new industrial America. The one thing above all others the old Southwest needed was a reasonably cheap way to move bulky freight along its internal rivers; the steamboat promised to be such a machine.[27]

Already the cotton gin was functional in the expanding cotton belt, but both it and the bale press needed substantial refinements before they could fully process the increasing volume of cotton growing on the newly cleared farms.[28] In this era there was a much broader application of steam power to turn all kinds of mills. By 1812 Oliver Evans's steam engine was in operation, and soon foundries in Pittsburgh, Cincinnati, and Louisville were casting engines adapted to a variety of uses.[29] In time this engine was to play a major role in exploiting the resources of the southwestern frontier. For instance, the introduction of the steam-powered sawmill in the years of rising population growth resulted both in commercializing the forests and in revolutionizing domestic construction.[30]

The flood tide of settlers after 1815 created an almost insatiable demand for even more social, political, and administrative adjustments. In the postwar era the backwoods county authority became a centralizing social and political and economic institution in the old Southwest. In areas well removed from the seat of territorial and state governments it was the arm of government responsible for what passed as law and order, and for what gave a semblance of organization to the thrust of population expansion.[31]

On 29 June 1815, Governor David Holmes introduced the second phase of this process of frontier political expansion when he proclaimed the creation of Monroe County out of the area defined in the Fort Jackson treaty. In his proclamation the governor enjoined new settlers "to be obedient to the laws, and to respect the rights which have been secured the Creek Nation of Indians by the treaty aforesaid."[32] Later he sent Judge Harry Toulmin an explanation of his action, along with a supply of civil commission blanks to be used in the appointment of county officers.[33] This action was to be repeated hundreds of times along the American frontier; in fact, by 1815 it had already been advanced beyond the experimental stage.

Organizing the new county in the Creek territory was a modest step at least in efforts to exercise an orderly control over land registry. Both in Washington and the Southwest there was well-nigh hopeless confusion over the validity of titles in the variegated land grants, over the determination of prior occupancy, and even over the precise location of much of the land in question.[34] Addition of the Creek cession compounded the confusion and rapaciousness which earlier had characterized the occupation of British and Spanish lands. Areas of Spanish West Florida immediately east of the Pearl River and along the Tombigbee were troubled by the uncertainties of sustainable land claims. Settlers along the latter streams who panicked and fled their homes during the early moments of the Creek War left behind a hopeless tangle of unestablished claims some of which later led to bitter social and political disputes. This border emergency involving a major Indian tribe and its lands was to constitute one of the most interesting chapters in southwestern frontier history, a condition which was to be eloquently documented by petitions and official communications.[35]

Everlastingly on hand in this era of southern frontier history was that faceless vandal, the land squatter, who appeared wherever new blocks of territory were freed of foreign and Indian claimants. By the successful acquisition of West Florida from Spain, and the annexation of Creek territory by the Fort Jackson Treaty of 1814, the squatter menace was compounded.[36] In December 1815, the federal land office in Washington instructed Colonel Benjamin Hawkins to drive illegal settlers off the Creek lands on the assumption that by means fair or foul they thwarted legitimate land sales.[37] In taking exception to the order, Judge Toulmin pleaded eloquently that

> The government can form no conception of the distress which numberless poor families will endure, who have settled on the Cahauba—the Alabama and elsewhere—if they are obliged to abandon their possessions. They have been nearly broken down in coming thro' an extensive wilderness to settle a new country—and in procuring provisions, before they could raise a crop. What a

merciless stroke upon them will it be, after they have raised corn—after they have with infinite difficulty procured a little stock;—to drive them back to Tennessee or Georgia.[38]

Judge Toulmin said that this population growth was a buffer against Indian raids from East Florida.

When President James Madison proclaimed his famous interdiction against squatters on 16 December 1815, he stirred up a tornado of communications.[39] Clabon Harris, a semiliterate protester, responded to the presidential proclamation by noting that there were five hundred families already in Monroe County and that they were three hundred miles away from any state. He claimed what he considered authority higher than the president's when he pointed out that "General Jackson encouraged us to Settle on the allerbarmer—there is a number of People from North and South Carolina & Georgia and a grate number of them has sold there Carages and Waggons & &- and Now how to get back only God knows— there is also a Number of Poore widows that has lost there Husbands in the late war with the British and Indians and is Not able to Move of—"[40]

In their self-pitying petitions to president and Congress, the new wave of pioneers advancing into the old frontier after the victory at Horseshoe Bend monotonously portrayed themselves as poor and hard-pressed people who found themselves trapped inside thousands of square miles of virtually impenetrable pine forests, where they were deprived of the civilizing amenities enjoyed by other Americans. No doubt in beginning life anew they did lower their standards and ambitions to the primitive level of digging and cutting a livelihood from forest and soil with such crude implements and materials as they were able to import over wilderness roads or devise. They adapted their lives to the barest log cabin and backwoods mode of rudimentary subsistence.[41]

Movement into the old Southwest by poorly conditioned and equipped settlers entailed heavy human sacrifices. One family that moved across the sprawling west Georgia and Mississippi territory was that of Gideon Lincecum; this oft-cited family advance westward may be considered characteristic of hundreds of others who moved away from the older eastern states. The Lincecums started their westward hegira in South Carolina; they crossed Georgia by slow stages between crop seasons, and moved onto the opening cotton lands in Mississippi along the Tombigbee. On the way they lingered "to get up their wind" for the next move.

Gideon Lincecum was a fairly well educated man and in off-crop seasons he taught school in the wilds of west Georgia along the headwaters of the Ocmulgee. He described his students as children of drunken cow drivers and "the coarsest specimens of the human family I have ever seen." The family had originally planned to enter the Tennessee Valley through northern Georgia but veered instead southwestward through the pine forests to present-day Tuscaloosa and then to the site of Columbus on the Tombigbee. While crossing the five-hundred-mile wilderness in March 1817, the Lincecums subsisted on deer and turkey meat, which they found plentiful. En route west they lingered once more, this time on the Black Warrior, where they became conditioned to settle farther west.

In season the southern woods were, according to Lincecum, productive of edible muscadines, persimmons, and nuts. Wolves howled menacingly about night camps, and rain and hail pounded their camps mercilessly. "Our wagons," he said, "being the first that ever traveled that untracked forest we had difficulty to make sufficient roads for them to pass." Stream crossings were arduous at best, and often threatened defeat. When at last the trail-weary wanderers reached the fertile Tombigbee bottoms, Mrs. Lincecum ecstatically exclaimed, "Who could look at this fat game, so easily obtained, this beautiful river with its handsome dry bluff, and gushing spring water and be otherwise [than happy]?"[42]

An almost unbroken procession of emigrants plodded trails onto the southern frontier in the years 1815–40. An early observer along the Federal Road between Augusta on the Savannah River and Fort Stephens on the Tombigbee kept count in 1816 of the number of emigrants he met. He saw 3,840 individuals who said they were bound for the Alabama. They traveled in 162 carts, 141 wagons, 10 stages, 14 gigs, and 2 coaches. He also met 27 droves of hogs, 29 droves of cattle, and 2 flocks of sheep.[43]

In this era of heavy migration of settlers in search of new lands all across the American West no pioneers took on the precise characteristics of those who crowded into Alabama, Mississippi, northern Louisiana, and eastern Arkansas and western Tennessee. These emigrants moved almost by a formula, and proceeded to settle in their new homes within the general pattern of the established social and political order they had known earlier. They brought with them an attachment for the old local political process, and a desire to create new counties and develop new courthouse rings of power. By 1828 thirty-three counties had been formed in Alabama, eighteen in Mississippi, three in west Tennessee, and five in the Jackson purchase area of far southwestern Kentucky.[44]

Whether emigrants to the southwestern frontier came from upriver Kentucky and Tennessee, or from Virginia, the Carolinas, and Georgia, they brought with them in their cultural baggage either formal or remembered plans for crude double-log "dogtrot" Carolina-style houses. In the ranks of emigrants were men skilled in the use of poleaxes and broadaxes, the drawing knife and the foot adze, and other elementary tools. They were adept at the crude art of stacking grass and mud-bat chimneys, which were only slightly less flammable than the surrounding woods.[45]

For the extraordinarily modest female members of the frontier household, there were usually hand-hewn poster beds screened in with homespun curtains or coverlets. Rough tables bore the score marks of the broadax and the adze. Riven board shelves were supported on wall pegs, and the most recent addition to the family was cradled in a segment of a hollow log.[46]

The famous frontier preacher Hamilton W. Pierson described the homes of frontiersmen whom he visited. He said a log house of less than fifteen feet square, in one instance, contained a loom, a narrow table, a couple of chairs, two benches, and a corner bed. The gaping fireplace in the front end of the room seemed about to gulp down humans and contents. The hospitable family shared their coarse fare of barbecued shoat, ashbed-roasted sweet potatoes, graham bread, bee-tree honey, and coffee. Men ate first, while the womenfolk served and looked on in silence. Substantially this kind of household was duplicated hundreds of times in the old Southwest.[47]

Coarse though the usual southern frontier fare may have been, it was usually abundant, and the stranger was welcome to partake of it. Though most of the region's families were poor by almost any economic standards, they nevertheless shared common aspirations. To the raw country between the Tennessee River and the Gulf of Mexico, they brought a kindred taste for food and a common vernacular. They relied heavily on an oral pharmacopoeia of folk medicine, lived by an emotionally charged religious fundamentalism, and were exposed to a minimal amount of learning and literature. The southern frontiersman possessed an innate capacity to endure privations, hardships, personal grief, and frustrations.[48]

Presumably every respectable settler sought "good" land, well watered by a bubbling spring and a live stream, and covered with good mature trees. From the outset they pitched into the laborious task of clearing away the forest, planting a first crop of corn in grubby and sprouty ground, and later trying to grow a cash crop of cotton, a garden, and fruits to sustain life. Along with their patch farming the pioneers frequently laid silent claim to adjoining public lands on which they grazed their rangy cattle and pine-rooter hogs.

Nowhere in the vast American hinterlands were the communal workings more used than among the settlers of the southern frontier. Neighbors cooperated in rolling logs, splitting rails, raising log cabins and houses, laying stake and rider fences, and working through-and-through in the plant-ing and harvesting of crops. Women shared many household tasks: they molded candles, rendered lard, boiled soap, spun and wove wool and cot-ton fabrics, sewed garments, knitted socks and sweaters, wove coverlets, and quilted comforters and quilts.[49]

By no stretch of the imagination were all the southwestern yeoman pioneers poor and ignorant. Among them were families who either possessed some wealth or set their aims socially and culturally above the average backwoods cabin level. Such a family were the Williamses of Raleigh, North Carolina, who moved to the western Tennessee Big Hatchie country in 1818. They traveled in a caravan comprised of carriages, wagons, horses, cows, and hogs. The women rode in a carryall, which also served as their sleep-ing quarters. Male members of the party slept in the woods. Traveling at the slow pace of six to eight miles a day, and being delayed frequently at swollen stream crossings, they finally arrived at their prearranged destina-tion. Like Noah and his ark, the Williamses were adrift in the backwoods for forty days and nights.[50]

Whatever else emigrants to the old Southwest brought with them in the way of social and cultural baggage, they fetched along a fervent belief in a personal God and an unwavering dedication to protestantism. Their religious philosophy was largely that of simple agrarian people who struggled eternally against economic and environmental odds set for them by the will of God. They accepted their poor economic state as a natural part of their religious beliefs, a philosophy propounded to them incessantly by backwoods preachers. John B. Boles has explained in *The Great Revival* that "[as] the huge majority of church goers were of the common sort, habituated to work and poverty, very likely the clergy ministered to their acceptance of a less than comfortable life by minimizing the importance of affluence in the long run."[51]

The old Southwest was fertile territory for literal-minded evangelists who searched out lost souls and prospective congregations. Earliest of these ser-vants of the Word was the indomitable Lorenzo Dow. He made his way through the coastal wilderness with the emotional fury of an April hur-ricane, subsisting on wild turkey meat, and feeding roaring camp fires to fend off wolves and bears. Jacob Young, himself a blustery campaigner, described Dow as being able to face down Calvinists and backwoods rowdies with equal fervor.[52] Next in line of the semiliterate brimstone merchants was Brother James Axley, who preached mightily against false pride, sin of any stripe, general debauchery, and, specifically, tobacco chewing, whiskey drinking, and cavorting with the girls. Drumming his well-worn theme of the folly of pride and vainglory—sins of the backwoods people—he aroused the ire of one Esquire Turnbull over that old bounder's frivolities—one of which was chewing tobacco in church! Axley, it was said, was "truly brought up in the wilderness, the God of Nature had endowed him with many excellent gifts. . . . He knew well how to divide the word of God, and give every man his portion in due season."[53] In all, an army of less flamboyant bearers of the Word labored to implant in the minds and hearts of southern frontiersmen a rugged Old Testament concept of the awesome powers of God.

It was not unusual for companies of emigrants from the old communities centered about country churches back in Virginia, the Carolinas, and Georgia to move to the Southwest in straggling parties after they had decided on some vague western area in which to make settlement. Some of them moved overland in mutual-assistance caravans, and in their new homes they attempted to reestablish cherished socio-religious-economic patterns. All across the frontier these nostalgic emigrants founded new Chesters, Columbias, Raleighs, Orangeburgs, Augustas, Richmonds, and Charlestons. They raised log churches and named them after their beloved old testamentary Salems, Enons, Lebanons, Calvaries, Shilohs, Pisgahs, and Zions. At laying-by time in waning summer they built brush arbors to shade their week-long revivals. In time they replaced long meeting houses with drab frame buildings, and laid out cemeteries in which to bury their dead, who bore the same surnames as those carved on tombstones in hundreds of country graveyards beyond the Savannah River.

One of the most dramatic scenes in the early southern backwoods was a camp meeting in progress with its fire pots and rich pine torches full ablaze, and a congregation droning through a hymn. Added to this crude Miltonic scene was a fiery evangelist, fanning the embers of hell to consume on the spot obstinate sinners and wrongdoers. Adding an extra cubic of emotional eeriness were the hysterical shrieks of over-wrought shouters, who loosed the cords of inhibition and gave free rein to orgiastic joy. Milton himself could have described no wilder scene. Brother Hamilton W. Pierson wrote

that [a] congregation, when assembled, seated, and engaged in their devotions, presented a scene not to be forgotten. The preacher, small in stature, stood upon a rude platform at the feet of massive columns of his pulpit [two trees]. The people were seated among the trees upon seats arranged without any usual regularity and order, but lying at all points of the compass just as they had been able to fall, the smaller trees among the larger ones. The voice of prayer and song ascended amid those massive, towering columns, crowned with arches formed by their outstretching branches, and covered with dense foliage.[54]

In the next century this rock-ribbed protestant region came to be known as the "Bible belt" of the nation, with ramparts that were nearly unassailable.[55]

The folk ways transported to and modified on the southern frontier revealed themselves historically in many forms; in social and religious attitudes, in provincial and regional politics, in the nurturing of a pronounced type of American ruralism, and in a heritage of common blood-stock origins. In later years yeoman of the region flocked to the Confederate Army, but even so some asserted an astonishing independence in their loyalties. After the Civil War they resisted the excesses of radical reconstruction, and shared the subsequent woes of the one-crop-credit-ridden system of a region caught in isolated economic travail.[56] Consistently, the statistical profile of the region of the old Southwest remained fixed in such categories as nativity, economics, social mobility, and cultural progress. The region became the breeding ground for an outflow of emigrants who moved on westward along the parallels over which they or their forebears had traveled earlier.

Remarkably, the great human tide that flowed and billowed into the old Southwest with such initial vigor produced few or no frontier idols of the stature of Daniel Boone, Simon Kenton, George Rogers Clark, Jedediah Smith, Kit Carson, and Joseph Reddford Walker.[57] The yeoman emigrant was the regional hero, and his soul-wearying border experiences were of course far less colorful than those of Boone, Carson, et al. He stoically accepted the sacrifice and deprivation that fell so abundantly in the gray area of his life. Perhaps the southerner's saving grace in the backwoods was his expansive ability to poke fun at himself and his neighbors. The brashness and greenhorn uninhibitedness of individual characters in the region captured the attention of contemporary genre writers. The legacy of their colorful writings is rich literary documentation, which has been dredged repeatedly by contemporary interpreters of the Old South.

Authors on the old frontier produced such classics as A. B. Longstreet's *Georgia Scenes* (1835), Joseph Glover Baldwin's *Flush Times in Alabama and Mississippi* (1839), Johnson Jones Hooper's *Some Adventures of Captain Simon Suggs, Late of the Tallapoosa Volunteers* (1846) and *Widow Rugby's Husband, a Night at the Ugly Man's and Other Tales of Alabama* (1851), and George Washington Harris's *Sut Lovingood: Yarns* (1867). The *New York Spirit of the Times* and the southern country newspapers carried a continuing flow of folk stories and humorous matter depicting the antics and crudities of southern frontier life.[58]

All the nineteenth-century authors depicted the southern frontier yeoman as a rough and grotesque character of natural greenness. Nevertheless, they preserved a rich human overview of conditions of social development in a state of forest and wilderness isolation that fundamentally influenced the molding of the rural southern personality. The impact of frontier physical conditions, folkways, economics, the exploitation and wastage of natural resources, and the constant fulminating of local politics made deep imprints upon the regional turn of mind. Frontier conditions entrapped beneath the cover of the great southern virginal forests lingered for a much longer time than on many other segments of the American westward movement.

The literary legacy of the frontier was revived in the twentieth-century writings of Caroline Miller, Marjorie Kinnan Rawlings, James Street, Brainard Cheney, possibly Thomas Stribling, and many others. In Mississippi, William Faulkner and Eudora Welty have drawn rather generously upon their section's pioneering experiences. Faulkner's people, in the main, were lineal inheritors of the folkways and foibles of forebears who negotiated trails and indifferent roads to lay claim to lands on the sprawling southern frontier from the Carolinas to the Mississippi. Running through Eudora Welty's marvelous short stories is a variegated thread of robust folklore and backwoods vernacular of pure natural strain.

There is, however, an intellectual paradox in the historical treatment of human adaptations to the ways of life on the raw virgin lands of the old Southwest. One searches with too meager rewards in the major general histories of the South for either discussion or description of the impact of the forest resource on the course of formative regional events. In fact, an uninitiated reader might assume from these works that the great Piney Woods and the hill forests scarcely existed. Even Thomas Perkins Abernethy, in his solid work *The South in the New Nation, 1789–1819*, gives the subject too slight attention. W. Clement Eaton, Francis Butler Simkins, and Robert S. Cotterill all but ignored the woods and their impact upon regional civilization. This comes close to being true even of Frank L. Owsley's *Plain Folk of the Old South.*

In the current rash of books and articles that attempt to define the "southerner," and to analyze his character and mores, his personal distinctiveness, and his place in American history, there is no material mention of the bearing of the great forest on the shaping of regional character and bent of mind. This fact stands in sharp contrast to historical interpretations of the historical backgrounds of the Great Lake states and the Northwest. In good measure, it was the socially isolative grip of the backwoods that accounted for the retention of a homogeneous population, black and white, over such a broad span of time; for the shaping of enduring institutional patterns; and for the formulation of narrow political attitudes.

Whatever may have been the sins of omission and commission regarding the forests in the southern backwoods during most of the nineteenth century and the earlier decades of this century—and there were many—the region which once comprised the broad southern frontier has survived to bask under the bright rays of a new rainbow of promise in the renewability of its riches. The bountiful timber resources of the southern frontier—which pioneer settlers recklessly laid low to build dogtrot houses, double-log barns, corn cribs, and worm-rail fences; despoiled with wildfires; and sold for fractions of their worth to cut-out-and-get-out lumbermen—are now being reclaimed and cherished. The frontier bequeathed many legacies to this generation of southerners to be searched out and revered as hereditary beginnings, as productive of distinctive regional traits, and as the human bonds with region and land. Nature, fortified by better conservation and economic renewal policies, has given the modern tenants of the old Southwest a second opportunity to enjoy and profit from the resources of the region which their forebears penetrated nearly two centuries earlier with such high expectation of gathering the fruits of this far-off Eden.

Notes

1. "The Forests of the United States" in U.S. Bureau of the Census, *Tenth Census* (Washington, D.C., 1882), 532. A note of despondency and of the impact the great southern pine forest had on settlers was sounded in 1812, when a petition in that year informed the Congress "That for not less than five years back we have met with little more than one tide of woe pressing back on another. The good people, after getting here & battering with the difficulties incident to a wooden wilderness, instead of meeting an asylum, or rural retreat, we have one continued scence [sic] of poverty, anguish and distress." "Petition to the Congress by the Inhabitants of the Territory," in *The Territory of Mississippi, 1807–1817,* vol. 6 of *The Territorial Papers of the United States,* ed. Clarence Edwin Carter (Washingon, D.C.: Government Printing Office, 1938), 6:vi, 345–47.

2. Edwin Ruffin, "Southern Agricultural Exhaustion and Its Remedy," *DeBow's Review and Industrial Resources, Statistics, etc.* 14 (January 1853):43.

3. Ibid.:34–48. An excellent microcosmic view of soil conditions in parts of the Old South is the twentieth-century soil survey by M. Earl Carr, F. S. Welch, G. A. Crabb, Risden T. Allen, and W. C. Byers, U.S. Bureau of Soils, *Thirteenth Report: Soil Survey of Fairfield County, South Carolina, 1911* (Washington, D.C.: Government Printing Office, 1914), 479–511, 593–643, 859–96, 1003–81; maps nos. 11, 14, 21, 24, 25. Subsequently the National Soil Survey completed investigation of conditions all across the old Southwest.

4. Ascribed to Daniel Clark, Esq., "Remarks on the Population and Culture of Louisiana," *Literary Magazine and American Register* 7 (1807):45–57. Reproduced by Eugene Schwab with

the collaboration of Jacqueline Bull, *Travels in the Old South*, 2 vols. (Lexington: University Press of Kentucky, 1973), 1:120.

5. William Barrett to Acting Secretary of War, 12 March 1817, in *The Territory of Alabama, 1817-1819*, vol. 18 of *The Territorial Papers of the United States*, ed. Carter, 18:70-71.

6. "Petition to Congress by Inhabitants of the Territory," 30 Dec. 1812, in *Territory of Mississippi*, ed. Carter, 6:345-47.

7. M. B. Hammond, *The Cotton Industry: An Essay in American Economic History* (Ithaca, N.Y.: Cornell University Press, 1897), 34-66; A. B. Moore, *History of Alabama* (University, Ala.: University of Alabama Press, 1934), 139; Frank L. Owsley, *Plain Folk of the Old South* (Baton Rouge: Louisiana State University Press, 1949), 23-76.

9. *DeBow's Review of the Southern and Western States* 12 (June 1852):600.

10. In September 1794, Andrew Ellicott wrote President John Adams: "This like all other new countries, is settled by people of the three following descriptions, Viz. persons of ambition, and enterprise, who have contemplated an encrease of fame, and wealth, others who have fled from their creditors, and some, (not a few) from justice." Carter, *Territory of Mississippi*, 5:4. In October 1808, the Secretary of the Treasury wrote Thomas Freeman: "You will perceive that the great object of the President is to discriminate between settlers who lay no claim to the land, and will either become purchasers, or submit quietly to the laws, and those who under pretense of pretended Georgia titles, intend either forcibly to occupy the lands, or to extort money from ignorant Settlers. Against the last description, the president intends to cause the law, to be rigorously carried into effect, both by prosecuting for the penalties, and by removing them by force." Ibid., 5:659. Ephriam Kirby wrote Thomas Jefferson, 1 May 1804: "This section of the United States has long afforded an asylum to those who prefer voluntary exile to the punishments ordained by law for heinous offenses. The present inhabitants (with few exceptions) are illiterate, wild and savage, of depraved morals, unworthy of public confidence or private esteem; litigious, disunited, and knowing each other, universally distrustful of each other." Ibid., 5:323. Especially revealing are Harry Toulmin's letters to William Lattimore, 28 Dec. 1815, and to President Madison, 20 Jan. 1816, in ibid., 6:618-22, 641-47.

11. Thomas Freeman to the Secretary of the Treasury, 9 July 1811, in ibid., 6:205-6; Return J. Meigs to Louis Winston, 12 Jan. 1815, in ibid., 6:492-93; Secretary of the Treasury to Nehemiah Tilton, 10 June 1811, in ibid., 6:200.

12. Josiah Meigs wrote to Lewis Sewall, 5 Sept. 1816, "That a Mr. Coleman bid a high price for land at a sale and forfeited. Then pretended to have a certificate." Meigs said, "If he occupies those lands, he is an intruder & come within the scope of the President's Proclamation." Ibid., 6:702. Thomas Jefferson, on 22 Oct. 1808, declared "That the sales of lands of a certain portion of the public lands contained in the District West of Pearl River, in the Mississippi Territory, should take place on the Second Tuesday in January 1809," ibid., 6:200. Mitford M. Matthews, ed., *A Dictionary of Americanisms on Historical Principles* (Chicago: University of Chicago Press, 1951) 1625-26, defines the term "squatter."

13. Characteristic of such settler petitions was a "Memorial to Congress by Citizens of Pearl River," 1 Sept. 1815, in *Territory of Mississippi*, ed. Carter, 6:550-52.

14. "Petition to the President and Congress by Intruders on Chickasaw Lands," 5 Sept. 1810, in ibid., 6:106-9.

15. Richard Peters, ed., *The Public Statutes-at-Large of the United States of America* (Boston: Charles C. Little & James Brown, 1846), 2:305.

16. Governor Holmes to the Secretary of the Treasury, 29 July 1815, in *Territory of Mississippi*, ed. Carter, 6:543-44; J. L. Moore to Edward Tiffin, 24 Aug. 1812, in ibid., 6:318-19; Governor Holmes to William Conner, 27 Aug. 1812, in ibid., 6:320.

17. Judge Toulmin to the President, 6 Dec. 1810, in ibid., 6:149-51.

18. This complex subject is treated in Isaac J. Cox, *The West Florida Controversy, 1798-1813* (Baltimore: Johns Hopkins Press, 1918); A. P. Whitaker, *The Spanish-American Frontier, 1783-1795* (New York: 1927), and *The Mississippi Question, 1793-1803* (New York: D. Appleton, 1934); Cecil Johnson, *British West Florida, 1763-1783* (New Haven: Yale University Press, 1943).

19. Mary J. Welch, "Recollections of Pioneer Life in Mississippi," *Publications of the Mississippi Historical Society* 4 (1901):343-56.

20. Some of the travelers who penetrated the southwestern backwoods were Frederick Law Olmsted, *A Journey in the Back Country in the Winter 1853-1854* (New York: Mason Bros., 1860); Thomas Hamilton, *Men and Manners in America*, 2 vols. (Philadelphia: Carey, Lea, & Blanchard, 1833), vol. 2; Alex. Mackay, *The Western World; or Travels in the United States in 1846-47*, 2 vols. (Philadelphia: Lea & Blanchard, 1849), vol. 2; Margaret Hall, *The Aristocratic Journey; Being the Outspoken Letters of Mrs. Basil Hall Written during Fourteen Months Sojourn in America, 1827-1828* (New York: G. P. Putnam & Sons, 1831); Capt. Basil Hall, *Travels in America in the Years 1827-1828*, 3 vols. (London: Simpkin & Marshall, 1829); Sir Charles Lyell, *A Second Visit to the United States of North America*, 2 vols. (London: J. Murray: 1849); Francis Harper, ed., *The Travels of William Bartram* (Naturalist's Edition) (New Haven: Yale University Press: 1958).

21. Schwab, *Travels in the Old South;* Harry Toulmin, "A Geographical and Statistical Sketch of the District of Mobile" (quoting from *American Register* 6 [1810]:332-39), 1:90-91.

22. Frequent statements of population growth in the Old Southwest were made in the official correspondence. Specifically, "Census of Madison County," in *Territory of Mississippi*, ed. Carter, 5:684-92; Judge Toulmin to Joseph B. Narnum, 20 May 1809, in ibid., 5:732-33; "Population of Alabama, Census Taken under Act of Legislature and Furnished by the Secretary of Said Territory, December 23, 1816," in *Territory of Alabama*, ed. Carter, 18:3-7; Secretary Ware to William Lattimore, 15 Nov. 1816, in *Territory of Mississippi*, ed. Carter, 6:719-20, lists the population east and west of Pearl River; *Statistical Abstract of the United States*, 1920.

23. Judge Toulmin to William Lattimore, 12 Nov. 1815, in *Territory of Mississippi*, ed. Carter, 6:566-69; Israel Pickens to Josiah Meigs, 31 Jan. 1818, in *Territory of Alabama*, ed. Carter, 18:240; Postal Route Advertisement, 20 June 1818, in ibid., 18:354-55; Samuel B. Shields to the Secretary of War, 16 Nov. 1818, in ibid., 18:470-71; Acting Secretary of War to Daniel B. Mitchell, 3 Nov. 1817, in ibid., 18:186; Postmaster General to Bolling Hall and Thomas B. Robertson, 11 June 1813, in *Territory of Mississippi*, ed. Carter, 6:373-74; David B. Mitchell to the Secretary of War, 30 Sept. 1818, in *Territory of Alabama*, ed. Carter, 18:424-25.

24. Secretary of the Treasury to Josiah Meigs, 6 June 1817, in *Territory of Mississippi*, ed. Carter, 6:794-95; Secretary of War to Wade Hampton, 20 July 1811, in ibid., 6:213-14.

25. James Wilkinson to Juan Ventura Morales, 6 July 1803, in ibid., 5:219-20; "Memorial to the President and Congress by the Territorial Legislature," 21 Dec. 1807, in ibid., 5:587-90; "Memorial to Congress by the Territorial Assembly," 10 March 1818, in *Territory of Alabama*, ed. Carter, 18:268-69.

26. *DeBow's Review* (January 1850):94-95; Benjamin Casseday, *History of Louisville* (Louisville, 1852), 119-21, 141-42.

27. This fact was clearly reflected in "Memorial to Congress by the Territorial Assembly," 10 March 1818, in *Territory of Alabama*, ed. Carter, 18:268-71. Balthaser Meyer and Caroline Magill, *The History of Transportation in the United States before 1860* (Washington, D.C.: Carnegie Institute, 1917), 94-116.

28. James B. DeBow, ed., *The Industrial Resources of the Southern and Western States*, 4 vols. DeBow's Commercial Review (New Orleans, 1853-54), 1:122-24, 158-60; Lewis C. Gray, *Agriculture in the Southern States to 1860*, 2 vols. (Washington, D.C.: Carnegie Institute, 1933), 1:452-53, 2:704-5.

29. J. Leander Bishop, *A History of American Manufactures from 1608-1860*, 3 vols. (New York: Young & Co., 1868), 1:75, 112, 115, 145, 147-49.

30. Ibid., 1:99-100, 265; Victor S. Clark, *History of Manufacturing in the United States, 1607-1860*, 2 vols. (Washington, D.C.: Carnegie Institute, 1916), 1:176-77, 421-22, 522.

31. John Coffee to Josiah Meigs, 11 Jan. 1818, in *Territory of Alabama*, ed. Carter, 18:230-31; John W. Monette, *History of the Discovery and Settlement of the Valley of Mississippi*, 2 vols. (New York: Harper & Bros., 1846), 1:446-47; Timothy Flint, *The History and Geography of the Mississippi Valley*, 2 vols. (Cincinnati: E. H. Flint & William M. Farnsworth, 1832), 2:61, 505.

32. "Proclamation Organizing Monroe County," 29 June 1815, in *Territory of Mississippi*, ed. Carter, 6:538.

33. Governor Holmes to Judge Toulmin, 3 July 1815, in ibid., 6:539.

34. These cases were so numerous that a couple of citations will suffice. Lewis Sewall and Samuel Smith to Josiah Meigs, 31 May 1815, in ibid., 6:532–34; "Memorial to Congress by the Territorial [Mississippi] Legislature," 21 Nov. 1815, in ibid., 6:580–83.

35. Judge Toulmin to William Lattimore, Dec. 1815, in ibid., 6:584–91; "Memorial to Congress by Territorial [Mississippi] Legislature," 5 Dec. 1815, in ibid., 6:595–96; Monette, *Discovery and Settlement*, 1:402–3. "Memorial to Congress by Inhabitants of Amite County," 22 March 1816, in *Territory of Mississippi*, ed. Carter, 6:671–73.

36. Lewis Sewall to Josiah Meigs, 15 March 1816, in ibid., 6:668–69; Judge Toulmin to William Lattimore, 28 Dec. 1815, in ibid., 6:631–32; Toulmin to President, 20 Jan. 1816, in ibid., 6:641–47.

37. Judge Toulmin to William Lattimore, 28 Dec. 1815, in ibid., 6:631–32.

38. Ibid., 6:631; also, "Report of House Committee on Public Lands," 9 Jan. 1816, in ibid., 6:638–40.

39. *National Intelligencer*, 16 Dec. 1815; J. D. Richardson, ed., *A Compilation of the Messages and Papers of the Presidents of the United States, 1789–1897*, 10 vols. (Washington, D.C.: National Bureau of the Arts, 1891), 1:472–73.

40. Clabon Harris to the President, 20 Jan. 1816; Carter, *Territory of Mississippi*, 6:647–48.

41. William Darby, *The Emigrant's Guide to the Western and Southwestern States and Territories Comprising a Geographical and Statistical Description of the States.* (New York: Kirk & Mercein, 1818), 120–22; *View of the United States, Historical, Geographical, and Statistical; Exhibiting in Convenient Forms, the Natural and Artificial Features of the Several States* (Philadelphia: H. S. Tanner, 1828). Numerous petitions from the settlers in the old Southwest to the president and Congress, as recorded in Carter's compilations of territorial papers of Mississippi and Alabama plead poverty and economic and social oppression. Mary J. Welsh, "Recollections of Pioneer Life in Mississippi," *Publications of the Mississippi Historical Society* 4 (1901):343–50. Classic contemporary descriptions of life in the Piney Woods are found in J. F. H. Claiborne's "Rough Riding Down South," *Harper's New Monthly Magazine* (1862), and his "A Trip through the Piney Woods," *Publications of the Mississippi Historical Society* 9 (1906):487–538.

42. Gideon Lincecum, "Autobiography of Gideon Lincecum," *Publications of the Mississippi Historical Society* 8 (1904):459–60, 465, 470.

43. J. G. deRoughlac Hamilton, ed. *The Papers of Thomas Ruffin*, 3 vols. (Raleigh: Edwards & Brougham, 1918), 194–95.

44. Flint, 2:479, 505; Richard H. Collins, *History of Kentucky*, 2 vols. (Covington: Collins & Co., 1874), 2:108–9, 292, 342.

45. Justus Wyman, "Geographical Sketch of the Alabama Territory," Transactions of the Alabama Historical Society (Montgomery: Department Archives and History, 1898–99), 3:107–27. H. W. Pierson, *In the Brush; or, Old Time Social, Political, and Religious Life in the Southwest* (New York: D. Appleton & Co., 1881), 10–20, 78–80; W. H. Sparks, *The Memories of Fifty Years* (Philadelphia, 1870), 61.

46. A. B. Moore, *History of Alabama*, 4 vols. (Chicago: American Historical Society, 1927), 1:183; Frederick Law Olmsted, *Journey in the Back Country* (New York: Mason Bros., 1860), 140, 230–31; Frank L. Owsley, *Plain Folk of the Old South*, 31–43; Flint, 1:216–19.

47. " 'Movers' in the Southwest," *Dollar Magazine* 17 (January 1851):21–22; Schwab, *Travels in the Old South*, 2:394–97, 411–14; "Interior Georgia Life and Scenery, by a Southern Traveller," *Knickerbocker Magazine* 34 (August 1849):113–18.

48. G. M. Weston, *The Poor Whites of the South* (Washington, 1836), 1–7; J. C. S. Abbott, *South and North* (New York: Abby & Abbott, 1860), 119–21, 142–43; D. R. Hundley, *Social Relations in Our Southern States* (New York: Henry B. Price, 1860), 192; Frank L. Owsley, *Plain Folk of the Old South*, and his article, "The Pattern of Migration and Settlement of the Southern Frontier," *Journal of Southern History* 11 (1947):147–76; Thomas McCarroll Prince, "The Southern Pine Forests," *DeBow's Review* 18 (January 1855):188–89.

49. F. D. Srygley, *Seventy Years in Dixie* (Nashville: Gospel Advocate Pub. Co., 1893) 127–43; A. B. Moore, *History of Alabama*. (University of Alabama, 1934), 186–87; William C. Ward, "The Building of the State," *Transactions of the Alabama Historical Society* (1899–1903):53–72; Welsh, "Recollections," 343–50.

50. Joseph P. Williams, *Old Times in West Tennessee, Reminiscences—Semi-Historic—of Pioneer Life and the Early Settlers of the Big Hatchie Country, by a Descendant of One of the Early Settlers* (Memphis: W. G. Cheeney, 1873), 7-37.

51. John B. Boles, *The Great Revival, 1787-1805: The Origins of the Southern Evangelical Mind* (Lexington: University Press of Kentucky, 1972), 170.

52. Lorenzo Dow, *History of Cosmopolite; or, Writings of Reverend Lorenzo Dow* (Cincinnati: Applegate & Co., 1855), 57.

53. Jacob Young, *Autobiography of a Pioneer; or, the Nativity, Experiences, Travels, and Ministerial Labors of Rev. Jacob Young; with Incidents, Observations, and Reflections* (Cincinnati: Cranston & Curtis, 1857), 242-43. A graphic view of the state of religion in the old Southwest is William H. Barr, "Hiland Hubbard Mission to Alabama," Barr to the Editor, *Weekly Recorder*, 20 Oct. 1818, and Hiland Hubbard, "Report of a Missionary Tour, Read before the South Carolina Presbytery at Their Fall Session," *Weekly Recorder*, 11 Dec. 1818, 135-40, quoted in Schwab, *Travels in the Old South*, 1:197-201.

54. Pierson, *In the Brush*, 65.

55. Predominantly the great emigration brought into the old Southwest a staunch Calvinistic protestantism, which divided and subdivided into denominations, congregations, and evangelistic sects, all of them adhering to a more-or-less strictly literal interpretation of the Bible.

56. Consistently, the nativity tables in the United States decennial census reports revealed the overwhelming percentage of native southern and regional birth of the population. In more concentrated form of the population data are the summary tables contained in the 1920 edition of the *Statistical Abstract of the United States* (Washington, D.C.: Government Printing Office, 1921). In analyzing the statistical position of the South in all areas, Howard W. Odum, *Southern Regions of the United States* (Chapel Hill: University of North Carolina Press, 1936), emphasizes this fact in both text and tables. Especially pertinent to post-Civil-War conditions are Charles Nordorff, *The Cotton States in the Spring and Summer of 1875* (New York: D. Appleton & Co., 1876); Robert Somers, *The Southern States since the War, 1870-1871* (London: MacMillan & Co., 1871); Matthew Brown Hammond, *The Cotton Industry—An Essay in American Economic History* (Ithaca: Cornell University Press, 1897). A broader economic view of postwar life in the South is presented in E. M. Coulter, *The South during Reconstruction, 1865-1877* (Baton Rouge: Louisiana State University Press, 1947). Charles Otken's *Ills of the South; or, Related Causes Hostile to the General Prosperity of the Southern People* (New York: G. P. Putnam, 1894), despite its populistic point of view, gives an insight into the one-crop economy.

57. There were Benjamin Hawkins, Sam Dale, Pushmataha, and, maybe, Reuben, Samuel, and Nathan Kemper, and John and James Caller.

58. William T. Porter's *Spirit of the Times*, especially for the years 1836-60, ran a generous number of southern humorous folk stories. The author had access to the unusually complete file of this rare publication, which was collected by Louis Lee Haggin and is now deposited in the Keeneland Library, Lexington, Ky. The best general discussion of these Southwestern writers is A. P. Hudson, *Humor of the Old Deep South* (New York: MacMillan & Co., 1938).

Black Labor in Forest Industries of the Piney Woods, 1840–1933

NOLLIE W. HICKMAN

The Piney Woods soils of Mississippi and other southern states were large-ly unsuited for large-scale agriculture in the antebellum period. Generally thin, sandy, nutrient-poor soils characterize the land that bears a growth of pine trees.

The so-called cotton kingdom in 1860 did not include that section of Mississippi which was covered by a magnificent pine forest. Plantations and large slave ownerships were to be found only in a few localities along rivers and streams of the Piney Woods country. In the Mississippi panhan-dle, presently the six southeastern counties of the state, the number of plan-tations could almost be counted on the fingers of one hand.[1]

In the pine country population was sparse and farming was generally of a subsistence nature. Stock raising, hunting, and cultivating small one-horse farms were the prime pursuits of the population.[2] In what is today Stone County the largest of a few slaveholders owned only twenty blacks.[3] In what is today Jackson, Hancock, Harrison, and George counties, the picture was much the same.[4] Along the Mississippi gulf coast there were a very few sea-island plantations.

Because the Piney Woods lacked rich soils and large plantations, its black population was comparatively small. In none of the pine counties of the state did blacks outnumber whites in 1860.[5] The heaviest concentration of blacks was quite naturally found in the region of fertile soils. Only in recent times has a considerable black population appeared in Piney Woods country. Forest industries and urbanization have been responsible for this development.

During the 1840s commercial forest industries dependent on water transportation appeared along the gulf coast and the streams emptying in-to Mississippi Sound.[6] One of the early millmen, Calvin Taylor, operated sawmills at Handsboro from about 1845 until 1880.[7] From the beginning of his operation until the abolition of slavery Taylor used blacks owned by himself and slaves rented from others. Taylor provided shelter and food and paid twenty-five dollars a month for the labor of a slave. For one year's labor of a black female slave, Taylor paid the owner one hundred dollars. Occasionally a black slave ran away; such was the case with the slave Taylor rented from William Bond.[8]

Logmen who provided timber for lumbermen used slave labor to fell the trees, to transport logs to streams, and to raft timber downstream to coast mills. Logging operations were prevalent on all streams emptying into the Gulf of Mexico in 1860.[9] Goodman Hester and Alexander Scarbrough, logmen on the Biloxi River, used slave labor in their logging and rafting business in 1860.[10] In Perry County the Griffins used slaves in rafting timber down Black Creek and the Pascagoula River to Moss Point, Mississippi.[11]

The U.S. census data of 1850 and 1860 reveal the extent to which black slave labor was utilized by operators in forest industries and brick kilns in the three coast counties.[12] In 1850 George Kendall used 116 black men and 37 women in his brick kiln, which produced ten million bricks in the census year of 1850.[13] David R. Wingate, perhaps the largest slaveholding mill owner on the gulf coast,[14] owned 84 slaves at the mouth of the Pearl River in 1850. According to the U.S. census figures, operators of forest industries owned 200 slaves in 1850 and around 400 in 1860.[15] The Hand brothers, from whom the town of Handsboro derived its name, used their slaves in the production of steam engines and circular saws.[16]

According to local tradition, the work day began at dawn and lasted until darkness for six days of each week.[17] Labor in the small sawmills, those without labor-saving machinery, required workers of considerable physical strength and great endurance. In the coast mills, where both humidity and temperature were usually high, blacks were, perhaps, better adapted than whites for the ordinary operations required in the production of lumber. Most of the work involved such tasks as firing boilers, stacking heavy green lumber, and manipulating crude blocks of a log carriage. The tasks were relatively simple, although they required considerable physical strength; slave labor created, for the most part, a stable, dependable work force, free of absenteeism, that could be relied upon to labor constantly.[18]

One of the outcomes of the Civil War was the abolition of slavery. The war also administered a severe blow to what had been young, vigorous forest industries on the gulf coast. Although the forest industries languished for a brief period, sawmills resumed operations before Reconstruction ended. It is probable that Reconstruction in the Piney Woods was milder than in the cotton-growing sections of the state.[19]

By 1870 a new era of forest industries began to appear, which in time reshaped economic, political, and social conditions in the Piney Woods. In the antebellum period, the pine country in Mississippi was called the cattle country, but by 1900 the region came to be known as the lumber section. Rail transportation was the vehicle of change, since it made possible the development of large-scale forest industries that promoted the growth of population, towns, and cities, and the end of frontier culture.

If local tradition is correct, the transition of blacks from slavery to freedom in the Piney Woods was of little consequence to whites, mainly because they formed only a small percentage of the population, and also, slave ownerships were small. Blacks, as before the end of slavery, continued working in sawmills and in logging and rafting activities.

In most cases the position of blacks in forest industries differed little from their antebellum status. They were generally employed as unskilled workers, but a few played important roles in forest industries. Wesley Fairley, a former slave of Peter Fairley of Perry County, became a local Paul Bunyan. Fairley, weighing above two hundred pounds and fully seven feet in height, possessed great strength and endurance. He was unable to get shoes that would fit his mammoth feet. Consequently, regardless of weather, Fairley was always barefooted. From time to time he walked barefooted into the federal land office at Jackson, Mississippi, and purchased considerable acreages of land.[20]

It is probable that some time during the Civil War Fairley joined the Union Army and was assigned to guard the Confederate prisoners incarcerated on Ship Island, located a short distance south of the Mississippi gulf coast. One of the prisoners was Lorenzo Nolley Dantzler, who had grown up a short distance from Fairley's home. Fairley assumed responsibility for Dantzler's welfare and made frequent trips to the mainland to get food for his prisoner, who had become his friend. Later Dantzler credited Fairley with saving his life, and it was the beginning of a thirty-five-year personal and business relationship that ended with the death of both men.[21]

In the 1870s Dantzler acquired from his father-in-law, William Griffin, a small sawmill located at Moss Point. In about 1885 he built there one of the largest mills in Mississippi.[22] Fairley became one of the main suppliers of logs for the Dantzler mills. He bought timberland, conducted logging operations, and rafted timber down Black Creek and the Pascagoula River to the Dantzler mills. Fairley was, by common consent, the "creek runner" on Black Creek. He selected rafting crews and made all the decisions on log drives. He also bought timber from others and employed in his various operations a considerable number of blacks and whites. He was respected and liked by both races.

According to local tradition, Fairley prevented the bankruptcy of the Dantzler Lumber Company. The company had chartered a number of vessels to transport lumber to Dantzler's overseas customers. But unfortunately a long drought produced shallow water that made timber rafting difficult, if not impossible. With ships at anchor and no cargoes of lumber available, the company was faced with having to pay high, perhaps ruinous, demurrage costs. Fairley was equal to the emergency: using peaveys and spike poles, his large crew of blacks pushed log rafts through shallow water and over sandbars to their destination at Moss Point. Dantzler met his commitment and the company survived.[23] Fairley continued his relationship with the company until old age brought his retirement around 1900.

In a very real sense, Fairley was unique. Few other blacks were able to advance beyond the status of common labor. Israel Breland, of Perry County, conducted, on a minor scale, logging and rafting operations. Sandy Williams, a black Civil War veteran of the Union Army, was a logging contractor in Harrison County on Red Creek.[24]

Rankin Hickman, a white timber merchant, logging contractor, and creek runner, employed considerable numbers of workers of both races during the years 1878–1904. Blacks and whites on log drives down Red Creek and the Pascagoula River ate out of the same pots, slept in close proximity around campfires, and joined in singing at night. Wages were equal and skin color was of little significance to those of both races, who were often neighbors and longtime friends.[25]

On the coast in the 1880s, where lumbering was more advanced than in other parts of the state, the Noble Knights of Labor, a national labor organization, found fertile ground for their cause. Almost intolerable working conditions in the mills led both blacks and whites to embrace enthusiastically the cause of the labor union. Although both races joined the union, blacks and whites held separate meetings and each race had its own leader.[26]

The union organization at Moss Point demanded a twelve-hour workday, higher wages, and recognition of the union. Opposed by mill owners, workers ended mill operation with a work stoppage. Public opinion supported the workers and after a brief period of mill idleness, the owners capitulated to most worker demands. Mill owners, however, refused to recognize the union.[27]

Emboldened by their victory, in 1887 the Knights of Labor presented owners with a number of demands: ten-hour days, higher wages, and other benefits. Jean Brodean, president of the local black Knights of Labor union, in a speech to his followers, said that workers must be prepared to die if their just demands were not accepted. At first public opinion seemed to be favorable to strikers, but as incidents of violence occurred, and as rhetoric employed by laborers became increasingly inflammatory, public opinion turned against the workers. A newly formed committee of public safety used various means, including coercion and outright violence against labor leaders, to end the strike; striking workers failed to achieve any gains.[28] Probably the last gasp of the Knights of Labor came during a strike in Moss Point mills in the spring of 1900. About nine o'clock the mill whistle sounded and the workers came pouring out of the two Dantzler mills at Moss Point. There was violence, and three of the strike leaders were convicted of crime and sent to prison: the strike ended.[29]

Labor unions following the collapse of the Knights failed to gain a foothold in forest industries in Mississippi. The average white worker, usually reared on a small farm, was, perhaps, too independent-minded to accept the discipline required of a successful union. The black worker was another factor complicating unionization. Competition between blacks and whites for jobs of generally low or moderate skills discouraged cooperation of the two races. Owners understood the racial tensions and were said to use them to prevent labor solidarity and unionization. Not until after the 1930s was labor able to organize unions and then only to a very limited extent. Improvement of working conditions after the turn of the century resulted not from unions but from labor shortages and from competition between producers for workmen to operate the mills.

The tensions and hostilities between blacks and whites were dramatically demonstrated in the rise of the White Cap movement and the sporadic acts of violence perpetuated by the organization. The White Cap movement, a successor to the Ku Klux Klan, drew its support from the same element as had the Klan, namely, poorly educated whites from the lower strata of the population. The White Cappers were determined to keep blacks on the farm and to force mill owners not to employ workers of foreign origin.[30]

The Butterfield Lumber Company near Brookhaven, Mississippi, refused to fire black workers, and so incurred the wrath of the White Cappers, who burned the company's engine house.[31] In northeastern Jackson County the Gregory Luce logging operations employed thirty-one foreigners. The White Cappers posted notices near Luce's logging camp warning blacks and foreigners to leave their jobs or suffer bodily harm or death.[32] Near Van Cleave blacks employed by the L. N. Dantzler Lumber Company were threatened with death if they refused to quit their jobs.[33]

The improvement in the national economy, which began in the final years of the nineteenth century and continued down to 1907, plus the rapid growth of forest industries during the same period, produced an acute labor short-age in the pine country. Most of the expansion of forest industries resulted from mill owners from the northeast and naval stores operators from the Carolinas and Georgia who established plants in the pine country of the state. A northern mill owner moving to the state usually brought the key personnel and sought to recruit from the local population enough common labor to operate a mill. But the local population was unable to provide the army of workers necessary for the operation of large-scale forest industries.[34] Not until the Panic of late 1907, when large mills ceased operations, did the labor shortage end.

During the boom period black labor was a significant and necessary ele-ment in production of lumber and naval stores. In almost all lumber mills black men were often assigned jobs deemed dangerous to life and limb and tasks that required great physical strength and endurance. Moreover, the lowest-paying jobs were often those held by blacks. Few if any mill owners and foremen came from the black population.

Some of the most dangerous jobs in a sawmill were also those that re-quired men of above-average intelligence. The log carriage upon which logs were moved—with almost lightning speed—against the saw often split into sharp, pointed segments, endangering the blacks who operated the carriage blocks. Also, occasionally the bandsaw blade split into slivers of steel, fill-ing the space in which the carriage moved, sometimes wounding or killing the sawyers or carriage operators. Sometimes the carriage gears failed, and the carriage, traveling at great speed, hit a bunker and threw its operators up into the air, causing death or serious injury.

Almost always carriage operators working in unison had to make quick fractional calculations to determine the setting of the blocks for sawing the desired dimension of lumber. This required quick manual dexterity as well as the ability to use mathematical fractions.[35]

Another phase of lumbering monopolized by blacks was construction and maintenance of the logging railroads. Lifting railroad ties and steel rails and driving spikes required extraordinary physical strength as well as unusual endurance. In the hot, humid climate, one logging superintendent stated that in railroad construction blacks had no equals. They were, he said, in a class by themselves.[36]

John Saucier bossed the all-black section crew of the Finkbine Lumber Company. During the 1920s, one of his crewmen, a black giant, set the working pace of the crew. Often, when commencing work on an early sum-mer morn, he would sing out to the crew, "Lord, send me sunshine and I will send you a man." According to Saucier, his pacesetter burned out a lot of men who were either unwilling or unable to maintain the pace.[37]

All lumbermen were plagued by both the shortage and instability of labor during the lush period of lumbering, 1900–1907. S. C. Eaton, a lumberman near Hattiesburg, needed two hundred workers. He asserted that not a day passed without several blacks leaving the woods and mills. He reduced the hours of labor, increased wages, and gave free housing to workers, but all to no avail.[38]

In early 1907 an observer noted that not a single mill had enough workers. Following payday workers disappeared, returning to work only after their paychecks were exhausted. W. E. Guild, manager of the Finkbine Lumber Company at Wiggins and D'Lo, recommended the use of immigrant labor from northern Europe. They would, he said, save their money, work steadily, and become productive citizens.[39] J. J. White, mill owner at McComb, Mississippi, asserted that he had worked blacks when they were slaves and after they became free, and that they had become increasingly inefficient and unreliable: the higher the wages paid them the more unstable they became, he said.[40] Lumbermen seemed to agree that high wages paid blacks made them independent, and that they would work only enough to provide themselves with the necessities of life. One observer cited the high price of cotton as a reason for shortage of black labor in the sawmills. Given the choice, he said, blacks preferred picking cotton to working in sawmills.[41] I. C. Enochs, leader among lumbermen, attributed the shortage of workers to competition existing between cotton planters and mill owners.[42]

The state legislature, with the backing of Governor James K. Vardaman, enacted a drastic vagrancy law; however, it failed to solve the labor problem. The act, a modification of earlier legislation on the same subject, provided for imprisonment of from ten to twenty days for all idle able-bodied men. A second offense extended the time of imprisonment to ninety days and prohibited the payment of money to evade incarceration.[43] The vagrancy act worsened the labor problem. Blacks, perhaps rightfully, believed that the law was specifically intended to curtail their freedom and fled the state in considerable numbers.[44] Some lumbermen favored abolition of weekly paychecks on the ground that workers with money in their pockets would remain idle until the money was spent.[45]

Mill owners were far from unanimous, however, in their views as to the quality of black workers. Walter Barber, mill manager of Dantzler mills for more than thirty years, asserted that he knew black workers as a class to be both efficient and stable. He was especially impressed with the blacks who worked on sawmill carriages.[46] Another observer asserted that the average black, unspoiled by education and city life, was, if treated fairly, the best sawmill worker. He was as patient as an ox and as reliable as a steam engine. All he wanted was plenty of food and a chance to frolic occasionally.[47] S. S. Henry, a native lumberman, stated that he would rather have one black man than two whites, for a single black would do as much work as two whites. All the blacks want, he noted, is three square meals daily and a weekly wage payment.[48]

Supporting the contention that black labor was of high quality was the testimony of two German foresters who traveled through the pine country of the South in 1906. They said that only the black was acclimated to the subtropical South and his robust body withstood both heat and swamp fevers.[49] One foreman stated that in those jobs requiring great physical strength and endurance the black was superior to the white. They would, he said, stay on the job if given plenty to eat, a place to shoot craps, a place to preach, and good living quarters.[50]

Attempts to replace black with foreign labor proved disappointing. In the first place, only a few immigrants came to south Mississippi, and they remained only a short time. A few Germans came to Pearl River County and remained for only one day (the reason is said to have been "no beer"). The small number of Italians employed by Camp and Hinton at Lumberton proved unsatisfactory. The Norwegians at D'Lo left after a brief stay. The Danes who came to Wiggins likewise departed after a short period. With few exceptions, foreign immigrants, most of them from Northern Europe, avoided Mississippi, principally because of long, hot summers and the state's prohibition laws.[51]

From late 1907 to World War I in 1917 a long depression ended the labor shortage and created a surplus of unemployed. The lack of jobs brought out the latent animosities between the two races. When Camp and Hinton reduced wages at Lumberton, whites left their jobs and were replaced by blacks.[52] Angered by the company's action, whites with firearms forced blacks to quit working. At the Tatum mill near Hattiesburg, blacks were warned to stay out of the mill, and Tatum was told to fire all his black workers. But the owner stubbornly refused the crude attempt to coerce him and continued to employ blacks.[53]

Widespread unemployment and the concentration of considerable numbers of hungry blacks in towns produced fear in local white populations. Governor Vardaman, no friend of the blacks, called them a menace to society and demanded strict enforcement of the laws—particularly the vagrancy act.[54] One observer said that unemployed blacks resorted to theft on a small scale, but not to unusual acts of violence.[55]

Gradually, over the years, better working conditions developed, largely because of competition between mill owners for workers. The legislature enacted a ten-hour day for workers in factories, despite opposition by some lumbermen. The act did not apply to naval stores workers or to those employed in logging operation.[56] Phillip S. Gardiner, owner of the Eastman-Gardiner Lumber Company of Laurel, Mississippi, had reduced the workday to ten hours before the enactment of the law. Gardiner said experience had taught him that workers could produce as much in ten as in twelve hours.[57] The child-labor laws that aimed to regulate the labor of children were largely ineffective because no machinery existed to enforce the act.[58]

World War I and the postwar period to 1933 saw wages increase and overall living conditions improve, yet work hours remained unchanged. The depression of the thirties came almost simultaneously with the end of the big mill period, and created misery and poverty unknown to the region since the Civil War.

Although the great majority of black laborers in the Piney Woods from 1840 to 1933 were employed in lumbering, a sizable number were naval stores workers. Blacks constituted above 90 percent of workers employed in naval stores production. The naval stores industry derived its raw material from longleaf and slash pines found only in the southern and southeastern parts of the state. Naval stores had been produced from time to time on a small scale during and since the colonial period.[59] Only a few operations existed prior to the Civil War, one of these being the business operated by I. B. Ives and Francis Leech with slave labor on the lower Pearl River, at Napoleon. At Brewers Bluff, on the Pascagoula River, Thomas Gallaway and his slaves produced naval stores in the late 1850s.[60]

In the 1880s and early '90s, naval stores moved to Mississippi because of the exhaustion of virgin timber in the Carolinas and development of rail transportation. The migrating operators brought with them to the state hundreds of blacks who for generations had been naval stores workers. Joseph Simpson, accompanied by approximately one hundred blacks, came to Wiggins in 1900. Others with crews of blacks set up operations along the newly built Gulf and Ship Island Railroad around the turn of the century.[61]

In the longleaf-pine belt of the Piney Woods, virtually all sawmill operators conducted simultaneously a naval stores business. After the timber had been worked for not less than three years, the trees were sawn into lumber. Every aspect of naval stores production was, especially in large operations, conducted by blacks. Over decades a large number of blacks had come to form a unique socioeconomic group commonly known as turpentine workers. In many ways the status of turpentine workers was little different from that of slaves. Indeed, the slave system took care of the sick, aged, and infirm, but after age ended his working days, the naval store laborer lay around the quarters dependent on the charity of his friends for food and shelter until his death.[62] While there are no mortality statistics that deal specifically with naval stores workers, it is believed that their life span was shorter than that of workers in other occupations.[63]

Living usually in isolated villages out in the forest and having a standard of living lower than blacks in other occupations, the naval stores workers occupied what may be termed the "mud sill" of black society. Perhaps by design, the naval stores villages were usually located apart from agricultural communities and sawmill towns. Hence, turpentine workers had little contact with others not of their occupation; they lived in a world encompassed by the forest in which they worked and the village in which they lived. The village commissary, the boss, the village church, and the family were the realities of naval stores workers season after season, year after year.[64]

Because of the nature of operations used in naval stores production, workers were seldom paid wages. Chipping trees, dipping gum, boxing trees—the main tasks of naval stores production—were paid on a piecework basis. The chipper who cut streaks on the trees was assigned from seven to nine thousand faces to be chipped once each week. Beginning on Tuesday morning, the chipper usually finished his assignment late Friday afternoon and rested for the rest of the week. Dippers, including both women and children, were paid a certain amount for each barrel they filled with gum.[65]

The boss or manager of the turpentine operation wielded extraordinary power over the people of the village; even in matters of life and death he could be a determining influence. The boss hired and fired workers and decided the amount of goods one might purchase on credit from the village commissary. Enforcement of criminal law and punishment of the guilty were largely in the hands of the boss. If one worker killed another and the murderer was a good chipper, he might escape punishment completely. The boss settled disputes, punished infractions of the law, and kept peace in the village.[66]

The villagers lived in one-room unsealed huts that usually contained a bed, a stove, a table, and chairs. A centrally located pump provided the single supply of water for the entire village. Narrow streets separated rows of huts, built in close proximity to one another.[67] The average naval stores worker refused to live outside of the village. A request for housing away from the village was usually the first move of a worker who planned to leave and seek employment elsewhere.[68]

Over the years naval stores workers developed practices slightly different from those of blacks in other occupations. It is safe to say that naval stores blacks were little concerned with having their marriages legally sanctioned. Union between couples was a very simple matter; the couple requested the boss for a hut. He placed a bed, table, and stove in the hut and pronounced the couple man and wife. When separation was desired by the couple, if the boss approved, he had the furniture removed from the hut, thus ending the marriage.[69] At D'Lo, in 1917, most of those who were living together as married couples of the more than five hundred blacks had not had their union sanctioned by license or marriage ceremony. According to Simpson, he ordered all couples either to legalize their marriage or leave the village. Couples living together and having grown children now for the first time had their union legalized.[70]

The turpentine worker was rarely paid cash for his labor. Credit at the commissary was extended to all workers, who were encouraged to purchase goods in excess of their earnings, thus becoming permanently indebted to the employer. Workers, if paid at all, got company checks called "brozines," which could be used only to purchase goods from the commissary. In some operations workers received cash only at Christmas.[71]

Naval stores workers were a seminomadic people, rarely living in the same location longer than three years. As a result of their periodic movements from place to place, the naval stores blacks were never able to call any one place home. Children growing up in the villages lacked the opportunity to attend school for any length of time. The children, often unable to read or write, followed in the footsteps of their elders to become workers in an industry that provided little above the bare necessities for its participants for most of the period 1860–1933. Today, because of higher labor costs, there is not a single large naval stores operation in the state.

Forest industries have been the economic lifeblood of the pinewood sections of the state. Towns and cities grew out of forest industries during the last years of the nineteenth century. Labor both black and white provided the energy and muscle for forest industries. Black workers capable and usually hardworking made essential contributions to the economic evolution of the Piney Woods. In the words of one mill owner, they were as reliable as a steam engine and were always an important source of cheap labor for industry. Naval stores was, in fact, a black industry, and without the black man, could not have existed.

Notes

1. U.S. Bureau of the Census, Seventh Census, 1850, Schedule No. 1, Free Inhabitants, manuscript returns for Mississippi counties.
2. John F. H. Claiborne, "A Trip through the Piney Woods," *Publications of the Mississippi Historical Society* 9 (1906):523, 529; Frank L. Owsley, *Plain Folk of the Old South* (Baton Rouge: Louisiana State University Press, 1949), 72.
3. U.S. Bureau of the Census, Eighth Census, 1860, Schedule No. 2, Slave Inhabitants, manuscript returns for Mississippi counties.
4. Ibid.
5. Ibid., Schedule No. 1, Free Inhabitants, manuscript returns for Mississippi counties.
6. U.S. Census Office, Sixth Census, 1840, *Compendium* (Washington, 1841), 236.
7. Calvin Taylor and Family Collection, Department of Archives, Louisiana State University, Baton Rouge, Louisiana (hereafter "Taylor Coll."). The collection contains part of the Calvin Taylor Diary, all of the Serena Taylor Diary, journals, letters, and other papers.
8. Taylor Coll.
9. Ibid.; L. N. Dantzler Company Records, University of Mississippi Library (hereafter Dantzler Recs.). The collection contains journals, business records, deeds, wills, corporation reports, data on mill operations, and miscellaneous materials.
10. Dantzler Recs.; Taylor Coll., Journal No. 1.
11. Walter Barber, History of the L. N. Dantzler Lumber Company, typescript, 2; Wilmer Griffin, statement to the author, 2 May 1954.
12. U.S. Bureau of the Census, *Seventh Census* and *Eighth Census*, 1850, 1860. Schedule No. 2, Slave Inhabitants, manuscript returns for Mississippi counties.
13. Ibid., *Seventh Census*, 1850, Schedule No. 5, Products of Industry, manuscript returns for Mississippi counties.
14. Ibid., Schedule No. 2, Slave Inhabitants.
15. Ibid., *Eighth Census*, 1860, Schedule No. 2, Slave Inhabitants, manuscript returns for Mississippi counties.
16. Ibid.
17. John Clark, statement to the author, 6 June 1934. Clark was a logging contractor on the Biloxi rivers during the antebellum period.
18. Observations of the author during the late 1920s. The author noted the operation of a number of small sawmills in East Stone County.
19. U.S. Bureau of the Census, *Ninth Census*, 1870, Schedule No. 4, Products of Industry, manuscript returns for Mississippi counties.
20. John F. Hickman, statement to the author, 1 May 1954. Hickman was an acquaintance of Fairley; Barber, History of the Dantzler Lumber Co., 6.
21. Barber, History of the Dantzler Lumber Co., 4.
22. *Northwestern Lumberman* 26 (10 Oct. 1885):16; Dantzler Recs., Miscellaneous Papers.
23. John F. Hickman, statement to the author, 1 May 1954; Babe Fairley, statement to the author, 20 May 1954. Babe Fairley was the son of Wesley Fairley.
24. John F. Hickman, statement to the author, 10 June 1954.
25. Ibid.; Daniel G. McQuagge, statement to the author, June 1954.
26. Pascagoula *Democrat Star*, 9 July 1887.
27. Ibid., 22 Feb. 1889.
28. Ibid., 1 March 1889.
29. Ibid., 18 May 1900. John F. Hickman, statement to the author.
30. Pascagoula *Democrat Star*, 6 Feb. 1893; Governor John M. Stone Papers, vol. 2, Mississippi Department of Archives and History.
31. Ibid.
32. F. H. Lewis to Governor John M. Stone, 22 Nov. 1894, Stone Papers.
33. Walter Barber, statement to the author, 8 Jan. 1953.
34. *Southern Lumberman* 51 (25 Dec. 1906):57.
35. Walter Barber, statement to the author, May 1953; observations of the author, 1921.
36. *Lumber Trade Journal* 60 (1 Oct. 1911):18.

37. John Saucier, statement to the author, June 1933.
38. *American Lumberman* (16 June 1900):25.
39. *Lumber Trade Journal* 46 (15 Dec. 1904):15; Joseph Simpson, statement to the author, January 1953; *St. Louis Lumberman* 26 (15 Aug. 1905):52.
40. *St. Louis Lumberman* 26 (15 Aug. 1905):52.
41. *American Lumberman* (15 Oct. 1904):39.
42. Ibid. (16 April 1904):21.
43. *Mississippi Laws*, chap. 144 (29 Feb. 1904), 199–202.
44. *Lumber Trade Journal* 45 (1 June 1904):21; *St. Louis Lumberman* 33 (15 June 1904):30–31.
45. Ibid.
46. Walter Barber, statement to the author, June 1953.
47. *Southern Lumberman* 28 (1 July 1895).
48. Pascagoula *Democrat Star*, 4 Aug. 1904.
49. *St. Louis Lumberman* 39 (15 Feb. 1907):65.
50. *Lumber Trade Journal* 60 (1 Oct. 1911):18.
51. Joseph Simpson, statement to the author, 9 March 1954; *Southern Lumberman* 51 (25 March 1907):24E; *Lumber Trade Journal* 51 (15 April 1907).
52. *Lumber Trade Journal* 52 (5 Dec. 1907):39; ibid. 53 (15 April 1908):28.
53. Ibid.; *Southern Lumberman* 54 (11 April 1908):38.
54. *Southern Lumberman* 69 (25 June 1910):46.
55. Joseph Simpson, statement to the author, 9 March 1954; Alma Hickman, statement to the author, 1950.
56. *Mississippi Laws*, chap. 61 (15 June 1912), 48.
57. *Southern Lumberman* 71 (25 Oct. 1913):24.
58. *Mississippi Laws*, chap. 131 (20 March 1908), 137–38.
59. Carl E. Ostrom, "History of the Gum Namab Stores Industry," *Chemurgic Digest* 4 (15 July 1945):217; *Compendium Sixth Census*, 250.
60. Pascagoula *Democrat Star*, 8 May, 22 June 1889; Cyril Edward Cain, *Four Centuries on the Pascagoula* (Starkville, Miss. private printing, 1953), 148–49.
61. Charles Sargent, *Report of the Forest Trees of North America (Exclusive of Mexico)*, 7th Cong. 2d sess., H. Doc. 42, vol. 9 (1883), Serial 2137, Map opposite 580; U.S. Bureau of the Census, Tenth Census, 1880, vol. II, *Report on the Manufactures of the United States*, 141; Joseph Simpson, statement to the author, 9 March 1954.
62. Joseph Simpson, statement to the author, 9 March 1954; John Gary, statement to the author, September 1954; Gary, a black, was above seventy years in 1954. He had chipped timber in North Carolina, Georgia, Alabama, and Mississippi. Gary was intelligent and, for a turpentine worker, fairly well educated; Robert Newton, statement to the author, August 1954. Newton was a large turpentine operator for more than thirty years.
63. John Gary, statement to the author, September 1954; Joseph Simpson, statement to the author, 9 March 1954.
64. Ibid.; James O'Neil, statement to the author, May 1954. O'Neil managed the L. N. Dantzler Naval Stores business for more than two decades.
65. Ibid.; John Cross, statement to the author, 1954. As an employee of the U.S. government, Cross dealt with naval stores production in Mississippi.
66. Ibid.
67. John Gary, statement to the author, September 1954; Joseph Simpson, statement to the author, 9 March 1954.
68. Statement of O'Neil.
69. Statements of Simpson and Gary.
70. Statement of Simpson.
71. Statement of Gary; statement of O'Neil.

Sacred Harp Singing in the Piney Woods

JAMES C. DOWNEY

In 1900 the sounds of the Piney Woods were the steam-jenny calliopes, the rhythms of the double-faced ax, and the scream of millsaws rending the forest like a chorus of Valkyries. But when night came, men and women in the camps and neighboring communities turned their energies toward a kind of harmony that was new to an area accustomed to the spirituals and fuguing tunes of *Southern Harmony* and *Sacred Harp.*[1] The Piney Woods had its own distinctive musical sound that developed simultaneously with its towns and railroads at the turn of the nineteenth century. Sometimes called "rural gospel," or "shape-note gospel," the genre is best understood when compared to the folk music of the *Sacred Harp* tradition. It permeated both religious and secular functions with texts expressing the evangelicalism of its singers, and with music that was as lively and entertaining as a barn dance or minstrel show.

Shape note gospel or "seven-shape gospel" music was a product of blending together two diverse streams of American hymnody—the urban gospel songs of late nineteenth-century revivalism and the choral folk music of the southern states. Its purest form is the male quartet, with or without piano accompaniment. The sound forms the basic component in the style of the modern Oak Ridge Boys, the Statler Brothers, the Jordanaires, and numerous other popular singing groups. The style is carried over into soprano, alto, tenor, and bass texture, with the soprano serving as melody or lead, without losing the essential nature of the sound. The examples included with this article are classic examples of the form.

Mississippi, along with Alabama and Georgia, came to be the final resting place of a vigorous style of singing that dates back to the eighteenth century in England and America. It lies very close to the English folk tradition. It gave us the first generation of native composers like William Billings, Andrew Law, and Justin Morgan. After 1816 a new generation, led

by Ananias Davisson, William Walker, and B. F. White, institutionalized
it in the South in the singing schools where men and women learned to
sing from interlocking tetrachords sung to the syllables "fa–so–la" (see fig.
1). This method was an adaptation of a European solmization system dating
back to a tenth-century monk, Guido of Arezzo. Out of this folk tradition
came the sounds of the Piney Woods—shape-note gospel music.

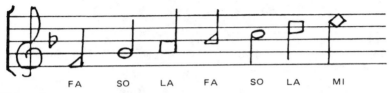

Figure 1

One can trace the tradition from 1801, when William Little and William
Smith published *The Easy Instructor,* a book of tunes in a notation of
geometric shapes, each representing a specific musical tone in the gamut
or scale. The system was widely circulated by a New England composer
and compiler, Andrew Law. In 1813, it was introduced into the South and
Midwest by John Wyeth of Harrisburg, Pennsylvania, who, with the aid
of music editor E. K. Dare, prepared the *Repository of Music: Part Second,* the first widely used tunebook to contain transcriptions of American
folk hymns.

Wyeth and Dare were imitated by Ananias Davisson, "Singing Billy"
Walker, and B. F. White, whose *Kentucky Harmony, Southern Harmony,*
and *Sacred Harp* became musical textbooks for the rural South and a
treasured repository of tunes transcribed from oral tradition and set for
choral voices in such a way that they preserved the tradition of the singers'
English and Scottish ancestors.

The *Sacred Harp* was the most popular collection used in Mississippi.
B. F. White organized "singing conventions," which used his book in their
monthly meetings and singing schools.[3] *Sacred Harp* was primarily used
above the Piney Woods, particularly in Calhoun and Chickasaw counties.
Reports of organized *Sacred Harp* singing in the state date back to 1853,
but the first records of a convention date from 1878.[4]

Numerous other collections were to be found in the state in the nineteenth century. One collection was compiled by L. J. Jones, Jr. (1816–97),
of Heidelberg, Mississippi. His book, *The Southern Minstrel,* was printed
by J. Lippincott in Philadelphia, Pennsylvania, in 1855. Tunes by Jones,
George D. McCormick, J. B. Yarborough, and W. P. Carter—all residents
of Jasper and Lauderdale counties at the northeastern corner of the

Mississippi Piney Woods—bear names of nineteenth-century communities like "Paulding" and "Oaky Valley." *The Southern Minstrel* was among the last and most western, geographically, of the four-shape publications to appear before the Civil War.

The publications showing the course of four-shape notation in the South, which culminated in the Piney Woods with L. J. Jones's *The Southern Minstrel,* are as follows:

Four Shape (Folk) Tradition: A Chronology

- 1801 *The Easy Instructor,* William Little and William Smith
- 1803 *The Musical Primer,* Andrew Law
- 1813 *Repository of Sacred Music: Part Second,* John Wyeth and E. K. Dare
- 1816 *The Kentucky Harmony,* Ananias Davisson
- 1835 *The Southern Harmony,* William Walker
- 1847 *The Sacred Harp,* B. F. White
- 1855 *The Social Harp,* John McCurry
- 1855 *The Southern Minstrel,* L. J. Jones

But the music of the Piney Woods does not sound like folk music. A piano is often heard accompanying the voices, and the singers read from seven-shape notation printed on pulp paper with a two- or three-color paperback cover. The pages resemble the popular music of the day, printed on a grand staff, not the octavo forms of the "long-boy" tune books of the singing conventions.

Seven-shape notation (fig. 2) simply extended the four-shape system, allowing each of the seven tones of the scale its own unique shape. The efficiency of seven-shape notation was ideally suited to the major tonality of American popular music, whereas four-shape notation served well the modal ambiguities of folk music.

Figure 2.   DO   RE   ME   FA   SO   LA   TI

Seven-shape notation can be traced to the publications of Joseph Funk and his descendants in the middle Atlantic states. Funk, a German immigrant to Virginia, published music for English and German settlers in the old tradition. He was greatly influenced by his English-speaking neighbors who sang the music in the Wyeth and Davisson collections. As the process of acculturation occurred, both groups came to share the same anthems and forms, including the camp-meeting or "Pennsylvania Dutch" spiritual. Funk's *Genuine Church Music* of 1832 became the most widely used compilation in the middle South. His life and the musical tradition he began has been immortalized in the Singers' Glen Festival held near Dayton, Virginia.

In 1846, Jesse B. Aikin published *Christian Minstrel* in Philadelphia in a new seven-shape notation. Funk's descendants tried unsuccessfully to obtain rights to use the patented system. In 1877, Aldine Kieffer, a grandson, obtained permission to use it in a new edition of *Genuine Church Music*. In 1870, using the new system, Kieffer began a campaign to educate normal-school students in the new method. He was hostile to proponents of the old style of the four-shape music. Through the periodical *The Musical Million*, the Ruebush-Kieffer Publishing Company spread the new notation and the new style throughout the South.[5]

The new church music carried by the seven-shape notation resembled most closely the urban gospel songs made popular in Great Britain and the northern areas of the United States in the Moody-Sankey revivals. New composers from the South began to write in the new style, sometimes retaining elements from the old tradition such as gapped (five-tone) scales, open final cadences, and some polyphonic byplay between voices.[6]

A. J. Showalter, another decendent of Joseph Funk, established a branch of the Ruebush-Kieffer Publishing Company in Dalton, Georgia. In 1888, he formed an independent publishing house to be the channel through which the new seven-shape gospel music would be carried into the Mississippi Piney Woods. Showalter continued to publish in the new notation and to advance the cause of "good taste" in the music of the South. He wrote over a thousand hymns in the new style, but only one is in use today, his pentatonic melody "Leaning on the Everlasting Arms" (fig. 3). In this and other southern "gospel songs," the appearance of the seventh scale degree is as a nonharmonic tone in the new "swinging" style. This serves to preserve much of the old gapped-scale sound of the folk tradition.

To spread the new system, singing schools similar to those of the older tradition were formed. The next illustration (fig. 4) appeared in *The Practical Music Reader*, published in 1904 by Ruebush-Kieffer.

Showalter was ideally placed to spread the new musical style. Two axes were formed between the Chattanooga area, dominated by the Showalter companies, and Dallas, Texas, the final center of publication of gospel music. The northern route extended through Lawrenceburg, Tennessee, into

Lean-ing on the ev-er-last-ing arms!

Figure 3

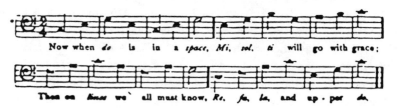

Figure 4

Arkansas. The main publishers were R. E. Winsett, of Chattanooga, James Vaughan, of Lawrenceburg, and the Hartford Music Company, of Little Rock. The southern route passed through Meridian, along the gulf coast, and through northern Louisiana to Dallas. The principal publishers were the Stamps-Baxter companies and the R. H. Coleman Company of Dallas.

Showalter was also located near the center of an intense religious revival, sometimes called the "Holiness revival," which swept the South, leaving in its wake new denominational alliances such as the Church of God and various pentecostal sects. The music of the new churches was rural gospel music in the seven-shape notation of the Showalter company. The music permeated traditional denominations, but it was the only musical style to be found in the new congregations.

Showalter had a direct influence in the Mississippi Piney Woods. His philosophical and theoretical positions are found in the manuals published by his company, *Class, Choir and Congregation* and *Rudiments of Music*. These were widely used throughout the state, even among the *Sacred Harp* singers. This fact may explain a unique feature of *Sacred Harp* singing in Mississippi. Historically, some conventions have used the seven-tone solmization—do, re, mi, fa, so, la, ti—to sing to the four shapes, which historian Buell Cobb described as "surely one of the unlikeliest stories of the shape note tradition in America."[7]

Other Showalter publications can be found in church libraries throughout the state. The earliest indication of this use was of Showalter's *Star of Bethlehem*, published in 1889. His *Rudiments* and collections, like the publications of Ruebush-Kieffer, were used in the Piney Woods in singing schools.

In 1910, C. C. Cunningham taught numerous singing schools around Picayune and Poplarville, sometimes using Ruebush-Kieffer publications. Beginning in 1914, there is evidence of Joe Cameron's activity in the Hattiesburg area, particularly a school held in the Lamar Lumber Camp at Oak Grove, just west of the city. Cameron, who is still remembered by residents, is reported to have used a wide selection of books throughout his life, including some publications by James Vaughan.

James Vaughan, who claimed that he invented the male quartet, founded his music company in 1912, although he had been active in promoting the new music long before. He was the first to produce recordings for a specific southern market. He bought WOAN, one of the first radio stations in the area. He sold his books by means of traveling male quartets who gave concerts on any occasion and sold Vaughan paperback gospel songbooks to churches and individuals. By 1964, Vaughan had published 105 different collections. Unlike the four-shape singers who wanted the old, "original" versions, there came to be a planned obsolescence in the collections of Vaughan and his contemporaries. The books were intended to be used for a few months and discarded when the next quartet arrived with the "new" or "improved" collection.[8]

In the lumber camps and towns where men lived in tents or boarding houses, the male quartet was a ready means of passing idle hours. Singing schools were taught in the camps and in community churches, where women's voices were added. It was customary for the members of a school or a church choir to have a photograph made, as items in the Piney Woods Collection at the University of Southeastern Louisiana will attest. Singers are shown standing or seated in ranks in military precision, holding their paperback hymnals before them.

Vaughan's books are to be found throughout the Piney Woods area, although their popularity seems to have been greater in the northern counties where WOAN brought the music into homes on early radio sets. Entire church choirs from towns like Macon often made trips to sing in the radio studios at Lawrenceburg and Jackson, Tennessee.

In Laurel, Mississippi, there are records of the Bush Brothers Quartet covering a period of thirty years. The piano came to be an integral part of the "rural gospel" sound in the early 1920s, and a distinct "gospel piano" style emerged. Nelda Holifield was the first woman to teach gospel singing schools in the area. She taught schools for various publishers all over the state. She was known in her hometown of Laurel as a piano teacher as well as a gospel singer.[9]

J. L. Roseberry of Hattiesburg founded the Roseberry Piano House in the early 1920s. His son Lloyd introduced various gospel publishers' collections into the store and was active in promoting gospel concerts. He said that gospel music accounted for 75 percent of his business in the forties and early fifties. Roseberry was the principal source of gospel-music publications in the Piney Woods area.

Val Sumrall and his brother, W. Herbert Sumrall, were active in the state gospel-music convention. W. H. Sumrall often scheduled the singing conventions in the auditorium of the Mississippi Southern College. He became the first dean of graduate studies there, while continuing to sing bass in a gospel quartet, and holding offices in the state convention.

A young associate of Showalter, J. B. Baxter, Jr., joined with Virgil O. Stamps in 1926 to form the Stamps-Baxter Music Printing Company. They relocated in Dallas, Texas, where they published, conducted schools for singers, operated radio station KRLD, and came to dominate the entire gospel-music business, not just that in the Piney Woods. Stamps-Baxter, like the firms of Vaughan and Hartford Music, encouraged composition in the new form. Thousands of new songs, written by those who had attended a gospel "singing school," poured in to be arranged by a contract composer, and to appear in one of their many paperbacks.

Two of the most prominent of the contract composers retained by the Stamps-Baxter companies were Videt Polk and J. B. Coats. Polk, founder and guiding light in the Gospel Singers of America, a summer encampment at Pass Christian, Mississippi, contributed hundreds of songs to the collections. He became the last president of the Stamps-Baxter Music Printing Company, which was eventually sold to Zondervan Corporation of Grand Rapids, Michigan. Polk, using youthful, talented graduates of southern colleges, gave excellent instruction to the young people who assembled each year at Pass Christian. He also incorporated into the curriculum the values of a conservative, early nineteenth-century America where God and country, moral living, and self-fulfillment found expression in gospel music.

The Rev. J. B. Coats was the most revered of the Piney Woods gospel-song composers. He lived his entire life between Laurel and Hattiesburg, becoming pastor of his home church and serving that congregation until his death. His church, Summerland Baptist Church, and his home became stopping places for gospel singers traveling through the Piney Woods area. His son, Edsel Coats, in his master's thesis at the University of Southern Mississippi, "The Singing School in Mississippi," vividly describes the period from the late 1930s to 1961, when his father was not only the busiest of the singing-school teachers in the area but a major influence on the music of the Stamps-Baxter publishers.

In 1951, Coats published *Mississippi Melodies*, a collection of 150 of his compositions, through the Stamps-Baxter company. The announcement of his death in 1961 was carried by the major news wire services. His life and its contributions to gospel music were eulogized in a Paul Harvey broadcast carried throughout the South.

Ward Hurt relocated to the Piney Woods from his home in Chattanooga. He established a furniture-manufacturing plant in Lumberton and served several terms as mayor of that city. He continued performing in gospel singing groups in Mississippi after his arrival. He organized numerous ensembles, singing conventions, and social functions built around the gospel-music sound as "the people's music." He organized a male quartet, the Bibletones, which preserved the old style while other groups were introducing new electronic instruments, drums, and various innovations that changed the basic sound and function of the gospel quartet. Hurt was a businessman who loved gospel music, not a teacher, writer, or agent for publishers. He, like W. H. Sumrall, exerted a strong influence on the style as it came to be known in Mississippi. He is introduced to audiences in the 1980s as "Mr. Gospel Music," a title that aptly describes a man of many accomplishments with a consuming fervor for the Piney Woods sound.

Shape-note gospel developed within the stream of publications beginning with Joseph Funk and culminating in those of the Stamps-Baxter companies. The following publications and events are significant:

Seven Shape Publications: A Chronology

1832	*Genuine Church Music*, Joseph Funk
1846	*Christian Minstrel*, Jesse B. Aiken
1877	*Genuine Church Music*, Aldine Kieffer
1877	*Musical Million*, Ruebush-Kieffer Co.
1884	A. J. Showalter Publications
1889	*Star of Bethlehem*, Ruebush-Kieffer Co.
1890	*Class, Choir and Congregation*, A. J. Showalter
1912	James Vaughan Publications
1926	Stamps-Baxter Publications
1945	Stamps Quartet Publishing Co.
1964	Sale of Stamps Quartet Publishing Co. to Church of God publishing corporation
1974	Sale of Stamps-Baxter Publishing Co. to Zondervan Corporation

Aldine Kieffer and A. J. Showalter would probably be troubled by the unexpected by-product of their efforts to "improve" the musical practices of their time with an efficient system of notation. The new musical genre that was developed in the hands of Vaughan, Winsett, Virgil Stamps, and

J. R. Baxter was to become a vital element in southern music in the twentieth century.

The culture of the Piney Woods of southern Mississippi developed simultaneously with the flourishing timber industry, its lumber camps, and, all too often, a transient population that erected towns overnight near the

Examples of Shaped-Note Gospel Songs

railroads and waterways only to abandon them as the sound of the millsaws moved south and west. Gospel music, the most characteristic expression of that time and place, testified to the energy and high spirit of a people whose religious faith and optimism made them sing, not about their troubles and trials, but of the goodness of the "promised land."

Farther Along

W. B. S.

W. B. Stevens
Arr. J. R. Baxter, Jr.

1. Tempt-ed and tried we're oft made to won-der Why it should be thus all the day long, While there are oth-ers liv-ing a-bout us, Nev-er mo-lest-ed tho in the wrong.
2. When death has come and tak-en our loved ones, It leaves our home so lone-ly and drear; Then do we won-der why oth-ers pros-per, Liv-ing so wick-ed year af-ter year.
3. Faith-ful till death said our lov-ing Mas-ter, A few more days to la-bor and wait; Toils of the road will then seem as noth-ing, As we sweep thru the beau-ti-ful gate.
4. When we see Je-sus com-ing in glo-ry, When He comes from His home in the sky; Then we shall meet Him in that bright man-sion, We'll un-der-stand it all by and by.

CHORUS

Far-ther a-long we'll know all a-bout it, Far-ther a-long we'll un-der-stand why; Cheer up, my broth-er, live in the sunshine, We'll understand it all by and by.

Notes

1. Walker, William. *The Southern Harmony and Musical Companion.* New Ed. Philadelphia: Ed. W. Miller, 1854; and While, B.F., and E. J. King. *The Sacred Harp,* 1844. For a list of editions, see Buell E. Cobb, *Sacred Harp: A Tradition and its Music.* Athens: University of Georgia Press, 1978.
2. For a discussion of the shape-note music in the South, see Gilbert Chase, *America's Music: From the Pilgrims to the Present.* New York: McGraw-Hill Book Co., 1955.
3. Cobb, *op. cit.*
4. Downey, James C. "Bound for the Kingdom" in *We Shall Come Rejoicing: A History of Baptist Church Music in Mississippi,* Ed. Gwen Keyes Hitt. Jackson: Mississippi Baptist Convention, 1984.
5. Eskew, Harry. "Shape Note Hymnody," *Grove's Dictionary of Music,* 6th Ed., ed. Stanley Sadie. New York: Macmillan, 1978.
6. For a detailed study of the "gospel hymn" of American revivalism, see James C. Downey, "Revivalism, the Gospel Song and Social Reform," *Ethnomusicology,* IX, 2 (May, 1965): or James C. Downey, "Mississippi Music: That Gospel Sound," in *Sense of Place: Mississippi,* eds. Peggy Prenshaw and Jess McKee. Jackson: University Press of Mississippi, 1979.
7. Cobb, *op. cit.*
8. James Vaughan of Lawrenceburg, Tennessee, was the principal publisher along the northern axis of seven-shape publishing. A detailed discussion of Vaughan may be found in "Shape Note Hymnody" in Grove's, *op. cit.*
9. Coats, Edsel. "The Singing School in Mississippi," unpublished master's thesis, University of Southern Mississippi, 1968.

Selected Sources

Baxter, Mrs. J. R., Jr., and Videt Polk. *Gospel Song Writers.* Dallas: Stamps Publishing, 1971.
Cobb, Buell E., Jr. *Sacred Harp: A Tradition and Its Music.* Athens: University of Georgia Press, 1978.
Downey, James C. "Mississippi Music: That Gospel Sound," *Sense of Place: Mississippi,* eds. Peggy Prenshaw and Jess McKee. Jackson: University Press of Mississippi, 1979.
————. "Bound for the Kindgom." In *We Shall Come Rejoicing: A History of Baptist Church Music in Mississippi,* ed. Gwen Keyes Hitt. Jackson: Mississippi Baptist Convention, 1984.
Fleming, J. L. *James D. Vaughan, Music Publisher, Lawrenceburg, Tennessee, 1912-1964.* Ph.D. diss., Union Theological Seminary, 1971.
Hall, P. M. *The Musical Million: A Study and Analysis of the Periodical Promoting Music Reading through Shape-Notes in North America from 1870 to 1914.* Ph.D. diss., Catholic University of America, 1970.

"A Creature Set Apart"
Pearl Rivers in the Piney Woods

W. KENNETH HOLDITCH

At what precise moment of her young life Eliza Jane Poitevent decided to become Pearl Rivers, to take for her pseudonym the name of that "laughter-loving stream" in South Mississippi beside which she spent much of her childhood, it is impossible to tell. The reason for her choice of that unique nom de plume is, on the other hand, no mystery at all; it lies revealed for any reader of the prose and poetry she was to publish from her late teens to the time of her death one month short of her forty-seventh birthday. In poem after poem, essay after essay, letter after letter, she speaks of her abiding love for "that happiest of places, the home of my childhood," that spot in the heart of the Piney Woods to which she returned through the years when, as she told friends and employees, "she must go back to nature for rest and peace and comfort."[1] No writer has been more devoted to his or her place of origin, but that, of course, seems almost an inevitable part of the makeup of a Mississippi writer, from Pearl Rivers to William Faulkner to Eudora Welty to Willie Morris. That sense of place of which Welty has eloquently spoken and written as it relates to fiction manifests itself clearly in Pearl Rivers's efforts in other genres.

What an amazing spectacle it must have been for the hardened and cynical reporters and other employees of the New Orleans *Picayune* when Eliza Jane Poitevent moved in the short space of two years from being a rural contributor to the newspaper to become its owner, publisher, and editor. Not only was she a woman, possessed of all the weaknesses and natural shortcomings most men of that time attributed to her sex, but her education was of the vague and idealistic variety dispensed at young ladies' academies of the day—in later years she herself disparaged her training as for the most part useless. Besides, she was young, and had come out of rural Mississippi to take on New Orleans, a city that prided itself, with some justification, on its sophistication and culture. It was not the first time

Pearl Rivers

The Historic New Orleans Collection

people beyond the boundaries of Mississippi had been astounded by what that state, with its reputation for being predominantly rural and backward, could produce; and it was certainly not to be the last. Those roots she never forgot, never shunned, and her devotion to the state of Mississippi and its people, to the Pearl River and the Piney Woods is amply demonstrated in three decades of her work.

It is difficult for people living in the liberated 1980s to imagine the daring required for a young woman from the southern country gentry to leave her family in southern Mississippi and become a resident of such a city as New Orleans, then, even more than now, the very symbol of urban sin and corruption. New Orleans in 1872 was still the capital of the state of Louisiana—the removal to Baton Rouge did not occur until 1877—and a bankrupt city under occupation. Federal troops were everywhere, and conditions very like martial law still existed. In contrast to its reputation as "the city that Care forgot," Reconstruction had converted the prosperous metropolis of the prewar years into a social and economic battleground where longtime residents struggled against exorbitant taxes and other forms of oppression to hold onto their property. Thousands fled the city during the decade after the end of the war, while others stayed to fight the carpetbaggers and the threat of newly freed blacks who occupied positions for which they were often ill suited. Organizations such as the Ku Klux Klan expanded and flourished; battles between them and the "invaders," white and black, were common; and a general atmosphere of lawlessness prevailed, making the period the darkest in the city's history. Hopes for the future seemed dim, and the once-great port languished like some backwater town, stale and brackish, in an era when northern cities expanded and prospered. This was the New Orleans to which the youthful Eliza Poitevent moved from her country home.

Another element of her daring in abandoning the idyllic purity of rural life for the temptations of the beleaguered city was the fact that she was accepting a paying position (she began at a salary of twenty-five dollars a week), and not as a teacher or a governess, acceptable occupations for a young lady of good station, but as a newspaperwoman. Journalists of the time had acquired a reputation, whether justified or not, for being a rough-and-tumble lot, little better in their manners or morals than riverboat gamblers or jockeys and other racetrack hangers-on. And a newspaper-woman? Did such a creature even exist? Not surprisingly, family members were passionate in their opposition to the move and, not surprisingly either, given the determination and strength she was to exhibit in the crises of the next few years, Eliza was adamant and had her way. She became a journalist, a professional, no longer merely a correspondent mailing her contributions in from the hinterlands, but a paid member of the staff of that previously all-male bastion, the New Orleans *Picayune*, a pioneer in a field hitherto almost closed to women nationwise.

Hardly had the small but dynamic woman settled in New Orleans and taken her place in the building affectionately referred to in newspaper circles as "the old lady of Camp Street" before she began to make her influence felt. She expanded the *Picayune*'s literary section, introducing fiction and sketches by such authors as Mark Twain, Joel Chandler Harris, and Bret Harte. She increased the number of poems and book reviews and had soon acquired a reputation as an energetic worker and a meticulously careful editor. Her own poems continued to appear frequently in the paper, and on 19 February 1871 her first signed piece was published. From that day until shortly before her death, her articles and columns of a variety of types, on a variety of subjects, were regular features of the *Picayune*.

It must have come as a considerable relief to her parents when Eliza and Colonel Alva Holbrook, her employer, were married 18 May 1873. The appearance of evil which had surely troubled them when they considered the spectacle of a young daughter of a good family working at a "common" job in the "wicked" city cannot have been totally offset by the fact that she was living in the home of her grandfather. That Holbrook was sixty-four and Eliza only twenty-three probably did not in any way cloud their relief, since such marriages were not unusual in a time when a large portion of the young male population had been annihilated in the Civil War. What may have given them pause, however, was the fact that Colonel Holbrook was a divorced man; and their concern in this regard, if it existed, must surely have been intensified when a month after the wedding the first wife entered the Holbrook home and shot at the new wife twice, and, when both bullets missed their mark, attacked Eliza with a bottle of bay rum. When Eliza fled, bloody, to the home of a neighbor, the melodrama continued as the first Mrs. Holbrook assaulted the furniture with an ax until she could be subdued. Her subsequent incarceration and trial were a sensation in New Orleans and received extensive coverage in the *Picayune*, which Holbrook had sold shortly before the wedding.

Despite this inauspicious beginning, the marriage seems to have been a successful one, if brief in duration. Holbrook in 1873 repurchased the newspaper and Eliza once again became a contributor, although she did not work on the staff during this period. In 1876, Alva Holbrook died, leaving his twenty-seven-year-old widow with a bittersweet legacy: the newspaper to which she was obviously devoted was hers, but its debts exceeded eighty thousand dollars and a libel suit of two hundred thousand had been filed against it. Her dilemma was a difficult if clear-cut one: she could declare bankruptcy or she could struggle to save the paper. Not surprisingly, given the initiative and determination and courage she had earlier shown in taking the *Picayune* position in the face of strong opposition, she decided to fight for her inheritance. Calling the staff together, she presented the facts in a straightforward manner some of them were to remember and record. "I am a woman," she told them. "Some of you may not wish to work for a woman. If so, you are free to go, and no hard feelings. But you who stay— will you give me your individual loyalty, and will you advise me truly and honestly?" Most remained to work for the first woman in the world ever to own and operate a big-city newspaper. Two years after Holbrook's death, Eliza married George Nicholson, an Englishman from Leeds who was business manager of the paper, and for the rest of their lives, they worked together to make the venture a success.

Under Eliza Nicholson's control, the *Daily Picayune* fought for reforms in the state government, in the police and fire departments of the city, and in the management of the state asylum at Jackson. Editorially the paper spoke out for prison reform, and when Louisiana became the fourth state in the Union to abolish the leasing of convicts to private businesses, Eliza and the *Picayune* had played a significant part in bringing about the change. In addition, she supported a public library for New Orleans, endeavored to have a public lecture series established, and offered encouragement to the French Opera House. Her sponsorship of those individuals and organizations active in the intellectual and literary life of the city was, Lamar Whitlow Bridges states, a part of what she called a "grand dream" to make New Orleans the "winter capital of arts and letters."[2] She added to the paper society coverage, a children's page, and any number of features designed for women, in the process turning the *Picayune* into a truly "family newspaper" as opposed to the male-oriented journal, typical of its time, which it had been before.

One historian of the *Picayune* under Eliza Nicholson's management has argued that she was probably not a feminist, judging from the paper's editorial stand in regard to suffrage and the fact that the paper's "attention to women's advances in the Gilded Age was also strangely mute in comparison to what one might expect in a journal owned by a woman, who herself was something of an innovator in Southern journalism."[3] It is, of course, easy after the fact to take to task those of a previous age for failing to advocate what we, possessed of more information and better perspective supplied by the passage of the years, see clearly to be right. Eliza Nicholson was a part of her age and therefore, as we are all fated to be, was shaped by it; and yet, it seems to me, the evidence for calling her an early feminist tends to belie this judgment in regard to her nonfeminist position. She argued in both word and example—and surely the latter is the more important of the two—if not for the equality of women, then at least for an acknowledgment that they were capable of much more than their position in the nineteenth-century American home and society had permitted them.

First as a journalist and later as editor and publisher of a major metropolitan newspaper—which she rescued from financial ruin and converted from a journal of limited appeal to one designed to entertain and inform a majority of the population—she demonstrated clearly what a woman could do in business, given the opportunity. Her poetry, her editorials, and her columns argued often for the humanity and rights of women. Poems, sometimes ironic, portray the suffering the female heart frequently was forced to endure:

> Only a heart, do not fear, my lord,
> Nobody on earth is near
> To come to the cry of the wounded thing,
> And God is too far to hear.

This early lyric foreshadows the majestic rage of the woman abused and scorned that is powerfully portrayed in Pearl Rivers's poetic masterpiece, "Hagar." Her prose writing argued more directly and openly for the rights of women. She supported better salaries for teachers, for example, and in 1888 she attacked the "useless education" being provided for women of the time. When Belva Ann Lockwood ran for President on the National Equal Rights Party ticket in 1892, the *Picayune*'s unnamed editorialist wrote that the time would come when it would be possible for a woman to become chief executive—this in an age when women were still without the vote. Women journalists, she wrote in 1879, were coming to prominence "slowly but surely," and men could "not fail to see that the influence of women who read the papers is increasing tremendously."[4] Although the newspaper's stand might not be as affirmative as the liberal of the 1980s might desire, Eliza's example and her occasional printed words always offered encouragement for the future.

One of the changes Eliza Nicholson effected in the paper was to expand considerably the coverage of news from the state of Mississippi. This resulted, Lamar Bridges observes, "partly no doubt because of her love of the state, but also because South Mississippi was a part of the circulation area." He is probably correct in this balanced evaluation of Eliza's motivation, for she was a businesswoman, and a good one; and poetry did not interfere with business. But consider her frequent remarks about the state that gave her birth. For example, in the essay in the *Picayune* entitled "An Idle Hour at My Desk" she asserts that "There are no people like our Southern people. No people so warm-hearted, so cultivated and so hospitable as the people of Louisiana unless it is the people of my own dear state of Mississippi!" Her heart, she says, beats "warmly for the people among whom I was born and with whom I was reared and with whom I would divide my last crust or my very last Picayune."[5] The concluding pun is typical of the wit that sparkles in her prose and contributes much of its charm.

How did she learn, one may wonder from the perspective of a century later, to run a newspaper so quickly and well, with little training, little education? Perhaps the judgment of one of her famous colleagues and protégées is as valid as any explanation. Dorothy Dix, who originated the column of letters to the lovelorn in this country, had been a neighbor of the Nicholsons and was hired by Eliza as a columnist when she was in financial need. Dix said of her employer that she was like "little Billee in Du Maurier's story, who knew things by the grace of God, without being told."[6]

When in 1896 Eliza Nicholson succumbed to an attack of influenza, only eleven days after the death of George Nicholson, she left the New Orleans *Picayune* in much better condition, financially and editorially, than she had found it twenty years before. She had rescued it from heavy debt and made it prosperous; she had enlarged it both in terms of the number of pages and in the coverage of news and the areas that interested her readers. Circulation had grown from six thousand to twenty thousand on weekdays and thirty thousand for the greatly expanded and diversified Sunday issue. The audience had grown not only in numbers but in types of readers; other segments of society, notably women and children, had been provided with reading matter of interest to them. Eliza Nicholson had established the reputation of the *Picayune* nationwide and in the process had made a name for herself as a journalist of note. Numerous awards from both American and international press clubs and from women's organizations make it clear that her position as a trailblazer in the field was widely recognized. She had indeed in a brief forty-seven years come a far distance from those early days on the banks of the Pearl River in South Mississippi.

It is unclear exactly when the first Poitevent ancestors of Pearl Rivers emigrated from France to America. Several genealogies prepared by members of the family at various times in this century, unreliable as such documents tend to be, give different accounts of the year when the American branch was established. One argues that Poitevents left France before Louis XIV's revocation of the Edict of Nantes in 1685. Another identifies Antoine Poitevent as part of that large exodus of Huguenots which was instigated by the Sun King's action and the subsequent persecution. Whatever the fact may be, it is true that there were Poitevents in the colonies in the last decades of the seventeenth century, most of them settled in the Carolinas. In 1835 John Poitevent, one of the descendants of Antoine, joined yet another exodus, of which my own paternal ancestors were a part, that westward movement from the eastern seaboard states to Mississippi in search of that new Zion or El Dorado of which another Piney Woods author, James Street, has written in *Oh, Promised Land*. This was the first period of tremendous growth for the state, of course, for in the two decades between 1830 and 1850, population in Mississippi expanded from 132,631, to 696,526.[7]

The first Mississippi Poitevent, John, settled in what is now Grenada County and is buried there in Pine Hills Cemetery. His son William James moved at some point to Gainesville, Mississippi, thus becoming the first Piney Woods Poitevent. He and his wife Mary Amelia Russ became the parents of eight children, of whom Eliza Jane, born 11 March 1849, was the third. One of the genealogies notes, without apparent recognition of the irony involved, that the elder Poitevents were buried in Gainesville in 1873 and 1896, but their bodies were moved to Picayune "after the NASA project was erected." So much for the promised land!

During Eliza's early years, her mother was an invalid and the child was sent to live with an aunt and uncle, Mr. and Mrs. Leonard Kimball, at their home near Hobolochitto. It was here that she spent most of her youth, a solitary child by her own account, but apparently not lonely; here that she formed her deep and lifelong attachment for the woods and the river that brightened her life and inspired much of her writing; here that she became, as she describes herself in "The Singing Heart," "a creature set apart." No doubt not only her love of nature and her creative introspection but also her resourcefulness and resilience in the business world have their roots in these early years and their experiences.

Whenever Pearl Rivers remembered her childhood and spoke of it or wrote of it, both the Piney Woods and the Pearl River figured significantly in the account. "I remember that old, dear home of mine, on the banks of the brown river, who was my fairy godmother," she wrote in "Indian Baskets." In one of the columns entitled "Leonard and I," which she wrote occasionally for the *Picayune*, this one dated in October 1886, she remarked that "there is no charm in nature that leads me back to that happiest of all places, the home of my childhood, by such pleasant paths as the magic music of the cricket's flute." She had been recently in Virginia, and in a humorous touch typical of her best prose, she compared the crickets she had heard there to those of her own region: "Our Mississippi and Louisiana crickets are not so aristocratic as the 'F.F.V.'s' and do not live in stately brown fronts but in summer houses all year round. A bit of pine bark, a whisp of grass, or a big leaf, is the only roof our jolly crickets need."

When she moves from the specific object of nature that inspired her musings to contemplate the past, she does so by relating to her son the memories that haunt her and feed her soul:

> Speaking softly, with tears in my eyes, the echo of which Leonard is quick to catch in my voice, I take my child back with me to the beautiful home of my childhood in the pine woods, and tell him how happy and merry I was, although there were only two people and a cat in the house for me to love; how I made friends with all the wild things in the woods and all the tiny people in the grass, and how I once caught three crickets and carried them into my bedchamber to keep me company.

When Leonard inquired if they did indeed keep her company, she replied that they lived happily in a crack in the chimney corner all winter, and because she fed them, "they repaid me for my bounty with a serenade each night."[8] In a similar vein she states in an essay called "Bird Lore" that she has heard of Virginia bluejays stealing cherries and getting drunk on them; but they are "F.F.V.'s,' she says, while "the jays I know are Mississippians and Louisianians, and the worst that can be said against their morals is that they are 'suck-egg' birds, and do not hesitate to help themselves to an omelet when their succotash of caterpillars and Indian corn is scantier than their appetite."[9]

In another "Leonard and I" column, she writes, following her penchant for studying the small, seemingly insignificant in nature, about doodlebugs: "I used to think myself wondrous wise in wood and flower and bird and bug, and butterfly and caterpillar lore," she begins, "but I find that my education must all be got over again. My ignorance confronts me at the very doorsteps in the shape of doodles." She observes that any "southern boy or girl who has not fished for doodles, with a straw, lives in a city and is to be commiserated" for having missed "the most fascinating amusement that falls to a child's lot." In the same column she remembers and describes dog fennel and the red sumac and "nigger heads" and golden rod that filled the woods in which her childhood was spent.[10]

In "An Idle Hour at My Desk," Pearl Rivers recounts her encounter during a train ride from Opelousas, Louisiana, to New Orleans with a sugar planter from the Teche country. She marvels that after they had exchanged the requisite greetings, what he talked to her about was "a tiny, white, star-shaped bitter sweet flower that grows in the piny woods and that lies so close to the ground that I thought nobody but me and the grass and the birds had ever discovered it."[11] In another column she asserts that she knows all about Indian baskets "from the time they were tender, juicy canes rustling their long leaves on the banks of the Pearl River, or green palmettoes, spreading their broad hands in benediction over the dark waters of Bayou LaCroix."[12] Such remarks, which appear frequently in the prose writings of her mature years, indicate the extent to which the memories of her Piney Woods childhood remained a real presence and influence all of her life.

She learned during those idyllic years on her aunt and uncle's farm to ride horses, something she continued to do as an adult. In one *Picayune* column she recounts having received a request from some schoolgirls asking how to ride horseback gracefully. "I know nothing of riding horseback gracefully as an art, dear girls," she writes, "but I used to be a sort of cowboy in petticoats long years ago, and I can tell you all about the natural way of riding." Her first such experience, she recalls, occurred when she was seven and rode the old carriage horse, so broad backed and long maned that she needed no saddle or bridle, to the creek in order for him to drink. As a result of this experience, she is convinced "that if a girl wishes to establish an intimate acquaintance with a horse, and acquire a perfectly good seat on his back, she should take her first lesson without saddle or bridle." She continues to describe other childhood experiences with the horses on the farm:

> I was not allowed to ride any of the horses except old Bald—how well I remember him—until I was 10 years old, and then I was promoted to the pommeled dignity of a saddle and pony of my own, and allowed to take the dog every evening and ride away to drive the milk cows home. Ah! those long, merry hunts for the cattle through the piny woods, with nobody but my pony and my dog to keep me company! We traveled for miles, sometimes, before we heard the faint tinkle of the leader's bell, and I learned to give that peculiar musical "who-er, whoo!" that is shouted by the cowboys of the piny woods.[13]

Sometimes, she says, the pony balked at jumping a log or stepped into a hole and fell, taking her with him, "but I never got hurt, and I owe my suppleness and ease in the saddle to those cowboy exploits in the piny woods." She continued these cattle-hunting expeditions, she recalls, until she was fifteen and was sent away to boarding school "to learn—I must almost say nothing that has been of much use to me as a woman."[14]

Pearl Rivers's childhood memories as they appear in her verse tend to be more generally romantic and less descriptive of regional flora and fauna than in her prose. In a long poem entitled "Myself," however, published while she was still living in Mississippi, she refers to swallows, bees, minnows, ants, butterflies, spiders, ground moles, hares, fox squirrels, a speckled hen, and a pony; and to Cherokee roses, water lilies, briars and brambles, daisies, pitcher plants, chinquepins, whortleberries, and violets. The poem is a typically romantic account of how a child is educated by nature, à la Wordsworth; in this instance it is specifically the flowers who instruct the ten-year-old girl in the gentle words and modest grace that "maidens all should wear." The nineteen-year-old poet begins by describing herself as a child living with her aunt and uncle in the woods near "a laughter-loving stream" in a "rambling, old log house" with two "quaint old chimneys," low and narrow windows, and chinks through which the sun could shine. The ten-year-old Eliza is portrayed as simple, wild, carefree, solitary but happy, a "merry roguish elf," who "played 'keep house' in shady nooks," waded in the stream, rode the pony, became sunburned, and tore her dress in "frolic wild and free." Unable to master geography, grammar, or mathematics from her "vexing books," she was, however, "quick to learn" the names of all the birds, where the speckled hen had nested, and other lessons of nature which she observed with "wonder-loving eyes."[15]

The *Picayune* for 23 February 1879 contained a poem called "Pearl River," in which Eliza created for that stream near which she had been born a legend to explain the name she shared with it. The verse is rather bad, far inferior in quality to her best lyrics and her two late dramatic monologues. The romantic excesses and strained meter bespeak the typical newspaper verse of the day, written under pressure to meet a deadline. The subject matter, however, makes the poem integral to any study of the influence of the Piney Woods region upon Pearl Rivers and her work. In a headnote she states that in the absence of any "Indian legend associated with Pearl River," she has determined to give to "the river I love so much a legend of my own making." Her native stream, she says, had its origin in "a hilly north county" where the Great Spirit gave a pearl to Tonka, an Indian girl. Her tears for the "past glory" of her nation melted the pearl, and, in legend, she weeps, the pearl melts, and the river flows on forever.

> In old Mississippi, God give her
> His blessings! are many old towns
> Peeping over high bluffs at my river
> To see if it smiles or it frowns.

She proceeds to list the Mississippi towns past which it flows—Jackson, "gray Monticello," and "marshy old Pearlington," before it finally moves through the "gates of the swift Rigolets" and is "lost in the blue Pontchartrain." Her river, she concludes, is fairer than those that "spring from a mountain," for its foundation is "a maiden's pure bosom" on which a pearl is eternally melting.[16]

One of the most revealing documents in terms of both Eliza Poitevent's life with her second husband, George Nicholson, and of her devotion to the Piney Woods of her youth is an undated letter contained in the Nicholson archives of the Historic New Orleans Collection. Headed only "Old Home—Friday Morning," it is addressed to "Uncle Knick," her affectionate name for George Nicholson. The contents reveal that the letter was written in August, probably in 1877, about ten months before her second marriage. She describes how pleased "Aunt Jane" and "Uncle Fred" are to have her visiting in the home in which she had spent a large portion of her childhood. As for herself and her response to the homecoming, she writes,

> I feel more natural, more like my *old self here* at home today than I have felt for years—everything is so pure, so peaceful and quiet that it makes me feel near to God once more; and I must try to keep near to Him. I love every inch of ground on the old place. If I had twenty girls I would like to raise them up right here just as I was brought up. I am sure that it was the pureness and peacefulness of my childish life that gave me strength of character to live through my troubles. To live above the earth was second nature to me, and so self sacrifice came easy.[17]

Nicholson, she continues, has spent only one night at the Old Home, but even that was sufficient for him to feel its "pure influence." She, on the other hand, had spent twenty years in this "Blessed home of innocence" before going "out into the world" and being "caught in the whirlpool of Slander!" The last is an allusion, of course, to her marriage to Alva Holbrook, a divorced man, and the bizarre attack inflicted on her by his first wife.

She comments humorously on Nicholson's plan to run a steamboat up the Hobolochitto and tells him that now is the time, since the "log men are busy with their logs" and that Uncle Jack says that he will be glad to be captain of the vessel. She reminds Nicholson, however, that he is now "commander of the old Ship 'Picayune,'" and that he must "bring her safely into port. God grant that you may be spared to do so!" In a very personal tone, she confides that Aunt Jane thinks it unwise for her to "go out" with Nicholson, since people might talk, and "it would kill her to have me slandered again." Aunt Jane has admonished her to "go out" only with single men, but, Eliza adds, when she returns to the city, she intends "to work so hard that I shall not find time to go out with anyone—married or single." She speaks very knowledgeably of business matters, demonstrating the extent to which in the space of approximately one year she has adapted herself to her position of power and responsibility. She has determined, she goes on to say, to return to the Piney Woods home more often but for shorter stays, and Nicholson must learn to "smook (is this another Englishism?) to console yourself for the loss of the 'widder up town.' " She has decided to leave her birds at Old Home and is even considering leaving Mat, her beloved dog, but doubts that she can, since he loves her "so devotedly" and might forget in two months. "I must have something to pet," she writes. "I never was without a pet of some kind as far back as I can remember, and it would not seem natural not to have something to care for and attend to." She concludes this lengthy epistle, composed at four different times over a two-day period, by assuring "Uncle Knick," who will in less than a year become her husband, "that he is being thought of occasionally."[17]

The letter is a remarkable document in terms of its revelation of the character of Eliza Poitevent. Not only do we learn of her love for the native plot of ground on which she was reared, but her devotion to George Nicholson is clearly demonstrated. Unfortunately, few of her letters are extant, although many of the communications which she received from a variety of people, famous and unknown, have been preserved. What they reveal, as do the letter just quoted and her more formal writing, is a woman of immense charm and resourcefulness and intelligence who, in an age not conducive to such accomplishments, made a position and a name for herself in a man's world. It cannot be denied, of course, that fate assisted in her achievement: had she not inherited the *Picayune*, what she did with it would have been impossible. But the way in which she rescued the paper from its debts and appropriated it for her own is something that few women and not many men would have been able to accomplish.

One of the most delightful and humanitarian elements of Pearl Rivers's personality, developed during her Piney Woods childhood, was her love of animals, clearly demonstrated in her August 1877 letter and in the column about horses. As a young woman, she often wrote with a pet canary named Billy Button perched on her finger, and Mat, the dog to whom she refers in her letter to Nicholson, was for years her almost constant companion. When Mat died, she wrote one of her better-known poems, "Only a Dog," in which she endeavors to explain the value and appeal of such a pet to those who are not dog lovers. In a letter dated 4 January 1895 to a Mrs. David Morgan of New Orleans, Eliza Nicholson refuses the offer of a dog named Jerry to replace Mat. "I love dogs better than I do people—as a race—and I know that I would soon learn to love Jerry as I did my little Mat." She must decline to accept him, she says, because she and her family are away from home six months of the year, and it would be necessary to leave the dog behind with servants. She describes her menagerie at Bay St. Louis, where the Nicholsons kept a summer home, on the very boundary of those Piney Woods she loved. "We have a lot of tramp dogs over here that I have taken in because they had no homes. They fare pretty bad when we are away, but that is better than being a cur, and homeless, and kicked about. Since I lost my little Mat I do not take a dog because I need him—for I do not want to love another dog—but because the dog needs me. That is the way it is with the poor tramps I pick up, but fine bred little Jerry can find a home anywhere."[18]

When Pearl Rivers was gone, New Orleans had her to thank not only for an excellent newspaper but also for various ordinances and organizations intended to protect animals. She wrote that she believed New Orleans to be the worst city in America in terms of how it treated various animals, and set about early in her career to alleviate that situation. In the *Picayune*, she instituted a weekly column entitled "Nature's Dumb Nobility" in which she addressed those concerns, and she organized the Louisiana Pioneer Band of Mercy, designed to teach children kindness to animals. In February 1885, she was active in the founding of a New Orleans branch of the Society for the Prevention of Cruelty to Animals; she was responsible for the installation of the first watering troughs for horses in the city; and many *Picayune* editorials urged that cockfighting be outlawed. Her activities in defense of animals extended to her personal life as well, for if she observed men abusing horses, she would snatch the whip from their hands and berate them for their insensitivity. Her achievements in the field gained national recognition when the American Humane Association commended her and the *Picayune* in 1886 and 1887 and elected her to their executive council. The child from the Piney Woods had learned well the lesson of respect for and love of animals.

Another perspective on Pearl Rivers's early life in the Piney Woods is offered in a 27 January 1876 letter from her brother James, who lived in Tampico, Mexico, from which he shipped tomatoes to St. Louis, Chicago, and New York. He had heard that Aunt Jane was ill (ironically she was to outlive Eliza) and wrote nostalgically that he once reverenced her as an "angel from heaven," his "beau ideal of loveliness and beauty." He recalled fondly what a pleasure it was

> to feast at her sumptuous table on fried venison steak with milk gravy and cookies and other sweets that old grandma Cook had made. And my memory is very

clear about . . . the broad fireplace and the leaning oaks over the door where
the China sign board's sweet song used to open the curiousity shop to all. And
I shall never forget our attempt to introduce the pigeon house pigeons and all
into Uncle's *political* sanctuary and the flight of the birds and the consequences
which followed, and I hope to have the chance to talk with you and her about
all old times with its [sic] many pleasures and the many blessings we have received
ought to at some extent relieve our many sorrows.

James goes on to describe his business transactions and reports proudly
that in New York "today Delmonico's table is supplied by me." His letter
provides proof that the idyllic life in the Piney Woods which Pearl Rivers
remembered from her childhood and recorded in her writing was not the
fanciful creation of one person but a situation close to the fact.[19]

That Pearl Rivers spoke often and lovingly not only to friends but also
to interviewers and other people she met of her devotion to the Piney Woods
region is indicated by the fact that every biographical sketch I have examined
refers to her childhood there in terms that must have originated with the
subject herself. An article in Frank Leslie's *Illustrated Newspaper,* for example, describing her as "a slender, soft-voice little woman" and "the little
lady in a big chair," commends Eliza's warm welcome, her "gentle conversation and frolicksome wit." She is, the author reports, from "a fine old
Huguenot family" and grew up

> in a rambling old country-house near the brown waters of the Pearl River. She
> was the only child on the place; a lonesome child with the heart of a poet, and
> she took to the beautiful southern woods and made them her sanctuary. . . .
> She is the poet-laureate of the bird and flower world of the south. Her poems
> and fantasies about the birds and flowers and other small-folk of the pine-scented
> Mississippi woodlands are the very airy ephemera and cobwebs of poetic
> thought—so dainty that they might have been etched with a thorn on the petal
> of a dog-rose bloom.[20]

An undated newspaper item clipped from its unidentified source and
preserved among Eliza Nicholson's papers records that she is "summering
at Sewanee," a common practice in those days among certain affluent New
Orleanians. She is known, the writer continues, as "the little poet of the
Piney Woods" because she "was born in the heart of that lonely pine forest
that stretches like a sombre veil across the State of Mississippi." When
"her genius had outgrown her environment," she moved to New Orleans
to become "one might perhaps say the first woman in the South to earn
money any way except by teaching" and to represent "the world's conception of a strong minded woman." Another unidentified clipping reports that
she is visiting in Massachusetts one summer: "She was a Miss Poitevent,
daughter of Capt. Poitevent, an old Mississippi River steamboat captain,

and was born in one of the 'cow counties' of Mississippi."[21] Finally, the biographical sketch by Nat Burbank that appeared in the *Twentieth Century Review* describes her childhood home as "a rambling old house known as 'The Bridge' . . . in the charming Pearl-river country."[22]

Repeatedly, then, in her own work and in others' descriptions of her, Pearl Rivers's connection to and love of the Piney Woods is sounded. If environment counts at all, hers was a childhood that ably prepared her for reaching her full potential in a world in which she, in effect, created her own place. The simplicity and innocence of that background she portrayed romantically in one of her best-known early poems, "The Singing Heart," in which she describes herself as "the merriest child of all," so gentle that "timid wild things knew my call."

> An ignorant child—Latin and Greek
> Were unknown tongues to me;
> But I was quick to catch and speak
> The tongue of flower and bee.

She describes herself as thanking God for flowers and birds while the more orthodox said grace over meat and drink. She "roamed the piny woods," she says, with a wild and free heart, unaware of why she loved God and Nature; but now she has come to realize that it is the fact that her heart "was singing all the time" that contributed to her peace and contentment. This early communion between the child and nature, she believes, like William Wordsworth, to have functioned in a beneficial and therapeutic way in her adult life:

> The world has bruised the singing heart,
> It has wept tears like dew;
> And Slander, with a poisoned dart,
> Has pierced it through and through.
>
> But singing hearts are hard to kill,
> And God made mine with wings,
> To fly above all earthly ill;
> And so it lives and sings.

That her memories of childhood are idealized in no way alters the fact that it was to the Piney Woods region of her youth that Pearl Rivers returned again and again through her adult life for consolation and strength and rest.

Mississippi and the Piney Woods and New Orleans, and women in general, can all take pride in the "little woman" at the big desk who saw what had to be done and did it. Small and shy and quiet, she chose to place herself in a position where she had to be strong and assertive and outspoken on occasion. The *Picayune*, like many formerly important American newspapers, has fallen on bad times in recent decades, but for half a century it was a great journal, largely because of the shaping hand of Eliza Nicholson. Various agencies of government in New Orleans and Louisiana and numerous philanthropic organizations bear the enduring mark of the work of "the whistling girl," as she called herself, from Mississippi's Piney Woods.

The week after Eliza Nicholson's death, one of her employees, Catherine Cole—whose career as a newspaperwoman was made possible by Eliza's example—recalled her employer and friend with affection. The two of them had recently spoken of eternity, Cole reports, and Pearl Rivers had remarked, "I am not afraid to go, for long since I have had my money's worth."[23] Certainly, she gave full measure in return for what she received.

Notes

The papers and other effects of Eliza Nicholson have been donated by her descendants to the Historic New Orleans Collection. I wish to thank the personnel of the library and archives of that collection, especially Susan Cole, for their invaluable assistance in my research and for permission to use the photograph of Mrs. Nicholson. —W.K.H.

1. New Orleans *Daily Picayune*, 16 Feb. 1896.

2. Lamar Whitlow Bridges, "A Study of the New Orleans *Daily Picayune* under Publisher Eliza Jane Poitevent Nicholson" (Ph.D. diss., Southern Illinois University, 1974), 160. Bridges provides a very thorough analysis of the newspaper's development under Pearl Rivers's editorship and of the significance of her contribution.

3. Bridges, "Study," 230.

4. New Orleans *Daily Picayune*, 30 March 1879.

5. New Orleans *Daily Picayune*, undated clipping, Historic New Orleans Collection, New Orleans, Louisiana.

6. Harnett Kane, *Dear Dorothy Dix: The Story of a Compassionate Woman* (Garden City, N.Y.: Doubleday, 1952), 48.

7. *Atlas of Mississippi*, ed. Ralph D. Cross and Robert W. Wales (Jackson: University Press of Mississippi, 1974), 37.

8. New Orleans *Daily Picayune*, undated clipping, Historic New Orleans Collection.

9. New Orleans *Daily Picayune*, 1 June 1890.

10. New Orleans *Daily Picayune*, undated clipping, Historic New Orleans Collection.

11. "An Idle Hour at My Desk," New Orleans *Daily Picayune,* undated clipping, Historic New Orleans Collection.

12. "Indian Blankets," New Orleans *Daily Picayune,* undated clipping, Historic New Orleans Collection.

13. New Orleans *Daily Picayune,* undated clipping, Historic New Orleans Collection.

14. James Henry Harrison, *Pearl Rivers: Publisher of the Picayune* (New Orleans: Tulane University Department of Journalism, 1932), 9.

15. New Orleans *Daily Picayune,* undated clipping, Historic New Orleans Collection.

16. New Orleans *Daily Picayune,* 23 Feb. 1879.

17. Historic New Orleans Collection.

18. Ibid.

19. Ibid.

20. Galley proof, undated clipping, Historic New Orleans Collection.

21. Clippings, undated clipping, Historic New Orleans Collection.

22. Clipping, undated clipping, Historic New Orleans Collection.

23. New Orleans *Daily Picayune,* 23 Feb. 1896.

James Street
Making History Live

THOMAS L. MCHANEY

That Mississippi bible, the 1938 WPA *Mississippi Guide*, tells me that during the Great Depression the Piney Woods was "a rather haphazard and irregular triangle, whose scenery of stumps, 'ghost' lumber towns, and hastily reforested areas [told] its saga. Strong men and women have been reared here, but the earth has been neither fecund enough to facilitate their getting away from it nor sterile enough to drive them away. It was a pioneer country; and now that the forests have been ravished . . . it is pioneer country once more." The settlement of Laurel was singled out as typical of the early Piney Woods lumber camps, "rowdy in character and forlorn in appearance."[1]

It is good to see plentiful evidence of human progress. For while the strong men and women in this area may remain rowdy, they do not appear to be forlorn, and the country itself has been restored to forestland and prosperity. If one travels through the Piney Woods to Hattiesburg via the Southern Crescent from Atlanta, following the old route of the New Orleans and North Eastern, as I did, one is struck by the way the landscape unravels as the land declines from low hills into pinelands and dissolves into bogues, creeks, and little rivers with ancient names. It is not a bad way to spend a day, and if I do not know as much about the Piney Woods as some of the contributors to this volume, at least I have had the chance not merely to imbibe its lore, geography, and spirit by reading about it in fiction and history books but also to see it directly from two important perspectives, that of the innocent pioneer from just a little farther north and that available to the railroad traveler, both views representing forces important to the development of the region.

My part, as an outlander currently from Georgia who spent all his childhood summers in the industrial north—that is, Tupelo—is to describe the career of Piney Woods author James Street. And my introductory quota-

tion from the *Mississippi Guide* is appropriate to my subject, for Street
was a native son whom ambition and opportunity sent away from the Piney
Woods, yet his memories, reflections, research, and writing about the region
remained perhaps his strongest assets as a successful commercial writer,
proving that the land was indeed fecund in more ways than the authors
of the *Mississippi Guide* perhaps realized.

I have deliberately chosen what, I suppose, looks like a cliché for my
title; but since one can pronounce l-i-v-e two ways, I have a loophole: by
the title, I intend to evoke both the conventional "Making History Live"
with a short *i* (that is, come alive and be palatable to the fiction reader)
and the more colloquial "Making History Live" with a long *i* (that is,
animate, current).

This mild and gimmicky verbal razzle-dazzle aims to emphasize
something about the ironies and ambiguities in the writing of James Street
and in the work of all authors who take history as the starting point for
romantic—that is, imaginative and heroic—fiction. I hope to explain later
what I mean by this. But at this point I must sketch Street's career, for
though he is known to some, and his books are still found on library shelves,
his career and major works are not much remembered, not even by red-
eyed devotees of the late-night channels, where Susan Hayward, Van Heflin,
and Boris Karloff are likely to turn up in the film version of *Tap Roots*.

As far as I can determine, only two scholarly critical essays have touched
on Street since his death in 1954: an article about Newt Knight's rebellion,
which considers *Tap Roots* as one of its examples[2] and a survey article in
Notes on Mississippi Writers, which looks at Street's career and lists the
first appearance of his publications but which commits such oversights as
listing *By Valour and Arms*, a fictional account of the Confederate ironclad
Arkansas and the siege of Vicksburg, as an expansion of "The Biscuit
Eater."[3] Although the author of the survey article attempts to document
Street's popularity by citing the numerous editions and printings of Street's
works and by listing favorable reviews in the national and southern press,
one can safely claim, nonetheless, that Street's work has not attracted
scholarly attention. I will not remedy all this neglect, nor am I qualified
to do so, and probably I run the risk of perpetrating some new errors or
legends of my own, but perhaps I can at least generate some interest in
his career, draw a few conclusions from his work—and even suggest an idea
for a future project.

James Street was born in Lumberton in 1903 and raised in Laurel and
Meridian, where his father served as assistant federal attorney. He claimed
to have started his career in journalism at a very early age in Laurel, and

though his family was Roman Catholic, he became a Baptist minister in his early twenties, after marrying the daughter of a Baptist minister. He served several churches in Missouri, Mississippi, and Alabama before leaving the ministry (and eventually the denomination) to return to journalism. He reported for some of the best newspapers in the South, including the Arkansas *Gazette*, and worked for the Associated Press in a number of southern cities. But like many bright Mississippians he wound up in New York, and in the wake of the success of his 1936 book of essays, *Look Away!*, he retired from the daily grind of journalism to Old Lyme, Connecticut, and devoted himself to free-lance writing, a career that soon succeeded.

His short stories and essays began to appear in that then best of all possible markets, the *Saturday Evening Post*, and in *Collier's, Good Housekeeping*, and *American Magazine;* and his novels, even with the restrictions of wartime publishing, began to reach an increasingly wide popular audience and to receive serious and generally favorable reviews in the *New York Times, Herald Tribune, New Yorker, Atlantic Monthly, Saturday Review*, Boston *Transcript*, and Springfield *American*, as well as in such southern newspapers as the Memphis *Commercial Appeal*, the Atlanta *Journal*, and Atlanta *Constitution*, and the New Orleans *Times-Picayune*.

Obviously Street's background and migrations as a working journalist and AP man did not hurt him among the newspaper fraternity, and he was beneficiary, as were so many southern writers of the period, of those regional brethren who worked in the New York reviewing media. Street's books were reviewed in New York by other southern writers (Hamilton Basso, for example). And his career coincided with a deep national interest in the South: politically—the era of Huey Long (for whom Street worked briefly as a public relations man) and Gene Talmadge; economically—the nation's "number-one economic problem"; and literarily—the so-called southern renaissance. This is not to say that Street's writing did not make its own way, for it did. He was probably among the most financially successful southern writers of his time—a condition that, especially during the depression and World War II, unfortunately did not bring the kind of fortune it might bring today, and he was a popular critical success, too, though not lacking negative reviews. His novels sold quite well, even became best sellers; many of them went into multiple printings (I have seen an eighteenth printing of *Oh, Promised Land*, dated May 1967) and second or third editions, including the inexpensive house reprints that were the paperbacks of their day. Several of his works were made into films, including the aforementioned *Tap Roots*, which, according to students of film, remains a minor classic motion picture.

After the war, Street moved to Chapel Hill, North Carolina, where his children attended the university and he made one of a small professional writing community there that included the dramatist Paul Green, like Street a liberal southerner, and Betty Smith, the transplanted New Yorker who had made the tree grow in Brooklyn.

Some of Street's best work—and the germ of much that would come later—is in his first book, *Look Away!* Subtitled a "Dixie Notebook," and qualified, in his short foreword, as "a newspaperman's unorthodox notebook of Dixie," *Look Away!* contains boldly journalistic recitations of stories told to Street by his father, a lawyer and judge in southern Mississippi, or by "Aunt Mattie, a flabby old Negro woman who nursed me through childhood and who amused me with bedtime stories of her adventures as a slave and as a voodoo woman." It also recounts contemporary events he saw as a reporter who, as such, felt constrained not to tell in the newspapers all he saw; as he said, "Newspapers in the South really do not like such stories. Some of them are not pretty."[4]

Look Away! is dominated by matter-of-fact reports of violence, including several south Mississippi lynching stories (national antilynch laws were being considered at the time) and thumbnail accounts of such south Mississippi phenomena as Sullivan's Hollow and the story of Newt Knight's secession from the Confederacy. These pieces are punctuated by slightly debunking tales of the legends of Casey Jones and John Henry—the kind of brash journalism that substitutes a less-well-known legend for one that is more widely known. There are tales of conjuring and tornadoes, the story of a wild man of the swamps, and anecdotes about backwoods independence, the rivers, and the land. Arkansas and the Sea Islands of Georgia get into *Look Away!*, but the book is, to steal another popular title of the day, Mostly Mississippi[5] and, within Mississippi, mostly about Piney Woods.

In a letter quoted by Jennie Gardner of the Memphis *Commercial Appeal* in July 1942, Street wryly remarked that his first book was entitled *"Look Away!"* and everybody did. The facts are rather different: The Memphis *Commercial Appeal* announced (16 February 1936) the book's appearance (and noted unsuspectingly that a novel by Margaret Mitchell of Atlanta entitled *Gone with the Wind* was scheduled for April publication). New Orleans novelist Hamilton Basso observed in the *New Republic* that Street "writes about these dismal and tragic affairs with a kind of feature-story nonchalance that often becomes extremely irritating."[7] The New Orleans *Times-Picayune* was more charitable, noting that Street displayed a "gift for history, that is, unrecorded history," and that the book was, in spots, "essentially Faulknerian."[8] Carl Carmer, who had written *Stars Fell* on *Alabama* (1934), reviewed *Look Away!* for *Books* and pointed out its shortcomings as well as its values: it is written, he said, in the "kind of journalistic English which some newspaper editors, particularly those in the South, call 'good reporting.' It makes use of forced simplicity, unnecessary repetitions, and the point of view of the Sunday-feature writer. That his stories suffer so little from it is a credit to his powers of selection and to the strenuous spirit which animates the whole book.'"[9]

These judgments, taken together, are a fair sampling of the kind of treatment Street's work would receive during most of his career, and they also seem to me a just appraisal of his strengths and weaknesses as a writer of essays and fiction. He had the tough, experienced newspaperman's iconoclasm and social and political liberalism that may have derived from his attorney father and even from life in and knowledge of the traditions of the Piney Woods. His more-than-fair treatment of racial matters also may have come from his loving memories of the old black woman who told him stories, from his ministerial training and work, and from his revulsion from racial and social injustice. He had clearly witnessed a great deal that might provoke a liberal reaction during more than a decade of work as a southern journalist in a violent and frustrating period. Yet he did not paint a bleak and negative picture of his region, for he also had a fund of powerful positive memories of its people and land.

When Street turned his talents to fiction, he brought all his journalistic equipment and his inherited and observed lore with him, plus—as more than one of his contemporary reviewers remarked—the gifts of a natural storyteller. To these things he added extensive research and a good hand with the ingredients of popular-historical fiction as it has been written from the time of Sir Walter Scott—including the American breast fixation. He was also skilled in the titilations—all puns intended—of the breast fixation in American popular entertainments. Among his blood-and-thunder romances, it is a rare book in which bosoms don't swell dangerously within their corsets, touching the lives and bodies of his impressionable male characters.

As a fiction writer, Street had a gift not only for storytelling but also for character delineation. He had a weakness, or perhaps just a commercial instinct, for the predictable contemporary plot. He knew how to use the sure-fire formula of boy meets dog, boy loses dog, etc., and this was no mean achievement; Marjorie Kinnan Rawlings, for example, for years resisted Maxwell Perkins's advice to write such a story before she came up with the *The Yearling*. Street was a good bit quicker coming up with his classic about the biscuit eater.

In a career that spanned only some eighteen active years of fiction writing, Street's name appeared on thirteen novels. However, several of them are self-imitations, sequels to more successful work, padded versions of successful short stories, and posthumous constructions by others. Despite his output, and with a couple of minor classics to his credit, Street has not made it into the academic literary canon, and probably will not. Yet he remains an interesting writer, and certainly one important to the history and spirit of the Piney Woods region of Mississippi. Street clearly loved and knew his home region with that instinct that gives back to a writer the country he has left or the country that has, simply through time and circumstance, left him, giving it back in memories that tickle the nose, burn the flesh, make pictures in the mind, stir passions that still prickle and lift the flesh, and evoke images that are the seeds of fiction.

Look Away! came out, as noted, the same year as *Gone with the Wind.* It appeared also in the wake of such reminiscent Mississippi works as Stark Young's *So Red the Rose* (1934) and *Feliciana* (1935). Hardly to be neglected are Faulkner's *Absalom, Absalom!*, also published in 1936, and his *The Unvanquished*, published in 1938. This is also apparently the time that Eudora Welty, at the prodding of an agent, turned her attention to historical materials as well, specifically the tales of the Natchez Trace that get into *The Robber Bridegroom*, 1942, and *The Wide Net*, 1943.[10]

Street was obviously quick to see the novelistic possibilities for using the places that he knew and the subjects that interested him, but it took him several years to complete his first novel, *Oh, Promised Land.* In some ways this was the typically large (over eight hundred pages) and panoramic historical blockbuster of that publishing era, the kind of book that still comes from the pen of writers like James Michener. *Oh, Promised Land,* which appeared in 1940, is the first of the series of Dabney family chronicles that Street wrote (the most well known of this series is the 1942 *Tap Roots*). Street has been taxed (for instance, in John Bettersworth's 1959 school history of Mississippi) with romanticizing the story of Newton Knight and greatly exaggerating the circumstances of the Jones County rebellion from Mississippi during the Civil War. However, in *Oh, Promised Land* (and for that matter in the more successful sequel, *Tap Roots*) Street clearly announces that historical fact is not his object, but rather fiction, fiction freely created from the exploits of historical personages. He relies upon a good deal of Piney Woods and south Mississippi history, to be sure, drawing from the works of J. F. H. Claiborne, for example: The Sam Dabney of *Oh, Promised Land* owes much, at least in appearance and outline, to the General Sam Dale of Claiborne's interesting "first-person biography" of

1860, and the Fort Mims massacre during the War of 1812 and Dale's famous canoe fight with Creek warriors figure prominently and climactically in Street's novel. Once he has settled in the Piney Woods, Sam Dabney takes on the characteristics of Tom Sullivan, the patriarch of Sullivan's Hollow. Then, in *Tap Roots*, the fictional Sam Dabney's illegitimate nephew and adopted son Hoab is given the role of old Newt Knight, but with a great deal of glamorous and exaggerated detail thrown over the family, the family seat, and the entire matter of Union sympathy in the Piney Woods. Street's character Keith Alexander in *Tap Roots* is drawn from the life of Alexander Keith McClung, and even a hasty survey of the history and characters of the region turns up probable candidates or prototypes for other characters. Street's noble Indian, Tishimingo, who appears in both these early Dabney novels— or Lebanon novels, as they are called from the name the old patriarch gives his secluded tree-filled valley—borrows characteristics from both the Choctaw Pushmataha and Greenwood LeFlore, while the suave, part-French, part-Indian villain Lake Flournoy of *Oh, Promised Land* is drawn freely from Greenwood LeFlore's less noble father, Louis LaFleur, and probably takes his surname from a historical Flournoy who was a general in the War of 1812 (and perhaps also from a distinguished but "scalawag" planter of the Reconstruction era).

I am not a good enough historian to probe these sources deeply, nor is that my purpose; the main point is that whatever their historical background, Street's fictions were meant to be romances—in the best sense of that word, and they hold up well as fictions, with vivid, consistent characters; fast-paced plots; and fully imagined settings and scenes. They are inspired by, rather than borrowed from, the history of Street's region. He has let history inform him, but not lead him, and he often takes a small element of recorded history and imagines and expands it into a major element of fiction. A principal image in *Tap Roots*, for example, is "The Tree," the ancient symbol of family and land that stands in front of the Dabney house in the Piney Woods. A version of that tree appears in *Oh, Promised Land*, however, long before Sam Dabney has reached the Piney Woods hollow where his roots will become permanent. At the end of *Oh, Promised Land*, Sam, who is living in the vicinity of the Nanih Wayih Indian mound, looks out his cabin at the trees down by the river. "They once had seemed such big friendly trees. But now"—when he has suffered a number of losses—"they were small trees. There were big trees in the Bogue Homa." He prepares his family to go south, and as the Dabneys set out for Bogue Homa, Sam stops their caravan to run back and retrieve from beneath a grave's headstone the old conch shell that is a family memento; the grave is under the "Big Tree." From this and other images, it appears that Street knew where he was going when he began his first Dabney fiction, and that he took the image of the tree from the story of old Newt Knight and his small-scale rebellion against the Confederacy. In the version of the tale that Street tells in *Look Away!* there is, at the end, the tree on which many of Knight's followers were hanged. "He never forgot that sycamore tree where his followers were hanged," Street writes,[11] and goes on to claim that it was also the tree, many years later, where he himself saw his first lynching.

Street was often accused of stretching the longbow about his own life and exploits, as well as about others', so we might doubt the convenience of one tree to link Newt Knight to the reporter of the 1920s lynching. But in the big trees of the Piney Woods, of course, hangs the region's whole history. The giant longleaf pines made the region remarkable in the beginning and tragic during the period of rapacious deforestation, something that Street works his way toward in the third Dabney novel, *Tomorrow We Reap*, where among the issues are the depredations of a Chicago-based lumber company and the use of steam-powered timber "skidders"—which one can see pictured in *Hattiesburg: A Pictorial History*, a fine photographic memoir of Hattiesburg, published in 1982 by the University Press of Mississippi—that sped deforestation and also destroyed the young second-growth pines.

To judge by the image of the Big Tree at the end of *Oh, Promised Land, Tap Roots* was already conceived as Street was working on his first Dabney novel, and he brought out the more successful sequel within two years, publishing two other novels in the interim, the book-length version of "The Biscuit Eater" (redone with illustrations, mainly for the young readers' market) and *In My Father's House*, a rural tale told through the voice of a boy, Little Hob Abernathy. It took him quite a while longer to complete the Dabney series, however, and he appears to have lost heart or interest in it. The book editor of the Memphis *Commercial Appeal* reported in 1942 that Street was slowed down by William Alexander Percy's *Lanterns on the Levee*, which appeared in 1941; he liked Percy's work so much, Street said, he didn't want to finish his own.[12]

Finish it he did, however, after some digressions: to write a very stirring and realistic account of river warfare in *By Valour and Arms* (which centers on the activities of the Confederate ironclad *Arkansas* during the siege of Vicksburg); to write the first of his two novels on a modern liberal and idealistic Baptist minister named London Wingo (*The Gauntlet*, 1945); and to publish a collection of short stories.

With help, however, the Dabney novels were finished. James Childers, a Chapel Hill neighbor and novelist, is given joint credit with Street for

Tomorrow We Reap, 1949; and the last novel, *Mingo Dabney*, is dedicated to Childers, "who helped me in so many ways." Like the forests of the Piney Woods in the same era, however, the Dabney novels that carry through the turn of the century appear to have lost the rich resources of the past: José Martí, the Cuban revolutionary, and a beautiful lady compatriot come on the scene toward the end of *Tomorrow We Reap*, and the most spirited of the Dabneys, Mingo, leaves Lebanon (Street's poetical name for the Piney Woods) to join the movement in Cuba, which is the subject of the novel that bears his name, *Mingo Dabney*.

I will only give brief mention to Street's other books. *The High Calling*, 1951, is the sequel about London Wingo, the Baptist minister; *The Velvet Doublet*, 1953, is an ironic first-person account by one of the voyagers who sailed with Christopher Columbus to the New World; *Goodbye, My Lady*, 1954, is a variation on "The Biscuit Eater," a different but similar boy-and-dog tale made from short stories that had appeared earlier in magazines. The posthumous works, assembled or completed by others, are *Captain Little Ax*, 1956, *Pride of Possession*, 1960, and *James Street's South*, 1955, edited by his son James Street, Jr., an anthology of lively essays about places and things in the South, many done for *Holiday* magazine. In addition, there are iconoclastic short histories of the Revolutionary War and the Civil War—he closes the latter with a note to the reader:

> I will not answer acrimonious letters. I will not answer the challenges of my sources unless the complainants list their sources for challenging me. I will ignore Southerners who call me a renegade, Southerners and Yankees who call me a biased hillbilly, a Jim Crowing poll-taxer, a reactionary, a fascist, a Communist or an egghead. Don't write me that line that you learned your history at your grandma's knee. Grandma's knee is a rightly nice place to pray, but it's a poor place to learn history.[13]

As I have said, the germ of Street's best work is in *Look Away!* but his best writing is in the fiction. His tales of boys and dogs have been well received, and a contemporary reviewer may have had part of the key to that success when he said that Street was effective in stories about "the forests and swamps which are women and the world to a youngster."[14] Street evokes this in the expanded *Goodbye, My Lady:* "Some day the swamp winds, the home sounds so long remembered, would feel for the strings to the boy's heart and bring forth only the echo of the melody of what used to be—the beauty of the sprouting years, the hope of longing, then the misery of loving something that must grow old."[15] Street's work in this line followed Marjorie Kinnan Rawlings's *The Yearling*, which appeared in 1938, the year before "The Biscuit Eater," but there seems no real limit in the world to the allowable number of "classics" of boy life, which may, in fact, as the aforementioned reviewer guessed, speak to all men's loves and losses in something like the forgotten and sublimated language of fairy tale.

Street's two novels about the Baptist ministry are well done, and they certainly ought to be important to anyone who would like a realistic, not a pietistic and sentimental, insight into the contradictions of man trying to serve God and his fellow men at the same time. His historical novels are hot and cold, weak and strong. As noted, contemporary reviewers seem to have pretty well hit the mark with Street's work: that he was a natural storyteller whose gift was spoiled, or weakened, by the application of aspects of the conventional thriller. But *Tap Roots* was greeted by the New Orleans *Times-Picayune* as a "welcome surcease from the 'magnolias and lace' crimes so frequently perpetrated upon Southern locales."[16] And Paul Engle in the *Saturday Review of Literature* observed that "the history and the personal stories are cleverly mingled, and where the stories weaken the history is always there, fascinating and naive."[17] Of *By Valour and Arms*, the *New York Times* critic said, Mr. Street "knows how to make the dust fly in the library stacks."

In fact, despite the love elements and the heaving bosoms of some scenes, Street's novels contain very strong stuff, the kind of understated but detailed realistic scenes of land and naval battles that one finds in the excellent but largely unread post–Civil-War novel by James W. DeForrest, *Miss Ravenal's Conversion from Secession to Loyalty* (1867), the kind of thing that Cooper and Melville, in their prefaces, warned their "fair" or "faint" readers against taking up. Like the American romantics who repeatedly plead for understanding and latitude, Street wrote explanatory prefaces, too. It is not easy to write historical romance for an audience that believes everything it reads in the papers, and then wants historical fiction to stick to the facts. "I want it understood," Street writes in his preface to *Tap Roots*, "before my home folks shut and bar the front door, that all citizens of Jones County did not fight the South." He makes it plain that he is aware of the small part played in the drama of the Civil War by Newton Knight, that he knows when and how the story was exaggerated, and he says that he has "taken many liberties. I had to," perhaps hinting that reality is seldom good enough for fiction.

History can be the stuff of fiction, certainly, but the writer who has a deep feeling and the experiences of childhood to wed him to a place and its past will often find himself using history not to tell the story of *the* past— not to make history *live* (i.e., to re-create it), but to tell the story of some past of his own—to make history *live* (i.e., to find his own human chords in it and touch or reveal them). And I wonder if this isn't what Street attempted, using the things he had learned to write of what he may never have learned, that perhaps none of us ever learns: the wellsprings of our loves and our losses, our awe and fear, our idealisms and our repudiations. Of course many things got in his way, not least those conventions of the big novel that, if they don't rule the marketplace, strongly dominate it. I find myself touched by Street's remark about his discouragement when he read *Lanterns on the Levee*. That is a romantic book, too. As a reviewer of *Tap Roots* said, "Romance by its very definition is inseparable from all recitals of desperate lost causes," and there were more lost causes in the South than the Civil War. Percy wrote about his liberal father, and Street may have wished that in the humanity toward Indians and Negroes and in the iconoclasm and independence from southern hotheadedness that one finds among the Dabneys he had painted a more obvious picture of a father of his own. Perhaps when he read Percy he lamented that he had not written a truer, a more personal book. I don't know and have no business, in my ignorance, speculating. But I am nonetheless struck all through Street's work with the humanity of it, and I suspect that Mr. Street's time in the ministry was not simply a way to catch a pretty wife.

In *Tap Roots*, the Dabney servant Quint, who is not a slave, dies among those resisting the Confederates, the "first of the Dabney household to die," and, Street writes,

> In years to come, men would say that Quintus, a free man of color, a faithful servant, died defending the Dabneys, that he died serving a white man. But that's not true. Quint died trying to defend himself, with nothing to help himself except a knife, with no chore to do except notch bullets. He wasn't thinking of the Dabneys when he died. He didn't want to die. He was afraid of death. And in dying, he didn't beg mercy of [Reverend] Kirk's Jehovah or of Tishomingo's Aba Inki, but he screamed a cry to his gods of the Congo, pleading that they spare him and smite his enemies."[18]

In 1942, with America at war, these were interesting words, as were these words about Gar Rivers in 1944 in *Tomorrow We Reap:*

> Men who didn't know the gaunt Negro said he was hideous, and rightly named, ugly as any long-snouted garfish that ever sucked in the mud. [But] the few who really knew Gar didn't think of his looks at all. They remembered the pride in his voice, and honored him as a man enriched by loneliness and suffering; made strong in his spirit by a solemn, reverent determination to replace ignorance with knowledge. . . . He believed it was good to walk strong and upright before all men and refused to allow the years or the burden of his birth to weigh him down; but in the twilight, when there was no one to see him, Gar Rivers admitted by his gait and to his cane that time and the unkindness of man had sapped his body and forced it to bend.[19]

There are many occasions in Street's books when he manages to make what he writes about "rougher, more vivid, more understandable, and pitiable," as a reviewer of *By Valour and Arms* noted.[20] What he attempted was not easy; as Sam Dabney says, it takes time to make good whiskey and aristocrats, and to that we can add, and good novels. Street published fifteen books in eighteen years and did a good bit of journalism and commercial short-story writing besides. When he was truest to himself and to his past—which is very much tied up with the Piney Woods region—he did quite well, capturing not only the spirit and myth of this place as it evolved but also its lore and voices. There's a certain charm and up-to-date relevance to the following passage from *In My Father's House* (1941), told in the voice of a Piney Woods boy: "We always went up to Laurel on the Fourth for a patriotic rally and political speaking. I like to go to political speakings just to hear what the speakers call each other. It's funny about politics. If you meet a man on the street and call him a liar, he'll bust you one in the face, but it's all right to call a man a liar in a political speech. If you don't believe it, I'll show you a paper to prove it."[21]

Street is a sufficiently interesting writer to be read today. Someone casting about for a research project or a master's thesis would find plenty of good work yet to be done on his career. A study of his writing and its presentation and reception would also make an excellent chapter in a much-needed history or survey of the southern popular book of the period 1920–50. If such a study were done, Street's work, I think, would be found on the same side of the scale as the work of the heavyweights. He was tough-minded and compassionate, and he genuinely knew and loved much of what he wrote about. He had no illusions about his stature, however, and late in his life when he turned down an assignment and suggested to *Holiday* that they get William Faulkner to do a big piece on Mississippi, he did so, he later told a correspondent, because "you don't pinch hit for Babe Ruth." He must have known, however, that for a time, at least, he played in the same league.

Notes

1. Federal Writers' Project, Works Progress Administration, *Mississippi: A Guide to the Magnolia State* (New York: Viking, 1938), 6, 223.

2. Ovid Vickers, "Newt Knight and the Free State of Jones: Fact, Fiction and Folklore," *Mississippi Folklore Register* 14 (Fall 1980):75–81.

3. Ruth Cooper, "James Street: A Biographical and Bibliographical Study," *Notes on Mississippi Writers* 9 (Spring 1976):10–23.

4. James Street, *Look Away! A Dixie Notebook* (New York: Viking, 1936), v–vi.

5. Harold Speakman, *Mostly Mississippi* (New York: Dodd, Mead, 1927).

6. Jennie Gardner, "Book Ends," *Memphis Commercial Appeal,* 12 July 1942, sec. 4, p. 10.

7. Hamilton Basso, review of *Look Away!, New Republic,* 27 May 1936, 79.

8. Review of *Tap Roots,* New Orleans *Times Picayune,* 23 February 1936, sec. 2, p. 9.

9. Carl Carmer, review of *Look Away!, Books,* 23 February 1936, 6.

10. Noel Polk, conversation with author, 20 Jan. 1983.

11. Street, *Look Away!,* 24.

12. Gardner, "Book Ends," 10.

13. Street, *Civil War* (New York: Dial, 1953), 144–45.

14. Surrey Thomas, review of *Short Stories, Saturday Review of Literature* 28 (23 June 1945):33.

15. Street, *Good-bye, My Lady* (Philadelphia: Lippincott, 1954), p. 138.

16. E.A.D., review of *Tap Roots,* New Orleans *Times Picayune,* 12 July 1942, sec. 2, p. 9.

17. Paul Engle, review of *Tap Roots, Saturday Review of Literature,* 1 August 1942, 15.

18. Street, *Tap Roots* (New York: Dial, 1942), 527–28.

18. James Street and James Childers, *Tomorrow We Reap* (New York: Dial, 1944), 62.

20. Mary Ross, review of *By Valour and Arms, Weekly Book Review,* 24 September 1944, 6.

21. James Street, *In My Father's House* (New York: Dial, 1941), 71.

Bibliography

Street, James. *The Biscuit Eater.* New York: Dial Press, 1941.

_____. *By Valour and Arms.* New York: Dial Press, 1944.

_____. *Captain Little Ax.* Philadelphia: J. B. Lippincott, 1956.

_____. *The Civil War.* New York: Dial Press, 1953.

_____. *The Gauntlet.* Garden City, N.Y.: Doubleday, Doran, 1945.

_____. *Good-bye, My Lady.* Philadelphia: Lippincott, 1954.

_____. *The High Calling.* Garden City, N.Y.: Doubleday, 1951.

_____. *In My Father's House.* New York: Dial Press, 1941.

_____. *James Street's South.* Garden City, N.Y.: Doubleday, 1955.

_____. *Look Away! A Dixie Notebook.* New York: Viking Press, 1936.

_____. *Mingo Dabney.* New York: Dial Press, 1950.

_____. *Oh, Promised Land.* New York: Dial Press, 1940.

_____. *The Revolutionary War.* New York: Dial Press, 1954.

_____. *Short Stories.* New York: Dial Press, 1945.

_____. *Tap Roots.* New York: Dial Press, 1942.

_____. *Tomorrow We Reap* (with James Childers). New York: Dial Press, 1944.

_____. *The Velvet Doublet.* Garden City, N.Y.: Doubleday, 1953.

Piney Woods Politics
and Politicians

WILLIAM F. WINTER

When one speaks of the Piney Woods, one speaks of that considerable geographical area of Mississippi running south and east from Jackson to the gulf coast and the Alabama line. It was the section, depending on when one knew it, that consisted of thousands of square miles of virgin longleaf pine in the years around the turn of the century, or, tragically, by the 1930s, on most of those same lands, mile after dismal mile of stumps, broom sage, and scrub oaks. The latter scene was largely the result of a timber-harvesting system that relied on huge power skids that literally laid bare the land and a tax system that discouraged reforestation.[1] Because much of the timber acreage was in the hands of large corporations, most of them from out of the state, there developed an early political attitude that was marked by a distrust of big business among the struggling small farmers and retail merchants of the area.

Because it was not an area suitable for extensive row-crop farming or the growing of cotton, the plantation economy of the Natchez region, the Delta, and the black-prairie and brown-loam sections of the state was missing from the Piney Woods. As a result, tenant farming on a massive scale did not exist there, and there were fewer blacks than in the rest of the state. Most of the blacks were mill hands who followed the ever-moving supply of timber.

Since the development of communities in the area frequently centered on sawmill locations, the region is dotted with the remnants of once thriving towns that now exist largely in the memory of the older inhabitants. There was consequently not the permanent and stable community structure in many of these mill towns that marked the plantation areas of the state. For the most part the larger centers of population in the area today— the Hattiesburgs and Laurels—are almost totally twentieth-century cities, products of the economic and cultural factors that have marked the development of the urban South.

There was, therefore, even late into the 1900s, a kind of frontier aspect to the Piney Woods. It was an area marked by movement, economic instability and deprivation, transient community life, and a rugged and often violent reliance on individual action. There was a volatility that was characterized at times by radical responses to what were perceived as threats to local ways of life, as would be reflected, for example, in the bitter resistance to the enforcement of the cattle-dipping law and the ending of the open range.

All of those forces made for a special brand of politics that could be generally characterized as populist. It was a populism based on genuine economic needs, but after Vardaman it also had about it much of the race prejudice that permeated politics in those areas of the state where the black population was much higher. As a matter of fact, it is an interesting paradox that at the height of the massive resistance struggles in the late 1950s and early '60s, probably the highest incidence of Ku Klux Klan activity occurred in some of the predominantly white counties of the Piney Woods. In any event it was in this geographically distinctive area of sand hills, pine forests, and clear streams that some of Mississippi's most fiercely contested political battles were fought; out of the Piney Woods emerged some of the state's most colorful and flamboyant political figures.

It is obviously impossible within the limits of this paper to dwell in detail on all of the activity in more than a century of Piney Woods politics, nor can more than passing mention be made of all of the leading figures of that area. There are, however, certain individuals who, because of their contributions to Mississippi history, stand out in any consideration of the eventful story of the Piney Woods.

While he was not a product of the Piney Woods and paradoxically had his initial political base among the Bourbons of the Mississippi Delta, James K. Vardaman was among the first of the state's leading public figures to give voice to the concerns and emotions of many of the region's poorer whites. He strongly opposed efforts to ease the limitations on corporate landholding that had been written into the Constitution of 1890. When the 1906 legislature raised the ceiling on corporate-owned real property from one million to ten million dollars, Vardaman vetoed the bill on the ground that it would concentrate ownership of south Mississippi forestlands in the hands of a few.[2] But it was really his open and blatant appeal to race prejudice that made of Vardaman the example of political success that was to be emulated so often by others in years to come.

The *Clarion-Ledger* expressed the opinion that "[Vardaman] is only play-ing on the passions and prejudices of the populace in order to obtain of-fice." Vardaman himself, in arguing for better schools, said, "When I speak of educating the people, I mean white people." He then added, "The Negro is necessary in the economy of the world but he was designed for burden-bearer."[3]

Whatever the basis of support and in a race where all three candidates were from north Mississippi, after two defeats Vardaman won the nomina-tion for governor in the 1903 primaries over Frank Critz. He and Critz ran virtually even in the Piney Woods, and Vardaman won the race with large margins in the Delta.[4]

That same year, in a little-noticed race in Pearl River County, a young man with the resonant name of Theodore Gilmore Bilbo was defeated for circuit clerk by a one-armed Baptist preacher. Four years later, however, he was back on the ballot in a successful race for state senator. From that date until his death in 1947, Bilbo would be a part of the lore and legend of Mississippi politics. More than any other Mississippian, with the possi-ble exception of Pat Harrison, he was, for better or worse, the most talked-about, written-about, and thoroughly discussed politician from Mississip-pi in the first half of the twentieth century. His name became synonymous with the politics of the Piney Woods, with his native Pearl River County as his base.

He early broke into the state's consciousness as a result of the so-called Secret Caucus of 1910. That episode would call for a full chapter in its own right, and without going into the intriguing details it can be said that while Bilbo emerged as less than a hero to many of his Senate colleagues, he was regarded as a martyr by most of his Piney Woods neighbors. Although the Senate by a one-vote margin refused to expel him for his alleged role in the affair, it did adopt a resolution stating that "the Senate of Mississippi pronounce said Bilbo as unfit to sit with honest, upright men in a respect-able legislative body, and he is hereby asked to resign."[5]

The upshot of the matter was that Leroy Percy defeated Vardaman for the United States Senate, and set up the confrontations that made the long, hot summer of 1911 one of the most tumultuous in Mississippi political history. Vardaman and Percy would contest in a bitter race for the Senate, and Bilbo would offer for lieutenant governor. Bilbo had spent much of his time since the secret-caucus affair in speaking throughout the state. He delivered a speech which he entitled "Jim Vardaman, the Radical; Leroy Percy, the Conservative; Grandma Noel, the Sissy; Senator Bilbo, the Liar."[6] Anti-Vardaman leaders attempted to silence Bilbo by denying him access to public buildings, but these efforts only increased his popularity. In early July 1910, he appeared at a rally at Newton, where the well-known orator and prospective Senate candidate Charlton Alexander was scheduled to speak. When the officials in charge declined to permit Bilbo to speak, some of those in the crowd pulled a wagon into a nearby field, and just as Alexander began, Bilbo mounted the wagon and launched his own speech. The result was that in a few minutes the crowd had surrounded Bilbo and Alexander was left virtually alone.[7]

Early on, Percy had declined to appear on the same platform with Bilbo, leading Bilbo to say, "I have charged in and out of season that whiskey, women, gubernatorial patronage, the influence of the Republican administration, money and an unholy alliance or combination were all used to secure his election in the Secret Caucus."[8] Later, on July 4th at Lauderdale Springs near Meridian, Percy did find himself on the same platform with Bilbo. In one of the most tense scenes of that or any other campaign, Percy, in the course of his speech and after overcoming hecklers in the predominantly Vardaman-Bilbo crowd, turned to Bilbo, according to Will Percy years later in *Lanterns on the Levee,* and denounced him with "the most scathing denunciation I have ever heard from human lips . . . with avenging anger [he] blasted him with his own infamy."[9]

A few weeks before the primary Bilbo had denounced John J. Henry, the former warden of the state penitentiary whom Vardaman had fired, as "a cross between a hyena and a mongrel; he was begotten in a nigger graveyard at midnight, suckled by a cow and educated by a fool." A short time later Henry confronted Bilbo on a train between Starkville and Sturgis, and while one of his associates kept a gun on the other passengers, he pistol-whipped the senator, fracturing his skull.[10]

The results were predictable, however, and both Vardaman and Bilbo won in the first primary. The little man from Pearl River County was on his way, and the governorship became his in 1915. At the same time a Piney Woods neighbor from Seminary in Covington County had come home from an unlikely background as a law student at Yale to be elected to the legislature. At twenty-four, Mike Conner was a candidate for speaker of the House and, with Bilbo's backing, was elected over the Delta Bourbon, Oscar Johnston. Thus was to begin an association that would sometimes find these two Piney Woods politicians as friends but more often as bitter adversaries over the next thirty years.

In the war-year elections of 1918 two very interesting developments took place. Vardaman, to the consternation and dismay of many of his supporters, had been one of the "little band of willful men," as President Wilson scathingly referred to them, who had voted against a declaration of war against Germany. The following summer he was opposed by the young congressman from Gulfport, Pat Harrison. This created a prospective vacancy for that congressional seat, and in an improbable turn of events, Bilbo, even though he was little more than half through his term as governor, announced for Congress against, among others, the circuit judge from Hattiesburg, Paul B. Johnson. The results were that Harrison decisively defeated Vardaman, and Johnson won even more decisively over Bilbo. A critical issue in Bilbo's defeat was Bilbo's support of the cattle-dipping law, which Johnson had denounced from the bench and refused to enforce.[11]

The gubernatorial campaign of 1923 brought to the state the first of several contests between Bilbo and Conner; its opening was marked by one of the most bizarre scenes in modern political history. The year before, incumbent governor Lee Russell, who had served as lieutenant governor under Bilbo, was tried in federal court in Oxford in a suit brought against him by one of his former secretaries for seduction and breach of promise. Although the jury found in favor of Russell, Bilbo was sentenced to thirty days in jail and fined one hundred dollars for contempt of court as a result of his failure to obey a subpoena to appear as a witness in the trial. Upon being released by the judge after ten days in the Lafayette County jail, Bilbo used the steps of the Oxford courthouse to announce his candidacy for a second term as governor.[12] However, neither of the Piney Woods boys would win this race, which went to Henry L. Whitfield, former president of Mississippi State College for Women.

A rerun of the 1923 campaign insofar as Bilbo and Conner were concerned occurred four years later. This time Bilbo was victorious, and again he attempted to do what he had done successfully in 1916 by supporting a fellow Piney Woods representative for speaker of the House. His candidate was the redoubtable Hugh Barr Miller of Copiah County, but it was not to be a Bilbo victory. Tom Bailey from Meridian, with the support of the river county barons, won decisively, and Bilbo's fate was sealed. The "Big Four," as they were called, were in control, and the second Bilbo administration was largely a disaster.

As a result of public disenchantment with that administration, and with the Great Depression causing unprecedented misery for the state and the nation, Mike Conner finally came into his own by winning the governorship over another Piney Woods political figure, Columbia mayor Hugh White. A third candidate in the race was the former congressman Paul Johnson. As a matter of fact, gubernatorial politics for the next twenty-five years would be dominated with only rare exceptions by candidates from the Piney Woods. Even though they came from vastly different political styles and philosophies, Conner, White, and Johnson from the heart of the area and Tom Bailey from the fringe would occupy the governor's office for sixteen straight years, fighting it out among each other for the ultimate victory.

After a one-term interruption by Fielding Wright from the Delta, White came back to best Paul Johnson, Jr., in 1951 in what was one of the closest and most acrimonious races in Mississippi history. Then after four years of J. P. Coleman's leadership, Ross Barnett, who, as a native of Standing Pine in Leake County, has to be included as a Piney Woods figure, and Johnson gave the state eight more years of leadership from this area. Of the thirteen state administrations from 1916 to 1968, nine (counting those of Bailey and Barnett) were in the hands of governors from the Piney Woods.

During most of the early years of this same period, the United States Senate was occupied by one or both senators from the Piney Woods. Pat Harrison held forth from his election in 1918 to his death in 1941, at which time he was serving as chairman of the Finance Committee, and Bilbo occupied the other seat from 1934 until his demise in 1947.

It was during the 1930s that the unusual relationship between the two Mississippians resulted in one of the strangest episodes in Senate history. Upon the end of his term as governor in January, 1932, Bilbo found himself in the middle of the depression in need of employment, whereupon Senator Harrison was prevailed upon to help the former governor find a rather obscure position in the Department of Agriculture in a public relations capacity. Among his duties was the responsibility to preserve newspaper clippings of interest to the department. His job was derisively referred to by some of his detractors as the "Paste-master General."[13]

By 1934, however, the old warrior had his political equilibrium back enough to challenge and defeat the incumbent, Senator Hubert Stephens of New Albany. It was then that his battles began with his former benefactor, now his Senate colleague. Harrison, enjoying tremendous national influence and playing a major role in senatorial affairs, was up for reelection in 1936. Mike Conner, whose relations with Bilbo had been so strained that they refused to ride together in the inaugural parade marking the transition between their administrations, announced against Harrison, and Bilbo actively stumped the state in his (Conner's) support. The result was an overwhelming reelection victory for Harrison.

The following year, upon the death of Senate Majority Leader Joe Robinson of Arkansas, Harrison and Alben Barkley of Kentucky were the candidates to succeed him. Barkley, with the support of President Roosevelt, won the prestigious position by one vote. That vote was cast by Harrison's Mississippi colleague in favor of Barkley. Prior to the vote, Bilbo was approached by Senator Byrnes of South Carolina on behalf of Harrison. The Mississippian responded that he would vote for Harrison if the latter personally asked him to do so. The two Mississippians literally had not spoken to each other since the race of the year before. When advised of Bilbo's response, Harrison told Byrnes, "Tell the son of a bitch I wouldn't speak to him if it meant the Presidency of the United States."[14]

By 1940, when Bilbo came up for reelection, the two senators had buried the hatchet. The summer Bilbo was opposed by Hugh White, who had just concluded his term as governor and who was running with the support of his old adversary, Mike Conner. Governor Johnson was supporting Bilbo, and Harrison stayed out of the campaigning, although he voted for White. Bilbo was handily reelected and came back to the Senate to work on increasingly amicable terms with his Mississippi colleague.

After Byrnes nominated Harrison for president pro tem, Bilbo seconded the nomination, which resulted in Harrison's election.[15] The two Piney Woods senators remained on good terms for the remainder of their concurrent tenure, which ended with Harrison's death in the summer of 1941.

The final stormy chapter in the political career of the little man from Juniper Grove was written in the winter of 1946–47, when, after Bilbo gained reelection, his colleagues did not permit him to take his seat because of alleged improper relationships with certain war contractors. Plagued by terminal cancer and with the stormy battles behind him, the old senator was permitted to retain his staff and his salary but not to participate in Senate affairs until he slipped away into death a few months later, to be succeeded by a young judge named John Stennis, who could claim to be from the edge of the Piney Woods himself.

As a matter of fact, it could be claimed not only that Senator Stennis was a Piney Woods product but that his longtime colleague Jim Eastland was, too. Even though Eastland was elected to the Senate as a resident of the Delta, he had grown up in Scott County and had been one of Bilbo's floor leaders as a young legislator from that county. When he ran for the Senate for the first time in 1942, it was at the courthouse at Forrest that he opened his campaign before a crowd that was made up to a large extent of his Piney Woods friends and neighbors. He drew strong support throughout south Mississippi.

In the often heartbreaking and unpredictable game of politics, time, circumstances, and plain luck frequently prove to be the difference between victory and defeat, success and failure, the front row and the back of the room. This immutable fact of life prevailed, of course, in the politics of the Piney Woods. Some of the brightest and ablest of south Mississippi's political figures never quite achieved the ultimate goal of their ambitions but nevertheless contributed greatly to the region and the state. In fact, in some instances their efforts in the long run may prove to have been more constructive than those of some of their more heralded colleagues.

Among the most attractive of these were two Piney Woods figures of recent vintage, whose careers overlapped and occasionally clashed. They were Evelyn Gandy of Hattiesburg and her next-county neighbor, Carroll Gartin of Laurel. Gandy's public career began after her graduation from the Ole Miss Law School, as an aide to Senator Bilbo in his final years in Washington. She then came back home and launched a career that would gain her recognition as the premier woman politician in Mississippi history. Elected as a member of the legislature, as state treasurer, as commissioner of insurance, and finally in 1975 as lieutenant governor, she handled those responsibilities with great credit to herself and the state, but she was unable to be elected governor in 1979 and 1983, despite an impressive and valiant effort.

At about the same time that Miss Gandy was launching her career, Gartin became mayor of Laurel, and then in 1951 was elected lieutenant governor over his Piney Woods neighbor, Jimmy Arrington of Collins, himself a well-known and entertaining speaker. Three years later Gartin unsuccessfully challenged Eastland for the Senate, stayed around to be reelected lieutenant governor, and then, in a campaign dominated by talk of segregation, lost the governorship to Ross Barnett. Having staged a comeback by winning the lieutenant governor's office again in a hard-fought race with Miss Gandy in 1963, the handsome Gartin was planning another try for the governorship when he became the victim of a fatal heart attack a few days before Christmas in 1966.

No mention of Piney Woods politics could fail to record the significant career of two other longtime public officials whose careers were intertwined with that of Bilbo. The first of these was Willard Bond, appointed state superintendent of education by then-governor Bilbo in 1916 to succeed ("Corn Club") Smith, who had resigned to become president of Mississippi A. and M. College. Bond had been reared as an orphan deep in the Piney Woods, and his distinguished career, including twenty years as state superintendent, spanned sixty-one years. His was a persistent and effective voice for school improvement and consolidation during a time when the needs were great and the resources few. He was also a chronicler of life in south Mississippi during many of the turbulent events there. He writes with particular feeling of the attempted execution around the turn of the century of his friend Will Purvis, at Columbia, for a murder that a member of the White Caps later confessed to. Purvis was actually hanged for the crime, but when the noose slipped, he survived the execution and was later pardoned by the governor.[16]

The other figure of special note is Heber Ladner, for thirty-two years secretary of state and one of Mississippi's most beloved public servants. Ladner, from Pearl River County, wil be remembered not only for his many years of dedicated service but for his colorful and picturesque oratory, which marked him in the latter part of his career as one of the last of the old school of Piney Woods politicians.

There are many others who are now relegated to the ranks of the largely forgotten but who for a few shining moments enjoyed a place in the spotlight. One of the bright names of the 1920s was Congressman T. Webber Wilson of Laurel, regarded by some as the premier orator of the era. After serving three terms, he unsuccessfully challenged Senator Stephens in 1928 and thereafter dropped from political popularity, finally serving as a federal judge in the Virgin Islands.

One of the greatest upsets in the history of the state took place in 1964, when an obscure chicken farmer from Smith County, Prentiss Walker, running as a Republican, took advantage of the Goldwater sweep in Mississippi to defeat longtime Democratic congressman Arthur Winstead. It was the Republicans' first breakthrough in a major race since Reconstruction, but Walker's place in the sun was short-lived when he unsuccessfully challenged Jim Eastland for the Senate two years later.

There were many lesser luminaries who for sheer color and individuality were the equal of their more famous colleagues on the political scene. For instance, who can ever forget the inimitable Kelly Hammond, of Columbia, friend and confidant of Bilbo, member of the state legislature, candidate for governor in 1951, wearer of the gold horseshoe stickpin, and arm-waving orator who brought tears to the eyes of many who heard him speak. It was he who claimed that Bilbo had told him just before the senator died that he, Kelly, was to be his (Bilbo's) successor.

Then there was the tragi-comic character from Hattiesburg by the captivating name of Peachtree Harper. He derived his name from his early occupation of selling peachtree seedlings door to door, but achieved a certain amount of notoriety as a populist state senator from Forrest and Perry counties in the 1930s. Totally lacking in resources, he campaigned successfully by hitchhiking his way through his state senatorial district; and, buoyed by his upset victory in the 1931 primaries over the well-regarded

Lowrey Love, he launched a campaign for the U.S. Senate in 1934, using the same system of transportation. In the days before Senator Lawton Chiles of Florida made walking an acceptable way to reach the Senate, Peachtree did not fare well in his statewide venture, garnering only fifteen hundred votes in the race, which was ultimately won by Bilbo.

Whatever else may be said about the Piney Woods of the past, it has become today an intriguing amalgam of the old Mississippi and the new, the most productive and the least, the fastest growing and the slowest. Its politics, still tilted toward populism, nevertheless has seen economically conservative Republicans become strong forces, particularly in such cities as Hattiesburg and Laurel. In the future the region will probably become increasingly like the rest of the state politically, but what one hopes will not change is the sweep of clear streams and clean air, of green forests and crystal lakes, of room to work and room to play, and with it all, the commitment of the people to keep it thus. It is hoped that it is to these new goals, along with a commitment to education, that a new generation of Piney Woods politicians will turn.

Notes

1. Nollie Hickman, *Mississippi Harvest* (University: University of Mississippi, 1962), 256.
2. W. F. Holmes, *The White Chief: James Kimble Vardaman* (Baton Rouge: Louisiana State University Press, 1970), 147.
3. *Weekly Clarion Ledger,* 9 April 1903.
4. *Mississippi Official and Statistical Register,* 1904, 408.
5. *House Journal,* 1910, 1523.
6. Holmes, *White Chief,* 240.
7. Ibid., 242.
8. R. A. McLemore, *A History of Mississippi* (Hattiesburg: University & College Press of Mississippi, 1973), 2:57.
9. W. A. Percy, *Lanterns on the Levee* (New York: Knopf, 1941), 151.
10. Holmes, *White Chief,* 253.
11. McLemore, *History of Mississippi,* 2:71.
12. Ibid., 78.
13. Martha Swain, *Pat Harrison: The New Deal Years* (Jackson: University Press of Mississippi, 1978), 75.
14. Ibid., 159–60.
15. Ibid., 242.
16. Willard F. Bond, *I Had a Friend* (Kansas City, Mo.: E. M. Mendenhall, 1958), 40.

The Wood Dealer System

WARREN A. FLICK

Forestry and associated industries are among Mississippi's most important industries, and they are inextricably linked to many aspects of Mississippi life. One of the most important links, the wood-supply system, connects Mississippi's thousands of timber owners and even more thousands of woods workers to the forest-products industry. Historically, the wood-supply system has two parts, that used by the lumber and wood-products industry (including the plywood industry) and that used by the paper and allied-products industry. The system used by the paper and allied-products industry is known as the "dealer system," because of the role of one of the prominent players, the wood dealer. Wood dealers are independent businessmen who contract to deliver wood to the South's large pulp and paper mills. Their story—their origins, operations, and economic functions—is a fascinating example of how the potential for economic growth is realized in a free economy. It is also a story about how modern commercial development is shaped by a region's cultural and economic history.

There is very little formal research or writing on the dealer system; consequently much of this paper is offered as hypothesis. When forming hypotheses, one has license to use all of the impressions and understanding available, regardless of their direct verifiability, and so it is here. Some important sources are cited, but others are as informal as quiet conversation after dinner and are not cited. I interviewed three wood dealers in Mississippi in March 1984; these interviews provide some confidence that much of what exists elsewhere in the South also exists in the Piney Woods of Mississippi.

The wood-dealer system is part of a whole forest economy, and Mississippi's forest economy is large, vibrant, and growing. It is a bastion of free enterprise where independent businessmen of all kinds work toward their living. The Piney Woods are no longer the backwater of civilization. Instead, at the heart of Mississippi's economic life, they support an industry that makes a large contribution to the state's economy.

Forestry in Mississippi Today

How can an industry's contribution be assessed? Bowers, relying on Zinn, provides criteria.[1] They include the historical role of the industry; the amount of economic activity generated by the industry; the productivity of the industry; the industry's wage, salary, and other compensation charcteristics; its stability over time; and the degree to which it stimulates other business activity. In Mississippi, the forest-based industries rate high by most of these standards.

There is no doubt of the historical significance of the forest industries in the state. The Crosby Symposium itself is testimony, as is Nollie Hickman's classic, *Mississippi Harvest.*[2] While always changing, the industry has been an important part of Mississippi since the earliest frontier days, largely because of an enormous natural endowment of virgin pine forests. That forest and the capacity to grow additional forests has nurtured what is now Mississippi's largest manufacturing industry.

The lumber, plywood, and paper industries, the principal users of Mississippi's wood resource, had the largest value added in 1980 ($941.3 million) of any manufacturing industry in the state.[3] "Value added" is the difference between the value of finished products and the value of raw materials, that is, the value an industry creates by virtue of its activity. It is often thought to be the best single indicator of an industry's contribution to a regional economy. In 1980, the value added of the forest industries was 42 percent larger than that of the electrical and electronic equipment industry ($664.4 million), Mississippi's second largest industry in that year, and 45 percent larger than that of the apparel and textile industries combined ($648.0 million). While these census data are about four years old, they are consistent with trends back to 1972.[4]

More recently, many manufacturing industries have been adversely affected by the recession of 1981-82. The automobile industry and its suppliers suffered greatly, as did the forest products industries. But in Alabama and probably Mississippi and other southern states, the recession's effect was less severe because the industry's newest and most efficient mills, those least likely to be slowed, are in the South. As a result, employment in the forest-based industries was stable through the recession.[5]

The forest industry is one of the state's largest employers, and it offers a range of opportunities from the more highly skilled and highly paid workers in paper mills to unskilled woods and mill laborers earning relatively low wages. While the lumber industry has a history of low labor productivity and high quit rates, the paper industry tends to have the opposite.[6]

The employment range in the forest-based industries is suited to Mississippi, where there is a large, rural, relatively uneducated labor force.

Forest industries have larger economic multipliers than other manufacturing industries in Mississippi, with income and employment multipliers averaging 20 percent greater than other sectors of the state economy.[7] Similar results were found in Alabama, where the forest industries had income and employment multipliers about 9 percent larger than the all-economy average and about 28 percent larger than other manufacturing industries.[8] These multipliers measure the extent to which forest industries of the Piney Woods are linked to other aspects of Mississippi life. In a formal model, the links are purchases, and because forest-based industries purchase more of their raw materials from other Mississippi industries, expansion of the forest industries will have a disproportionately large ripple effect on the whole state economy.

Such economic and historical ties make forestry a member of the community in Mississippi, a familiar enterprise, an intimate neighbor. Forest-based industries tend, then, to be treated and judged differently than other industries. They become the subjects of myths, of emotion, of virtue, and of sin. They tie people to the land and to nature, giving them a cultural identity, a sense of place.

Mississippi and the Region

Mississippi's forest industry is part of an integrated regional forest economy. The paper industry tends to be dominant in Georgia, Alabama, and Florida. Lumber and plywood industries tend to account for a larger share of the economy in the western part of the South, particularly in Mississippi, Louisiana, Arkansas, and Texas.

Mississippi has one of the newest paper industries. The data in table 1 show that by 1970 Mississippi's pulp and paper industry was developing more slowly than that of other Southern states.[9]

TABLE 1
Number of Pulp and Paper Mills in the South, 1950–70

State	1950	1970
Alabama	4	13
Arkansas	2	6
Florida	8	10
Georgia	7	14
Louisiana	8	13
Mississippi	1	4
Texas	3	6

146

By 1984, however, Mississippi had eight mills, while the number in most other states had tended to stabilize at or near the 1970 figure.

The growth of a modern pulp and paper industry in the South may be viewed as a symbol of the profound change that occurred in the woods industries over the last hundred years. At the turn of the century, lumber was the principal product of the forest. The lumber industry was notoriously migratory, moving from one area of virgin timber to another, and finally to the West Coast to exploit its vast Douglas fir forests. The southern paper industry was insignificant.[10] By 1980, pulp and paper had become the dominant wood industry in the South, more than double the size of the lumber industry in many southern states. The same period witnessed the development of forestry as a profession and the realization on the part of industrial wood users that, in addition to being harvested, wood could be profitably grown in the South. The wood industry, especially the paper industry, became a permanent resident interested in the long-term future of the region.

Four major factors produced the rise of the southern paper industry. First, the technology of using southern pine for paper developed rapidly in the early twentieth century. Research at the U.S. Forest Products Laboratory in Madison, Wisconsin, during the first two decades of the century showed that southern pines could be used to make "kraft," the strong brown paper used for packaging. Research also demonstrated that southern pine could be used for newsprint and other white papers. Dr. Charles Herty, a chemist in Georgia who helped solve the newsprint problems, became an effective spokesman for the technological potentials of southern pines.[11]

Second, and somewhat later in the century, Inman F. ("Cap") Eldridge, an employee of the U.S. Forest Service, conducted a survey of the southern forests, measuring the extent, volume, and growth of pine timber. Besides being a careful timber appraiser, Cap was also an articulate advocate of southern forestry development.[12] He was soon astounding businessmen and other foresters with his findings of enormous acreages of young, rapidly growing pine forests. The cutover timberland left by the lumber industry had returned to pine.

Third, the U.S. economy was undergoing a revolution in packaging technology. Strong brown paper bags, especially those with a flat bottom, and paperboard boxes were providing cheap and effective means of packaging consumer and industrial products. With paper, packages could be made in many sizes, depending on market potentials. Uniform geometric shapes facilitated rapid handling, and, because paper was inexpensive, disposable packages were feasible for small, low-priced consumer items. Paper packaging created marketing opportunities that helped stimulate growth throughout the economy, and the nation's demand for paper soared.

Fourth, the South had water, labor, and transportation facilities, all needed by a growing paper industry. Southern rail and highway systems gave access to timberland across the South. Abundant rainfall and scores of major river systems made river transportation attractive and gave papermen many promising locations for new mills. The depressed agricultural and lumber economy of the 1920s and 1930s created thousands of unemployed rural poor, many of whom were accustomed to the rigors of outdoor work. In all, the South had a remarkable combination of resources for a growing paper industry.

The Procurement System

As the industry developed, it encountered a procurement problem, in that while physical access to the timber resource was easy, social and economic access was fraught with difficulties. A large pulp and paper mill might consume thousands of cords of wood, several hundred truckloads, each day. As the industry moved south it initially owned little timberland, and it depended on the hundreds of thousands of rural landowners across the South to sell their timber. Each landowner had to be dealt with individually. Only one day's wood supply for a pulp mill might well require negotiations with many landowners.

Once purchased, the wood had to be harvested, loaded onto small trucks, hauled to a rail yard, and loaded again onto rail cars; all of this was done by hand.[13] Railroads had to cooperate by supplying cars to locations scattered throughout the Piney Woods, then by pulling them to the mill when full.

Thus, the procurement problem is that of organizing and carrying out the wood purchases, logging, and transportation needed to provide a steady flow of wood to the mill.

A difficult problem anywhere, it proved especially difficult in the South, where landowners were suspicious of and reluctant to deal with outsiders; where racial barriers impeded the efficient operation of labor, wood, and land markets; where a heritage of independence, violence, resistance to central authority, and cultural isolation made woods labor frequently unreliable and difficult to manage. The formal business practices of the north—including adherence to contracts and schedules, deliberate planning of long-term activities, and the ability to distinguish business from personal matters—were not common in the rural South.

148

In the early days of the industry, mills were small, wood was relatively abundant, and the procurement problem was manageable. As the industry grew, pulp and paper-mill representatives found it more difficult to keep wood flowing to the mill. They gradually enlisted the help of local businessmen, perhaps a hardware store owner, a local mayor, or a county sheriff's brother—people who were socially established in the county and who could both purchase timber from landowners and coordinate timber harvesting and hauling. These men became wood dealers, and their assignment was to deliver a specified amount of wood to railroad cars, which would then be pulled to a pulp and paper mill. Dealers were independent contractors, not employees of the companies. In turn, they contracted with "producers," also independent contractors, who hired labor from backwoods settlements to cut and haul the wood.

This system of layered independent contractors became complex and important, yet remained almost unique to the coastal plain and piedmont regions of the South with their large, rural, unemployed populations, and to the pulp and paper industry, which used wood that could be harvested and loaded by hand. Over time the pulp and paper companies learned that dealers could deliver wood at lower costs than that of other wood-supply arrangements. The companies became dedicated to the preservation and expansion of the system. The system is especially important in the Piney Woods of Mississippi because an estimated 85–90 percent of the wood delivered to pulp and paper mills is contracted through dealers.[14]

In the 1940s and '50s, a typical wood contract consisted of a phone call from the company procurement representative, who might order a hundred cords of wood from a dealer. Dealers were typically assigned territories, having what amounted to a license to represent a particular pulp and paper company in a specified geographic area. The dealer would contact local producers who he knew would be willing to buy wood from landowners, cut it, and deliver it to a rail yard. If the producer needed a truck or money to purchase timber, he frequently obtained a loan from the dealer who, in turn, may have had a loan from the pulp and paper company. When the company paid for the delivered wood, the dealer took a share for arranging the delivery and perhaps another share as payment on a truck used by the producer. The remainder went to the producer. The producer paid his labor, paid the landowner for timber, and kept whatever was left. As one early wood producer in southern Mississippi recalls, a producer was typically paid about $5.00 per cord of wood, $1.00 of which was deducted to pay for his truck, $2.50 of which was paid to the crew of two men, and $.50 of which was paid to the landowner, leaving about $1.00 for the producer.[15]

As the paper industry grew and competition for wood increased, the system evolved. Transactions became more complex and variable, depending on the potentials of all the parties. Dealers opened woodyards of their own, hired woods crews and other labor to help organize and run a burgeoning wood business, began delivering to more than one pulp and paper company, and diversified into other businesses such as trucking, retailing woods equipment, and so on. Dealer territories eroded and competition among dealers became widespread. Dealers began buying timber on their own accounts from landowners. Pulp and paper companies also began buying wood from landowners, sometimes competing directly with their own dealers. The web of financial interdependencies became as variable as people could imagine. Companies financed dealers and producers. Dealers financed producers and paid for timber in advance. Companies started purchasing land and growing their own timber, and dealers often contracted to harvest and transport the company's own timber to its mill. All of these activities were coordinated with the railroads, the inventory requirements of the mill, and, perhaps most important of all, the weather. While the rain in the South affords excellent growing conditions for trees, it makes harvesting and hauling wood impossible on many tracts of land during wet seasons.

As just described, the dealer system seems to be unmitigated chaos, and it is difficult to see how such a patchwork of ad hoc arrangements, all quite informal and each one individually unpredictable, could collectively become a dependable, smoothly operating, low-cost wood-supply system.

The meaning of the system is derived from the economic, legal, and cultural contexts from which it arose. Historically, the dealers facilitated access to landowners and timber.[16] Local dealers would know landowners and local laborers. They would know who might be capable of organizing a crew and getting some wood cut. They would be able to negotiate with local landowners and wood producers to obtain a favorable price for timber and labor. And all the arrangements were made consistent with local custom. It was a remarkably comfortable system.

Beyond facilitating access, the dealer organized and managed the local labor force. The characteristic indolence, resistance to central authority, tendencies toward violence, and stubborn independence of rural southerners could be exploited by a wood dealer. A large percentage of the pulpwood producers and their cutters were blacks who had left declining turpentine camps and share-crop farming. Dealers were prominent white businessmen who understood and endorsed the dependent, subservient role of rural blacks. Blacks were often in debt to their dealers for trucks and other equipment, a condition of peonage like that in the turpentine camps and sharecrop agriculture.[17]

Producers were generally poor businessmen. As independent contractors, they too were responsible for their own business planning and survival. They knew nothing of accounting, were unable to plan for market fluctuations, and were undisciplined in their use of money. Their continued reliance on a dealer was all but guaranteed.

The dealer system relieved the pulp and paper companies of the need to ensure that wood cutting and hauling were done in compliance with the myriad laws regulating and taxing such work. The major laws of concern are the Fair Labor Standards Act, the Federal Insurance Contributions Act, and the National Labor Relations Act, though there are several other federal and state laws.[18] Because dealers and producers were independent contractors, pulp and paper companies were not responsible for the accounting and tax collecting associated with the laws. While dealers would frequently comply with such laws for their direct employees, dealers were not responsible for producers. Producers were generally ignorant of the issue, incapable of completing the forms, or unwilling to pay the taxes. Federal and state governments could not monitor the thousands of small producers who left no paper trail. Therefore, much of the wood delivered to the mills was produced illegally and, by not bearing appropriate taxes and associated accounting costs, cheaply.

The dealer system provided pulp and paper companies with maximum flexibility to meet their wood-inventory requirements. When demand for paper declined, wood orders were cut, and when paper markets were good, wood orders were increased. The burdens of rapid change frequently fell on the dealers, producers, and landowners. To survive, dealers needed keen business judgment: being too heavily in debt to finance new equipment might mean disaster if wood orders were cut; yet being unable to respond to increased demand might well force the pulp and paper company to establish a new dealer in direct competition, perhaps selecting one of the existing dealer's best producers for such favored treatment. Having too much wood in need of cutting created large financial risks for dealers, yet having insufficient wood under contract might jeopardize a dealer's ability to respond to increased demand. Dealers sought arrangements with local landowners in which wood was purchased on a pay-as-you-cut basis. If orders were reduced, dealers and producers could stop cutting and buying wood.

For all of these reasons, wood markets and rural labor markets were known to be bare-knuckle business environments, where mistakes often produced brutal financial or personal consequences. The likelihood of mistake was significant. Given the business risks, dealers and producers had strong incentives to work quickly through a tract of land, often leaving it in poor

151

condition; most dealers were not trained foresters, and very few producers had any knowledge of forestry. A typical logging operation often involved "high grading," cutting only the best timber and leaving the rest. Such harvesting methods did virtually nothing to facilitate the establishment of a new timber stand, and high-graded areas became poor-quality, low-valued forests. Landowners had little recourse to damages because the contracts governing the conduct of dealers and producers were often minimal or nonexistent.

Wood dealers also represented pulp and paper companies with local politicians.[19] When a county road or bridge needed repair, when a producer needed to be bailed out of jail on Monday to work, or when a land title needed clarification, a good dealer could intercede and frequently obtain the desired result.

In modern times, dealers are diversifying in response to overlapping wood-product specifications. When the system started, the distinction between wood for paper and wood for lumber was sharp and clear. Technological improvements in the manufacture of lumber, however, have allowed that industry to use smaller wood. Plywood plants constructed in the 1960s and '70s added yet another set of product specifications to the wood business. Some timber that was especially straight and properly tapered could also be used for poles, and the number of pole-manufacturing plants grew. Each use of raw wood could justify a different price, so a financial incentive developed to separate the several types of wood on any given trace of timber, sending each type to the manufacturing facility capable of paying the highest price. Such product separation requires more sophisticated timber-harvesting systems and better knowledge of local and regional marketing opportunities. Dealers now typically deliver to more than one pulp and paper company. They own their own rail yards, operate several logging crews who use expensive equipment, and still contract with independent producers. In all, a system that started from humble beginnings has grown and diversified to meet the changing needs of a maturing forest-products industry.

The dealer system is a living example of the virtues and problems of free enterprise. The two great merits of capitalism are the impersonal character of the constraints it places on people and its unrivaled flexibility.[20] Individuals are free to enter, exit, buy, sell, produce, and adapt as they see fit. There is little mercy, however, for landowners, dealers, or producers who make mistakes. In the aggregate, the system is flexible in that it can move rapidly from nonadapters to innovators, always keeping its center of gravity near the most efficient and productive.

Its great faults tend to be its fragmentation and consequent lack of provision for the future, and its unsatisfying distributive consequences. Dealers played almost no role in developing modern mechanical logging equipment, and they have been slow to adopt it once developed. Logging systems costing half a million dollars or more and requiring skilled operators are simply too expensive for a small business with fluctuating wood orders, unless the system's value has been proved.

The unsatisfying distributive aspects of the wood-supply system are the seeming inability of an uneducated rural labor force to improve its situation. The pressure of competition forces each player to seek his maximum advantage. The least advantaged players, usually landowners, producers, and laborers, are traditionally ill equipped to negotiate profitable contracts.

The harshest aspects of the system have been already mitigated. The debt peonage of early years is much less common. Employment opportunities in other industries have expanded, and the negotiating positions of rural labor are gradually improving. Landowners are becoming more knowledgeable about timber and more aggressive in their marketing efforts. The woods industry's continuing expansion is causing increased competition and higher prices for wood and labor.

The wood-supply system of the Piney Woods is an understandable adaptation to the time and place and task. It helped facilitate the development of one of the South's most important industries. And the fact that it is a common system in neighboring states is a clear sign that Mississippi's Piney Woods are a vital part of an interdependent regional economy.

Notes

1. John R. Bowers, "The Alabama Forest Industries: Their Contribution to the State's Economy" (M.S. thesis, School of Forestry, Auburn University, 1979); Gary W. Zinn, "A Model for Analyzing the Contribution of Forestry to a Region" (Ph.D. diss., College of Forestry, Syracuse University, 1972).

2. University: University of Mississippi, 1962.

3. U.S. Department of Commerce, Value Added by Industry and State (preliminary statistics, mimeographed, 1980).

4. U.S. Department of Commerce, 1977 Census of Manufactures, Geographic Area Series (Washington, D.C.: Bureau of the Census, 1980).

5. Warren A. Flick, "Forestry and Alabama's Economic Recovery," *Alabama Forests* 26 (1983):2.

6. Bowers, "Alabama Forest Industries," 35–46.

7. Richard L. Porterfield, Thomas R. Terfehr, and James E. Moak, *Forestry and the Mississippi Economy,* Bull. 869, Mississippi Agricultural and Forestry Experiment Station (Mississippi State: Mississippi State University, 1978), 46–48.

8. Warren A. Flick, Peter Trenchi III, and John R. Bowers, "Regional Analysis of Forest Industries: Input-Output Methods," *Forest Science* 26 (1980):4.

9. Jack P. Oden, "Development of the Southern Pulp and Paper Industry, 1900–1970 (Ph.D. diss., Mississippi State University, 1973), 66–237.

10. Ibid., 17.

11. Ibid., 123.

12. Elwood R. Maunder, ed., *Voices from the South: Recollections of Four Foresters* (Santa Cruz, Calif.: Forest History Society, 1977), 91–92, 125–27.

13. Arthur Nelson, "Oral History of a Wood Industry Executive," interview with Warren A. Flick and J. Wayne Flynt, Auburn University Archives, cassette tape, 1978.

14. Lee Hopson, "Oral History of an Early Pulpwood Producer"; John Rollins, "Oral History of an Early Pulpwood Dealer"; Ben Stevens, "Wood Dealers in Southern Mississippi": interviews with Warren A. Flick, Auburn University Archives, cassette tape, 1984.

15. Hopson interview.

16. Jack O. Cantrell, "Effect of Mill Inventory Policy and Pulpwood Procurement Practices on Producer Income and Job Stability" (M.S. thesis, College of Forestry, Syracuse University, 1969); James E. Moak, "Some Factors of Pulpwood Procurement and Production Costs in Alabama" (M.S. thesis, Auburn University, 1978).

17. Jerrell H. Shofner, "Forced Labor in the Florida Forests, 1880–1950," *Journal of Forest History* 25 (1981):14–25; Pete Daniel, *The Shadow of Slavery: Peonage in the South 1901–1969* (Urbana: University of Illinois Press, 1972).

18. *How to Stay at Peace with Your Government* (Washington, D.C.: American Pulpwood Association, 1981).

19. Stevens interview.

20. Tibor Scitovsky, "Can Capitalism Survive?—An Old Question in a New Setting," *American Economic Review* 70 (1980):1–9.

Water-Powered Sawmills
and Related Structures
in the Piney Woods

M. B. NEWTON, JR.

When L. O. Crosby, Jr., was born, the forest industry of the Piney Woods
had already largely been transformed by the likes of his father. Since about
1880, the historic manner of harvesting the bounty of the great forests of
the Gulf South had come increasingly under development by modern, industrial lumbering operations. By 1907, the historic forms of lumbering
were largely displaced. Yet even at that date some relicts of the older mode
survived which the younger Crosby would surely have seen and for which
he probably would have developed some nostalgic appreciation. One way
to acknowledge the accomplishment of the L. O. Crosbys is to understand
what they superceded.

Throughout the first four-fifths of the nineteenth century, people who
operated mills in the parts of the Gulf South near the coast confronted a special difficulty. Their environment provided but scant slope, normally less than
eight feet of downhill descent per mile of travel toward the sea.[1] At scarcely
any place in the Piney Woods was there a mill of the kind romanticized in
calendar art. Nowhere in the Gulf South was there a mill that had the grand,
solemnly turning mill wheel with a diameter of twenty to thirty feet, like those
that might be seen north of Atlanta.[2] In a region where the streams slope only six to eight feet per mile, raising water high enough to pour over the top
of an overshot wheel fifteen feet in diameter would require a millrace of
uneconomical length. At eight feet of slope per mile and allowing for some
fall of water in the millrace, a fifteen-foot wheel would require a race more
than two miles long by straight-line measure. Over that distance, the race
would have to cross several small tributaries of the main stream. Such a crossing would require either costly trestles or circuitous canals that would run first
up, then down, the valleys of the small tributaries.

While such engineering works were completely possible in the early nineteenth century, they were just as completely impractical in the Piney Woods. No local market promised to repay the capital investment required for such construction. Instead, the person who hoped to operate a mill required another, less costly manner of harnessing the power of water flowing downhill under the pull of gravity. Customs whose origins lie in the dark recesses of European prehistory provided a means of capturing the last increments of the power of falling water during its last, gentle descent to the gulf.[3]

While documents show that a few expert millwrights did work in the antebellum South,[4] most of the mills actually built were erected by farmers and planters who had the general skill and competence that careful students of the Piney Woods plain folks have come to expect. The customary, or folk, mills were set in more-or-less out-of-the-way places, normally where a would-be mill operator happened to find a likely site on his property. Travelers through the Piney Woods commonly missed seeing or reporting the mills, leaving it to us to discover and reconstruct them today from a variety of documentary sources. Evidence of the old mills appears in the manuscript census, probate and succession records, surveyors' plats, and—best of all for the geographer—in the grandest of all documents, the landscape itself. Within a hundred or a hundred and fifty miles of the gulf in Alabama, Mississippi, Louisiana, and east Texas, any county may be expected to have sites of between ten and forty old mills, except in areas lower than about 30 feet above sea level.

One specimen county, St. Helena Parish, Louisiana, has yielded more than thirty millsites.[5] St. Helena lies generally between 50 and 375 feet above sea level and has stream slopes of 6 to 8 feet per mile. Some of these mills were discovered in the manuscript census where a miller was listed among the residents of households. Others appeared when a mill was mentioned in a succession or a land survey. Others were discovered in the field. Many of those mentioned in paper documents have subsequently been verified by field evidence (table 1). Initial inquiry into the mill geography of other counties suggests that comparable numbers will be found for the other Gulf South counties. We can expect the zone within 150 miles of the gulf and spreading from Alabama into east Texas to yield at least two thousand millsites.

The mills thus far examined produced minimums of between ten and twenty-five horsepower, figured conservatively. These two thousand mills could easily have produced a combined output of more than thirty thousand horsepower. To give that figure a modern comparison, thirty thousand horsepower hours amounts to more than forty thousand kilowatts, still figured conservatively. Such figures fall somewhat below estimates published in the nineteenth century.[6]

Mill Type and Location

The cultural geographer, attempting to understand the historic landscape, seeks types. A type is a recurrent form, a repeated pattern of building construction, for one example, that people use in their customary alteration of the surface of the earth. Emphasis falls on the form of tangible objects because these features are "dottable data"; that is, such dots entered on maps and graphs represent discrete, real objects.[7] This essentially fiduciary act, the equivalent of the historian's documentation, provides an assurance of a substantive basis for inference. Once a type has been established and its relations to culture and nature delineated, it can serve as direct evidence of past relationships.

Types commonly show some degree of variation, largely because people differ as to their intentions and understandings and as to the sites that they have for development. While individuals may occasionally create new solutions, three factors seem to diminish the role of such creativity. For one, the innovation may not gain wide acceptance because either it or its innovator fails to meet expectations of the other individuals in the region. More often, however, the innovator merely replicates a form from another region, albeit with perhaps some small change. Second, the effect of this cultural borrowing tends to become blurred in the historic landscape because forms may be borrowed from several directions and because subsequent borrowings get emplaced among earlier ones. The third factor working against the success of innovations is the simple success of older borrowed forms; older, working forms, already using the available space, work against the local innovator. Patient unstacking of types in space and time, however, greatly aids in understanding the unfolding of the cultural landscapes of the past and, by accumulation, of the present.

The type of mill that abounds in the gently sloping Gulf South consists of a model that has several variations, each understood at the time to serve useful purposes in its distinct context. The individual mill, through each of three variants, was understood as an application of a general form. Each variant form served to capture the energy of falling water in a distinctive setting.

Regardless of the variant used, however, the function of the mill is a separate consideration. A mill might serve as a sawmill, gin, or gristmill, or it might serve a combination of these functions. Some mills had tanneries attached, and at least one served to make ink. While the choice of the variant of the general type depended upon the mill owner's conception of the physical setting, the function depended upon his idea of what function would pay a return on his investment. It often happened that, having a suitable site for a mill, the owner would contrive to have the mill carry out several functions. The gristmill was the most common function, followed by ginning and sawmilling.[8] A large minority, however, combined at least two of these functions. The degree of combined functions seems to have been greatest in the midrange of milling successes. The largest mills generally served one or two functions, while the smallest usually served but one. The small, fortuitously situated mill owned by a man who operated a complex enterprise seems to have had the largest number of functions. Such a person was generally a farmer, merchant, and professional, as well as a mill owner.

Fortuitous situation includes much more than mere availability of waterpower. Despite widespread belief, in the Gulf South mills did not cause, or even significantly contribute to, the formation of towns. Scarcely any towns in the Gulf South can be traced to foundations at the sites of watermills, although a few had mills established after the town had already begun. Even villages and crossroad hamlets rarely grew up at the sites of watermills.[9] Fortuitous situation for mills in the Gulf South, by contrast with the common misconception, consisted of a suitable millsite located on a road in the midst of a generally successful farming region. For sawmills, the conditions were somewhat different: the suitable site commonly lay between the forest and the head of schooner navigation, but still at a ford or bridge. If the sawmill functioned as an adjunct to a gristmill, it would also require a surrounding small-farm population.

Fortuitous situation for such single-purpose mills as those devoted solely to sawing timber, ginning, or tanning depended less on the surrounding farmers and, thus, could be located more idiosyncratically. The operator of a large farm or plantation had little concern as to whether his mill attracted business. He cared more that the mill served his immediate desire to gin his own cotton, saving the cost of custom ginning. Similarly, the sawmill operator cared more that his mill occupied a site that let him effectively move his logs to the mill and his sawn timbers to market.

Gulf South Mills

Given that the Gulf South generally lacks both steep slopes and rocky outcrops, the would-be mill owner had little expectation of creating a major milling center. Rather, he had scarcely more than the hope of making a modest living as a lumberman, of supplementing his income as a small custom miller, or of reducing his costs as a farmer. Even with such limited goals, however, the mills established by some owners endured for generations as landscape features, some even becoming well-known landmarks. Many, however, lasted but a few years, perhaps no longer than the original owners' efforts to make them going concerns.

The basic concept of a mill site in the Gulf South includes a building, a dam, a wheel or turbine, and a situation, all of which have small variations. The various forms, however, share a general overall design.

The building commonly takes the form of a shotgun house or a covered bridge, though this is not to say that either of these forms dictated or suggested the form of the mill house. The building was in all known cases a long, narrow structure that had a gable roof with gables to the ends and the ridge perpendicular to the stream. Set across the stream, it used the high banks of an incised stream as its foundation.[10] Thus sited, it stood well above normal flood levels, but remained vulnerable to century floods. The miller and his customers entered the building from the bank, entering either gable end. The floor of the mill house stood commonly fifteen to twenty feet above the bed of the stream. With the milldam in place, the floor of the mill house stood about eight feet nearer the water surface. The floors of sawmills may have been closer to the water surface.

The mill works stood inside the mill house, the shaft extending through the floor to the wheel below (fig. 1). Flow over the milldam, directed into a single stream, turned the wheel. The power of the wheel was transmitted by the vertical shaft to the mill works on the floor of the mill house. While the power of the shaft could be transferred directly to the mill works, either by direct shaft drive or by means of cogged gears, it was perhaps more commonly transferred by one or more twisted belts.[11] Starting or stopping the mill was usually accomplished by shunting the water onto or away from the wheel by means of a gate controlled from the floor.

The choice of power wheel depended in part on the period of history. Earlier, the tub mill had been the only form available capable of producing the power required to run more than a very small gristmill. The tub mill, the precursor of the turbine, had rotors that were contained within a sheathing, or "tub," in such a way as to force the falling water over the blades without permitting it to escape to the sides. The water fell on the wheel from a height of six or more feet and escaped through the bottom of the wheel, which therefore had to stand mostly out of the water. While a fall of six feet could power a goodly gristmill, a fall of at least eight feet

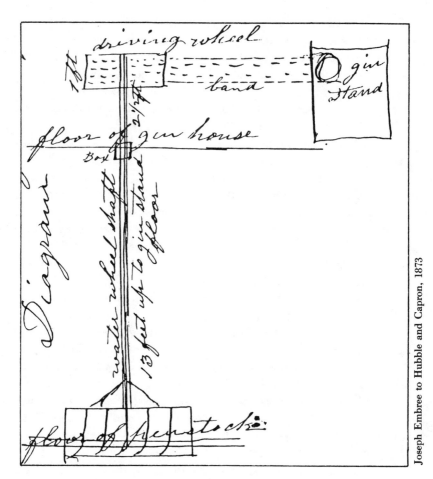

Figure 1. Sketch of band (belt) driven millworks

was required to power a rotary sawmill. A sawmill designed as a sash saw could, however, successfully use a six-foot fall of water.

The invention in 1827 of the turbine opened a new era of more efficient extraction of power from the energy of falling water. With the development of more effective iron casting, the new water turbine became increasingly effective as a landscape element. Improved engineering made the turbine more and more the effective choice for those mill owners who felt that they could compete in the emerging industrial age of the nineteenth century. For the Piney Woods, however, the Civil War and Reconstruction delayed development for a generation. The turbine gained increasing adoption in the last quarter of the century.[12] While the increased efficiency of the turbine theoretically permitted small mills to continue operation into the future, it generally favored the medium and large mills because they could profit even more from the improved designs. Soon both large and small water-mills of the Gulf South were to be overwhelmed by the introduction of steam and internal combustion engines.[13] However, for two generations straddling the turn of the century, the turbine renewed the vigor of the small mills of the Gulf South without noticeably changing the form of the mill house or the mill site.

The form of the mill house type and the details of engineering merge in geographical interest in the relations of these forms with the typical sites of milling activities. The minimal physical requirements include a fall of at least six feet—preferably at least eight feet—and a stable foundation protected from flooding. Mill owners repeatedly chose one of three kinds of site. Each of these presented special opportunities and distinct difficulties; the same mill house and choice of wheel, however, pertained in all three typical sites.

The most common site for a small mill in the gently sloping Gulf South was a small, tight meander of a modest upland stream. If the flow of the stream during the dry month—normally October or November—did not fall below 1 cubic foot per second, then the stream might afford a mill site. A farmer-miller might reckon that minimum flow by determining the size of a square box that would contain the dry-season flow. One such would-be miller wrote to Hubble, Capron & Co., turbine manufacturers, that his stream's dry-season flow would pass through a box 10 inches square, or 120 cubic inches at a flow of 1 cubic foot per second.[14] With a discharge of 1 cubic foot per second, a weekly discharge in the dry season would be 600,000 cubic feet. Wet-season discharge would, of course, be greater, and the presence of springs above the mill site would have stabilized the rate of discharge. All of these matters were understood by virtually any landowner of the late nineteenth century.

Given a dry-season discharge of at least 1 cubic foot per second, the next locational question concerned the geometry of the stream. The most common site at the lower end of a meander on an incised stream provided two important qualities. The incised cross-sectional profile provided for a restricted, channel-like storage pond. With an average slope of six feet per mile, a stream that has a normal floodplain of fifty feet wide by twelve feet deep would, with an eight-foot dam, store 1.3 million cubic feet of water. Such a millpond would have been a body fifty feet wide by seven thousand feet long. The narrow, incised profile would have minimized backing water onto otherwise useful land and would have provided a float surface for moving logs to the mill.

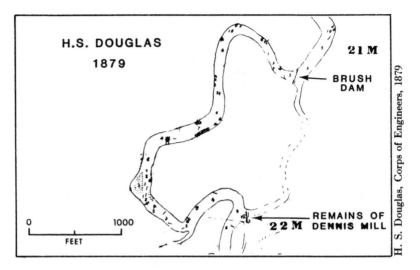

Figure 2. Part of the Amite River

The tight meander provided the opportunity to cut a diversion channel across the neck of the meander. Such a channel permitted excess water to leave the millpond and exit below the milldam. The mill site, thus protected from normal high water, could survive all but the most severe floods. This tight meander seems to have been one of the most important locational factors for small, upland mills on the gentle slopes of the Gulf South.

A second kind of site was used on small rivers with multiple, parallel channels. At such a site, the mill house was placed on the bank of the channel nearest the mill owner's house. The mill house straddled that channel, much as the same kind of structure spanned small, upland streams. A coffer dam shunted water into the chosen channel (fig. 2).[15] The height of the coffer dam sufficed to raise water to the height required, while still permitting floods to pass over the dam largely unrestricted. No millpond was created, but a four-foot dam standing forty-five hundred feet upstream would have produced a head of about nine feet, sufficient for significant operations. Such a mill remained safe from all but the most severe floods.

Something of a blend of the other two, the third kind of site appears on small, upland streams that have two or more prongs. Such conditions occur where the stream crosses a broad, gently sloping part of its valley. One channel was chosen as the site of the mill. A point near the lower end of the prong, where the channel was well defined and the banks firm, provided the seat of the mill. At the upper end of the channel, a coffer dam shunted water into the chosen channel. Excess water continued over the dam and down the unused prong to a point below the mill site. Thus the second prong removed the need for an overflow channel near the mill site.

The same kind of mill house and one of two kinds of mill works were usually used at all types of sites. Each combination could and did serve all the functions commonly expected of watermills. The general model and its variants were known to virtually every man and boy in the Gulf South.[16]

Areal Pattern

Because the operation of a watermill requires that the water falling on the wheel escape freely, the pond of one mill must not rise above the wheel of another. Such a constraint did not affect the kind of mill site that occupied a side channel of a larger stream, but did determine the minimum distance between the two types that occupied the smaller, upland streams. Given a slope of 6 feet per mile and a dam height of 8 feet, mills would have to stand not closer than 7,000 feet (1.33 miles) apart, measured along the main trend of the creek valley.

Along Darlings Creek, a left-bank tributary of the Amite River in St. Helena Parish, six mill sites occur at fairly regular intervals along the creek valley (figure 3). The sites stand far enough apart to prevent backwater from a lower millpond from rising above the wheel of a higher mill. Documents and fieldwork show that several of these mills operated at the same time. No other string of mills on a small, upland stream has yet been found, but careful search of the records and the landscape will surely reveal such cases.

Along the small rivers of the Gulf South slopes, a somewhat different regime existed. Many of these small rivers are—or were in the nineteenth century—spring fed and, as such, had fairly stable flows. Where these streams transited relatively narrow valleys, the pattern of mill sites would have been similar to that of the smaller creeks, about 7,000 feet apart. Where, on the other hand, the smaller rivers passed through broader segments of their valleys, the pattern of mill sites was often more dense. The upper Tickfaw in St. Helena, for example, had two clusters of closely spaced mills. Some of these occupied the mouths of tributary creek valleys and thus took the form of the small, upland mill. Others, however, occupied different parallel prongs in the main valley, thus raising complicated questions of priority in the positioning of coffer dams. These dams would have become a serious issue where one mill owner's coffer dam interrupted the movement of logs to another's sawmill.

The relation of the mill to the roads and other elements of settlement provides another aspect of areal pattern. So far, no mill site has been found

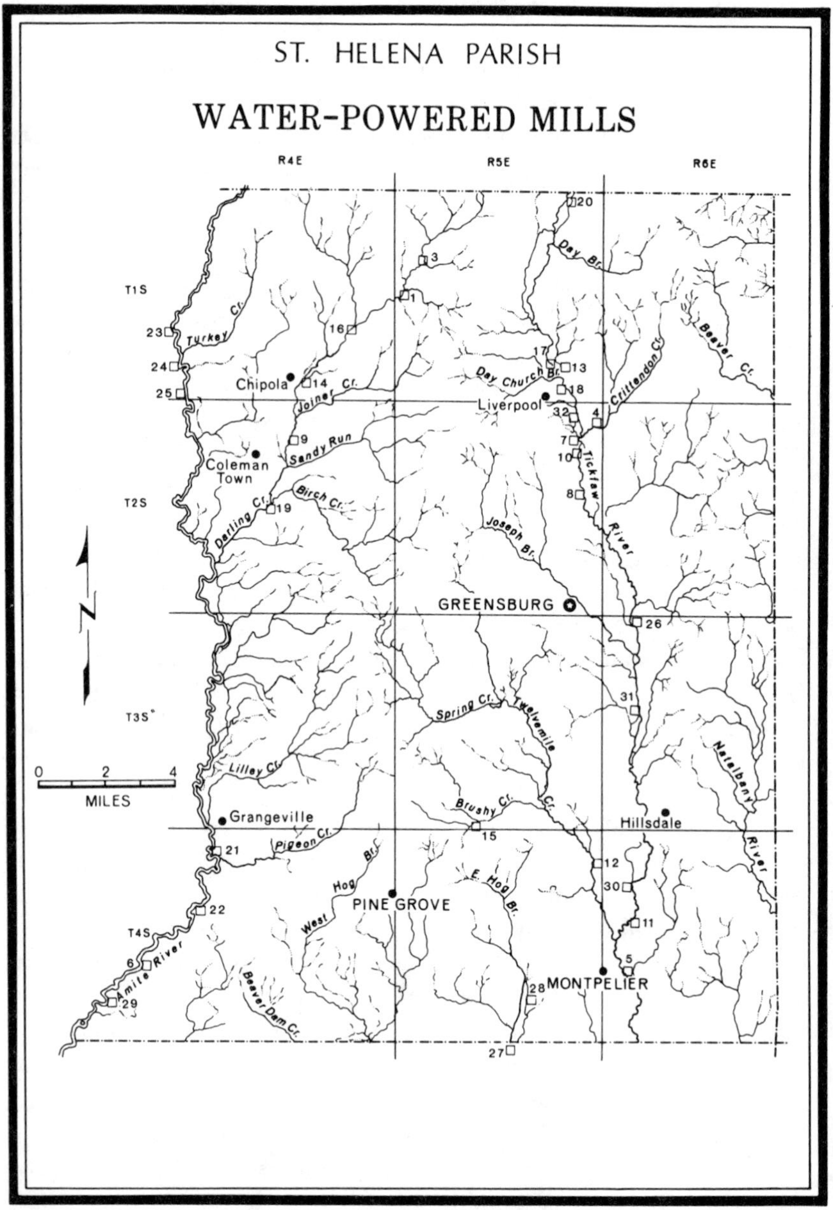

Newton, 1981

Figure 3. Water-powered mills, St. Helena Parish, Louisiana

that did not have a road serving its locality. Typically, the road crossed the stream at a ford just below the milldam. Such an arrangement facilitated the arrival either of customers or of the services required by the mill owner. Given a millpond of more than a mile in length, no road could easily have crossed the stream closer than 1½ miles upstream of the mill seat, unless it did so by a bridge. In many cases, then, the fortuitous situation for a mill included as an element a stream crossing a road.

Some mill seats occupy sites just below the juncture of several tributaries with the main creek valley. Such sites provide an additional advantage to those hoping to establish a ford. The steeper slope of the tributaries allows them to carry larger sedimentary particles (sands and gravels), which are dropped upon entering the less steeply sloped of the master valley. These coarser sediments provide improved footing for vehicles crossing the master stream. Such sites also provide for a single fording, whereas crossings at points higher up the valley would require fording the tributaries, as well as the main stream.[17]

Thus do both natural and human factors tend to make mill seats and roads appear in the same place. Despite these tendencies, however, no significant support can be adduced for the notion that mills promote the appearance of towns. Indeed, the evidence thus far in hand shows that mills—both individually and in clusters—stand quite apart from the nearby towns.

The Water-Powered Upland Sawmill: A Case

Across Lake Pontchartrain from New Orleans lie the Florida Parishes, so called for having once formed part of British and Spanish West Florida and, subsequently, the Republic of West Florida. Except for the lower-lying, southern portion of the Florida Parishes, the area belongs with the Piney Woods of southern Mississippi and Alabama, as well as North Louisiana and East Texas. Gently rolling, slightly hilly pine forests form the fabric of the landscape. Early settlers moved into these pine forests largely from Tennessee, Mississippi, Alabama, Georgia, and Carolina.

Except along the southern portions and along such streams as the Pearl and the Bogue Chitto in the east and the Amite and Tangipahoa farther west, relatively few slaves were introduced into the Piney Woods of the mid and eastern Florida Parishes. Few enterprises could have been classed with the large slaveholdings along the Mississippi. Rather, the region served as the home of small and middling farmers who generally owned few or no slaves. Masters and slaves alike concerned themselves with raising both food and feed crops and with procuring some sort of marketable produce, generally cotton. Some, however, raised stock, and even slaves were permitted to ride horses in managing the cattle.[18]

Somewhat surprisingly, perhaps, at least some "plantations" were logging and lumbering operations. North of Covington, seat of St. Tammany Parish, along the Bogue Falaya (a Choctaw word meaning "long creek"), a sawmill plantation was established in the early nineteenth century. The master in 1828 had sixteen slaves, thirteen of them males. The five occupations of these men included: blacksmith, sawyer, teamster, chopper, and laborer.[19] Such a list accords with what one ought to expect of a small, pre-industrial, Piney Woods sawmilling business. Documents show that from early in the nineteenth century until well after emancipation, the structure eventually known as Hossmer's Mill continued in business, albeit not without changes in ownership.[20]

Examination of the site of Hossmer's Mill reveals it to have qualities that we now expect. The Bogue Falaya at that point makes a fairly tight meander around toward the right (west) bank. The cross-section of the stream includes a normal floodplain about fifty feet wide and a higher, wider plain standing above the ten- to twelve-foot banks of the incised normal flood channel (fig. 4). During normal periods of high water, the Falaya remains largely within the twelve by fifty foot incised channel. The bed of the stream slopes six feet per mile.

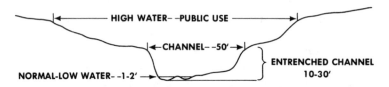

Figure 4. Cross-sectional profile of representative Piney Woods stream

The location of the mill seat can clearly and easily be seen in the characteristic timbers lying under the clear waters of the Bogue Falaya (fig. 5). The mill occupied a point on the lower arm of the tight meander, leaving a share of the meander to carry away the tailwater. The miller's house stood on the left bank, far enough back to place it above the normal flood zone. The neighborhood rural road forded the Falaya just below the mill, using the point bars on opposite sides to provide a convenient descent and ascent. Between the ford and the mill site, on the lower limb of the meander, there issued the outlet of the relief channel cut across the narrowest part of the meander. This channel functioned to shunt excess water from the millpond to a point downstream from the mill.

166

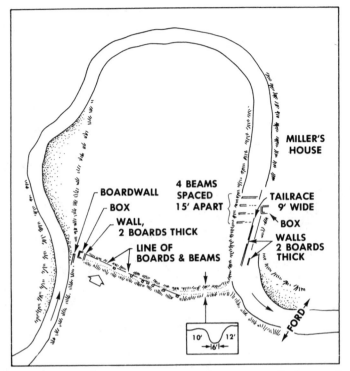

Figure 5. Site of Hossmer's Mill, Bogue Falaya, St. Tammany Parish, Louisiana

The milldam, which occupied the location of the timbers in the stream bed, was eight feet high. At the base of the dam, the pond was about eight feet deep. From that point for a mile and a third upstream the surface of the water was essentially level, but its depth gradually decreased. The pond was contained within the incised, normal floodplain of the Bogue Falaya, twisting and turning as its host channel curved its way along. If the gate on the top of the milldam remained closed or if more water came down the creek than was needed, the excess flowed to the right (west) through the relief channel cut across the neck of the meander.

During the normal week, the crew cut logs in the surrounding forest, floated them on the millpond to the mill, cut them into squared timbers, formed the timbers into rafts, and floated the rafts of timbers to the head of schooner navigation. On the Bogue Falaya, even the dry season provided discharge sufficient to run the sawmill all year.[21]

The rafts, made up of squared timbers, were assembled below the dam and held in readiness for Saturday, when they would be sent to market. Early on Saturday morning, the water held behind the milldam was released

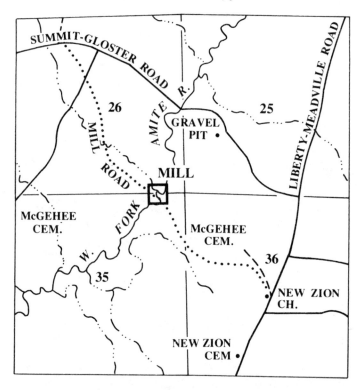

Figure 6. Setting of McGehee Mill, Amite County, Mississippi

and left flowing until evening. On the flood, the crew conducted the rafts to Covington, where the timbers were marketed to schooner captains. By evening, the rafts would have reached market, and the milldam would be closed. Even during the dry season, the millpond would have been refilled by Monday morning, and thus the mill ready to resume sawing timbers.

This neat operation continued from about 1820 until after 1884. Before the war, it was a slave plantation; afterward, it ran with free labor. It continued until the then new industrial lumbering that was spreading west from Florida overwhelmed the market that Hossmer's Mill had served.[27] Thus, by the time that L. O. Crosby, Jr., was born, mills like Hossmer's Mill had ceased operation, not because they did not work, but because they did not work well enough.

Associated Features

Finding and enjoying old mills absorbs the attention of both professional and amateur scholars. All too often, however, this worthwhile attention

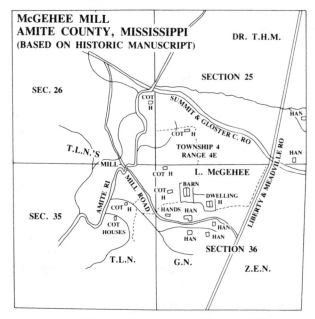

Figure 7. McGehee Mill and Farm, Amite County, Mississippi

focuses only upon the mill and the mill seat. To gain a fuller appreciation of the mill as part of the historic landscape, enthusiasts should seek to place the mill in the context that it occupied in its heyday.

Good fortune has preserved for us a record of McGehee Mill, located north of Liberty, Mississippi, on the West Fork of Amite River.[23] The family have in their possession a map made by an ancestor, apparently before the Civil War. The amateur cartographer's use of the regular sections as a frame for drafting allows us to relocate the places included in the map. Clearly portrayed are the Amite, the mill, associated roads, the owner's dwelling and barn, the houses occupied by hands, cotton houses, and some fences (fig. 6). To supplement the information on the map, a descendant recalls the mill in its last days.

Again, the mill occupied a tight meander on a stream sloping 8.3 feet per mile. The descendant recalls the dam to have been about as tall as a man, or about 6 feet. Such a dam would have created a millpond nearly 3,900 feet long, its upper end reaching the crossing of the "Summit & Gloster C[ounty] Ro[ad]." The upper end would have just missed backing water onto another, nearly ideal, site for a mill just upstream from the Summit-Gloster highway, although no such mill appears on the map. The descendant also recalled that the mill house had the form of a shotgun house set across the stream and using the high banks as a foundation. Adding complexity to the actuality of the historic landscape, however, the descendant also insists that the wheel of the mill was an overshot wheel six feet wide and six feet high. Such a wheel, while not conforming to the model, would have carried on the mill's functions.

The McGehee Mill served mainly for ginning cotton produced on the lands of the McGehee family and for grinding corn. Sawing was vaguely recollected. Considering the type of wheel and the limited fall of water, the only kind of saw works that could have served in such a mill would have been a sash saw, which requires less horsepower than a rotary saw. Examination of many historic structures in the region of the upper Amite does, in fact, support the suggestion that sash saws were commonly used in the nineteenth century. (Surveyors of standing historic structures sometimes confuse the evidence of sash-sawn lumber with that for pit-sawn lumber.)

To understand the historic importance of the McGehee Mill, then, we should have clearly in view that the McGehee family included several talented people; one neighboring McGehee was a doctor. These people

Figure 8. Artist's reconstruction of Hossmer's Mill, St. Tammany Parish, Louisiana

managed a complex enterprise, that included seven servant households, in addition to the McGehee house a dogtrot-plan structure of one and one-half stories. They raised cotton—and, of course, corn—on apparently more than six hundred acres, gathering this cotton into six cotton houses. The crop thus secured during the fall and early winter, the family could gin the cotton during the late winter. Corn, presumably gathered into the barn shown standing next to the McGehee dwelling, would have been ground as needed throughout the year. No records have yet told whether the McGehee Mill served others than the owner. The presence of a "Mill Road," however, made the mill accessible to neighbors (fig. 7).

In summary, then, the McGehee example shows that this historic mill should be associated with at least fifteen other buildings, two roads, and a millpond. If neighbors also used the mill, then other structures should be included in our portrayal and analysis of the historic mills.

During the nineteenth century, people in the Gulf South who wanted to build and operate water-powered mills faced limited opportunity. By custom, they carried in their memories a model of a type of mill that, also by custom, had one mill house form, two kinds of power wheel, and three site variants. The resulting structural combinations persisted through the change from tub mill to turbine, but declined in the face of competition from steam and internal combustion engines. The sites of most of these historic mills still produce power that today goes begging. By careful review of paper and landscape documents, the mill seats and their associated structures can be found so that we can fill out our conceptions of the historic landscape.

At each mill seat, custom and technics interacted with available natural features to influence the construction of mills. The special historic period amplified or decreased the likelihood of such mills' being built and of their success, once built. Custom and nature, mediated by technics and history, then, account for opportunity, while individuals account for initiation of structures in the historical landscape.

Notes

1. See, for example "Bude, Mississippi, 15' Topographic Quadrangle," in *U.S. Geological Survey*, 1962.

2. Donald Gregory Jeane, "The Culture History of Grist Milling in North Georgia" (Ph.D. diss., Louisiana State University, 1974). Jeane covers both the origins of mills and the specific applications of types different from those discussed here.

3. In ibid., 12–20, the facts and authorities concerning the European background of the rotary mill powered by water are reviewed concisely.

4. See, for example, Oliver Evans, *The Young Mill-Wright and Miller's Guide* (Philadelphia: Carey & Lea, 1832).

5. M. B. Newton, Jr., *Historic Standing Structures, St. Helena Parish, Louisiana* (Baton Rouge, La.: Department of Urban and Community Affairs, 1981), 22–26.

6. Herman Hollerith, "Power Used in Manufactures," in U.S. Bureau of the Census, *Census of Manufacturing* (Washington, D.C.: Government Printing Office, 1883), figures 1 to 4, following p. 8.

7. Carl O. Sauer, "Foreword to Historical Geography," *Annals of the Association of American Geographers* 31 (1941):353–64.

8. James L. Greenleaf, "The Rivers of the Gulf of Mexico in Louisiana and Mississippi, and the Tombigbee in Alabama" I-Statistics of Power and Machinery Employed in Manufactures, Reports on the Water Power of the United States, *Ninth Census of the United States,* pt. 2 (Washington, D.C.: Government Printing Office, 1887), 265–73.

9. Jeane, "Culture History," 106.

10. Patti Carr Black, *Mississippi Piney Woods: A Photographic Study of Folk Architecture* (Jackson: Mississippi Department of Archives and History, 1976), cover illustration. While Carr's illustration shows the shotgun-like form of a millhouse, the wheel mounted on the mill suggests late influence of calendar art.

11. Joseph Embree to Messers. Hubble and Capron, 1873 (correspondence in the possession of Mr. and Mrs. Stanley Morris, Clinton, Louisiana.)

12. Charles S. Sargent, *Report on the Forests of North America . . .* (Washington, D.C.: Census Office, Department of the Interior, 1884), 523–32.

13. Greenleaf, "Rivers of the Gulf of Mexico."

14. Joseph Embree to Messers. Hubble and Capron.

15. H. S. Douglas, "Chart of the Amite River, Louisiana" (made under the direction of Major C. W. Howell, Corps of Engineers, U.S.A., 1879, Cartographic Information Center, Louisiana State University, Baton Rouge).

16. Sargent, *Report on the Forests,* 532: "The ever-increasing consumption of timber at the mills upon the Pearl river . . . will prove a powerful stimulus to a people who, since the development of the lumber business in these regions, have almost completely abandoned their former agricultural and pastoral pursuits and now depend entirely for their support upon cutting pine logs, to supply this enormous demand. . . . This is true, too, of the region between the Pearl and Amite rivers . . . of eastern Louisiana, a region in which the forests are also particularly good."

17. M. B. Newton, Jr., "Route Geography and the Routes of St. Helena Parish, Louisiana," *Annals of the Association of American Geographers* 60 (1970):134–52, describes the forms of fords in different stream contexts.

18. Terry G. Jordan, *Trails to Texas: Southern Roots of Western Cattle Ranching* (Lincoln and London: University of Nebraska Press, 1981), 14, 29, 74.

19. St. Tammany Parish, Louisiana, Sheriff's Sale, 1839.

20. See various U.S. census reports and parish succession records for St. Tammany Parish, Louisiana.

21. Ramsey River Road Property Owners Association, Inc., vs. Charles E. Reeves, et al., First Judicial District, St. Tammany Parish, Louisiana, 1980; Ingram vs. Police Jury of St. Tammany, 20 La. Ann. 226 (1868).

22. Sargent, *Report on the Forests,* 529.

23. Manuscript map in the possession of Mrs. A. W. Jones, Sr., Liberty, Mississippi.

Vegetation of the Piney Woods

SIDNEY MCDANIEL

Southern Mississippi is divided into three major ecological systems: the coastal marshes and dunes, the alluvial bottomlands of the Pearl and Pascagoula river systems, and a complex of vegetation types under the influence of fire here defined as the Piney Woods. The Piney Woods include the eastern part of the longleaf-pine region and all of the coastal meadows as defined by Lowe.[1] The area is part of a larger longleaf-pine forest extending, with a few breaks, from the Savannah River in Georgia to central Louisiana.[2] It is included within the southeastern forest region described by Braun,[3] and the southern mixed-hardwood forest studied by Quarterman and Keever,[4] and it is equal, insofar as Mississippi is concerned, to the area of Kuchler's "Southern mixed forest"[5] and of what Eyde called the "longleaf-slash major forest."[6] It is also the same as the southwestern pine hills in adjacent Alabama.[7]

The total area of the Piney Woods in Mississippi is about thirteen thousand square miles.[8] The area of the region most distant from the coast is strongly to somewhat hilly and generally continues to be at least somewhat undulating until it reaches the Pamlico Plain (Lowe's "Coastal Meadows"[9]) near the coast. This latter area is generally quite flat and in places dotted with ponds and swamps. The climate of the region is warm temperate to subtropical with heaviest rainfall in the summer months (in contrast to northern Mississippi).[10]

Descriptions by early travelers and scientists of area vegetation may give us some idea of the appearance of the area prior to the changes of the late nineteenth and twentieth centuries. The earliest botanist to visit the area, in the late eighteenth century, was William Bartram, who, describing an area near the Escambia River in Alabama, noted that

> it is in fact one vast flat grassy savanna and Cane meadows, intersected or variously scrolled over with narrow forest and groves, on the banks of creeks and rivulets, or hommocks and swamps, at their sources; with long leaved Pines,

scatteringly planted, amongst the grass; and on the high sandy knolls and swelling ridges, Quercus nigra, Quercus flammula, Quercus incana, and various other trees and shrubs as already noted, inhabiting such situations. The rivulets however exhibited a different appearance; they are shallower; course more swiftly over gravelly beds, and their banks are adorned with Illicium groves, Magnolias, Azaleas, Halesia, Andromeda, &c. The highest hills near large creeks afford high forest with abundance of Chesnut trees.[11]

Bartram's statements probably apply equally to southern Mississippi. Noted Mississippi historian John F. H. Claiborne made a trip through the northern part of the Piney Woods in 1840. Of Greene County he wrote, "The growth of giant pines is unbroken for a hundred miles or so, save where river or large water courses intervene." Wayne County he described as an "extensive pine forest, covered over with a thin coating of soil, but affording a luxuriant growth of grass." Of Jones County he wrote:

> Much of it is covered exclusively with the long leaf pine; not broken, but rolling like the waves in the middle of the great ocean. The grass grows three feet high and hill and valley are studded all over with flowers of every hue. The flora of this section of the State and thence down to the sea board is rich beyond description. Our *hortus-siccus*, made up on this hurried journey, would feast a botanist for a month.[12]

The first detailed account of the vegetation of the Piney Woods was by E. W. Hilgard, who wrote in 1860 of the forest of the northern Piney Woods:

> The prominent forest tree of the region is the Longleaf Pine- (*Pinus australis* Micx, *P. palustris* L.), which near its borders, occupies only the higher ridges, but gradually descends until we find it on the very verge of the bottoms, although it very rarely occurs in the latter themselves. It is accompanied, in the uplands, by the Post Oak and Black Jack (either or both), and almost invariably, especially on the hillsides, by some Black Gum (*Nyssa multiflora*), also, most generally, by some Dogwood (*Cornus florida*).

> The herbaceous vegetation and undergrowth of the Longleaf Pine Region is hardly less characteristic than the timber. Whenever the regular burning of the woods, such as practiced by the Indians, has not been superseded by the irregular and wasteful practice of the settlers, the pine forest is almost destitute of shrubby undergrowth, and during the growing season appears like a park, whose long grass is often very beautifully interspersed with brilliantly tinted flowers.[13]

In describing the beech-magnolia hammock community of the region Hilgard listed essentially the same plant associates we see today. Of the more coastal "Pine Meadows" he wrote,

> After ascending the bluff, we strike a level meadowland, in which there is scarcely any distinction into upland and lowland. The ground is densely covered with

a growth of sedge-grasses (*Cyperaceae*), Cordrushes (*Eriocaulon villosum*) and a small species of *Xyris;* in the shallow depressions, both species of *Sarracenia* (Side-saddle flower and Pitcher-plant), the larger *Eriocaulon* (*E. decangulare*), the *Dichromena,* the long-leaved and short-leaved Sundew, several species of bright-tinted *Orchideae* . . . The undergrowth is formed altogether by diminutive Long Leaf Pines, averaging 25 feet in height by 2½ to 4 inches in thickness, which stand at considerable distances (40 or 50 feet) apart, so that their sparse tops scarcely interfere, with the view of the observer.[14]

From these and other early descriptions we can surmise an area above the coast of open forest of longleaf pine interspersed with hammocks of beech-magnolia and occasional branch swamps, broken only by the alluvial bottomlands of the larger streams: the closer to the coast, the more open the forest, and the more densely accompanied by a rich and unique herbaceous flora of savannas and bogs. Thus, it is apparent that the vegetation was not all that different from what can be seen from remnants today.

The vegetation of an area is the result of the interaction of time, soil, climate (including fire), and the species available. Because fire plays a special role within the Piney Woods, it deserves particular attention here. Prior to the advent of man on the North American continent, fire-adapted plants such as longleaf pine had already evolved. Lightning is known to cause fire today within the longleaf-pine region[15] and could have been a factor for many years, since today's weather patterns had their origins in the Tertiary.[16] Moreover, in prehistoric times there were no roads or fields to stop a fire once started,[17] so any fire could have burned over many square miles. It would not, then, have been necessary to have a lightning-caused fire in a given spot very often. The longleaf-pine forests probably burned at least five years out of ten. However, occasional periods of two to three fire-free years would have been required to give the seedlings a chance to get established.[18] With the coming of man to Mississippi around twenty thousand years ago, a new source for fire arrived. Moreover, fire was no longer restricted to times of lightning, primarily the summer months, but could occur at other times and places than previously.[19] Hilgard comments specifically that the Indians burned the longleaf-pine forest regularly.[20]

Within the Piney Woods region, certain vegetation types are especially dependent upon fire, namely longleaf pine and bogs or savannas. The beneficial effects of fire upon the longleaf forest type have been summarized by K. H. Garren.[21] Fire increases the germination rate of longleaf-pine seeds through production of bare soils and helps the survival of seedlings through the destruction of the brown-spot needle disease and of competing hardwoods. Burning decreases acidity in the soil and adds nitrogen, replaceable calcium, and organic matter. Fire increases herbaceous cover through improved seed germination and vigorous sprouting of perennials. Fire furthermore influences the kinds and percentages of the species present within this cover. Folkerts indicates that fire is essential for the well-being of the pitcher-plant bogs or savannas that occur along the Gulf Coast.[22] In these habitats fire is responsible for the removal of competing nonfire-type plants (most bog species have structures underground resistant to fire) and for the recycling of nutrients. The significance of fire for Mississippi bogs was determined by L. N. Eleuterius.[23]

Within the Piney Woods the climax beech-magnolia forest results only during an extended absence of fire and following the amelioration of the microclimate so that an intermediate or mesic condition results. The actual forest vegetation of this region is quite complex and is particulary related to the interaction of fire, moisture, and time. Within the Piney Woods differences of vegetation occur from north to south. In the northern part longleaf pine has been in some areas replaced by loblolly pine–hardwood; in the southern part (especially below Hattiesburg) loblolly pine plays a minor role, and the relationship of longleaf to slash pine is more important. I have tried to illustrate diagrammatically some of these relationships in the southern part of the Piney Woods in figure 1. Note particularly the longleaf pine–slash pine relationships and how each changes with time when fire is removed or restricted. It is of course impossible to show all variation within a forest type, but the relationships as shown can be a basis for understanding change within our area. Note that very local or nonforest types (bogs, savannas, Atlantic white cedar, and shortleaf pine) are not included. Also note that vegetation types are not necessarily sharply defined, that each is an event in time more or less grading into another. Thus the change in species composition may be gradual and those present at one phase may continue into another. Because of the past existence of various fire and moisture regimes the vegetation of our area is a mosaic of various vegetation types we see today.

The rest of this paper describes the major vegetation types of the Piney Woods. In many instances, names of forest cover types follow those recommended by the Society of American Foresters in Eyde's *Forest Cover Types of the United States and Canada*. Numbers are those established in Eyde's work.

Longleaf Pine (SAF 70)

The dominant species is longleaf pine, but it may be associated with lesser numbers of slash, shortleaf, or loblolly pines. Other common associates include dogwood, sweetgum, water oak, bluejack oak, sand post oak, black-

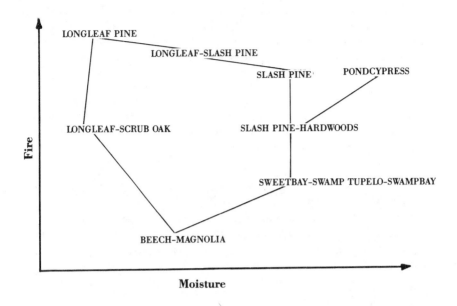

Figure 1. Relationships of forests in the southern Piney Woods region

jack oak, blackgum, persimmon, and sassafras. Gopher apple and poison oak are common shrubs. Herbaceous species are abundant, especially after burning, and include numerous legumes and composites. Fire is the primary reason for maintenance of this type, though where soils are exceptionally sandy there may be insufficient vegetation to sustain a fire. Moisture relationships usually vary from moderate to dry. In the absence of frequent fires this type may become longleaf pine–scrub oak (SAF 71), especially on drier sites. Areas which have greater moisture and hence are somewhat more protected from fire may, where a seed source is available, become longleaf pine–slash pine (SAF 83). In the northern part of the Piney Woods, some areas previously longleaf pine have become loblolly pine–hardwood (SAF 82). Where coverage is incomplete and sporadic, a longleaf-pine savanna may result.

Longleaf Pine–Scrub Oak (SAF 71)
This type is dominated by longleaf pine and upland oaks such as sand post, bluejack, and turkey oaks. There are some areas within southern Mississippi

which would fit within this type, mostly on drier sites. Other species that can be associated in this type with longleaf pine are sweetgum, water oak, black gum, and American holly. Fire is eventually necessary to maintain this type, or longleaf is completely replaced by hardwoods.

Loblolly Pine–Hardwood (SAF 82)

In the northern part of the Piney Woods loblolly pine–hardwood now occupies more area than any other forest type.[24] This is in part the result of old field succession and in part of succession from longleaf pine as the result of decreased burning after removal of longleaf pine. Longleaf and shortleaf pine are often associated, but by far the most common species of pine is loblolly. In our area common hardwood associates are post oak, white oak, water oak, southern red oak, black oak, black cherry, mockernut hickory, blackgum, sweetgum, and red maple. Common shrubs or small trees are blueberries (*Vaccinium arboreum* Marsh., *V. elliotii* Chapm., and *V. stamineum* L.), wild azalea, dogwood, French mulberry, and most abundant wax myrtle. The herbaceous species are similar to those of the longleaf-pine forest and include many composites and legumes, especially where burning has occurred.

Slash Pine (SAF 84)

The dominant species in this forest type, as the name implies, is slash pine. Major associates vary with site, but on wetter sites include sweetbay, swampbay, pondcypress, water oak, sweetgum, swamp tupelo, titi, and buckwheat tree. On drier sites longleaf and loblolly pines are sometimes found, as well as hardwoods such as sweetgum, blackgum, and various species of oak and holly. Saw palmetto is sometimes associated with this type on medium to wet sites.

In the coastal-meadows region slash-pine coverage is often not complete and results in savannas rather than a forest. The reasons for this are not certain, but more frequent fires preventing the establishment of seedlings and the existence of a hardpan in the soil inhibiting tree growth are possible contributors. The savanna type is discussed in more detail later.

Slash Pine–Hardwood (SAF 85)

Much of extreme southern Mississippi is forested with this type. As areas of slash-pine forest are protected from fire, hardwoods become more abundant and eventually become codominant. These species include sweetbay, swampbay, red maple, various hollies, titi, Carolina ash, sweetgum, water oak, and in some wetter sites buckwheat tree and pondcypress. In a few areas in Mississippi Atlantic white cedar is present. Fire is necessary for the continued existence of this type, but less frequently than for slash pines or longleaf pines. Hardwoods killed by fire may sprout rapidly from rootstocks to again form part of the community. Slash pine probably only reseeds itself in these areas after fire.

Sweetbay–Swamp Tupelo–Swampbay (equivalent to SAF 104)

Continued absence of fire in areas of slash pine–hardwoods results, particularly in wetter areas, in this forest type. It should be noted that, at least in our area, swampbay (*Persea palustris*) is present rather than redbay (*P. borbonia*). The combination of these three hardwood species may vary with some areas having considerably more of one species than of the other two. Additional associated species may include American holly, red maple, Carolina ash, southern magnolia, slash pine, loblolly pine, pondcypress, Atlantic white cedar, water oak, sweetgum and yellow-poplar. Shrubs and small trees include various hollies, titi, buckwheat tree, sweet pepperbush, numerous ericaceous shrubs, swamp blackhaw, wax myrtle, and poison sumac. Herbaceous species generally are very poorly represented except on edges, but do include the spectacular *Macranthera flammea* (Bartr.) Pennell with orange flowers.

Beech–Magnolia

Much of south Mississippi has the potential to become covered with this vegetation type. However, fire, a natural part of the environment, keeps most of the vegetation at a subclimax or successional stage. There are some areas of this type present, particularly where there is some feature that deterred fire in the past. More woody species are found in this community than in any other of our vegetation types. Some codominants include beech, sweetgum, southern magnolia, pine, spruce pine (especially in south Mississippi), occasionally loblolly, and various species of oak. Other kinds of magnolias are often present, and individual sites may have all of those native to Mississippi except umbrella magnolia. American holly, sweetbay, and star-anise are additional evergreen woody plants that may be present. Most of the deciduous species found within the Piney Woods may be present at one time or another in this forest, except those restricted to high, dry, or extremely wet sites. Generally the environment is more favorable for most species. Soil pH has been increased, moderation of soil moisture occurred, and generally soil organic matter improved. Herbaceous vegetation is best developed in the early spring or fall.

Atlantic White Cedar (SAF 97) and Pondcypress (SAF 100)

Both of these vegetation types are comparatively poorly developed in Mississippi and cover only a fraction of the area of the preceding types.

There are areas in eastern Jackson County where Atlantic white cedar makes up a substantial part of the forest cover. An excellent example may be seen from the interstate highway east of Pascagoula. There the primary associate appears to be pondcypress. In other areas, such as near Juniper Creek in Pearl River County, Atlantic white cedar is much less common and cannot be considered the vegetation type.

Pondcypress occurs sporadically throughout much of the southern part of our area, but rarely forms a separate vegetation type; rather, it is an associate in one of the more common types. However, in southern Hancock County I have seen areas of essentially pure pondcypress somewhat comparable to the pondcypress areas of Florida. Both of these vegetation types should be more carefully studied in Mississippi.

Shortleaf Pine (SAF 75)
Although shortleaf pine often is a minor component in upland forests in southern Mississippi, it is rarely found there as the dominant species. There are a limited number of areas, largely high gravelly ridges, which can be classified as this type. Within the Piney Woods common tree associates are loblolly pine, longleaf pine, post oak, sweetgum, and red maple. One site in the Devil's Backbone region of Pearl River County consists of an overstory predominantly of shortleaf pine with an understory of dogwood. Shrub or small-tree species characteristic are horsesugar, various blueberries, and French mulberry.

Shrub Bogs, Hillside Bogs, and Savannas
These three closely related vegetation types are similar to each other in species composition. Moreover, all three types frequently have large numbers of pitcher plants. Generally the shrub bogs and hillside bogs are somewhat wetter than the savannas. In fact, they may be so wet that they essentially shake when walked upon. Vegetationally the shrub bog may be defined as an area with bog vegetation, especially pitcher plants, surrounded or broken by areas of evergreen shrubs or small trees. The shrubs or small trees as stated are mostly evergreen or at least very tardily deciduous, the major exceptions poison sumac and pondcypress. Buckwheat tree and titi are often dominant in the shrub zone. *Myrica inodora* Bartr., another evergreen, is largely restricted to this type. The rarest woody plant of the gulf coastal region, bog spicebush (*Lindera subcoriacea* Wofford), was discovered in this habitat about twenty years ago. It was known only from a handful of sites in Mississippi and adjacent Louisiana, until recently discovered in North Carolina.

Hillside bogs are generally similar to shrub bogs, but are more open, lacking the break of intervening shrubs. Moreover, they have greater changes in elevation than the shrub bogs. Some hillside bogs are quite large and, especially after a winter burn, may be spectacular sights with literally hundreds of thousands of pitcher plants. The best examples of this type are located on a line just north of the Pamlico Plain and extending from about southern George County to northern Hancock County. In addition to pitcher plants the bog areas may be quite diverse in herbaceous species and include orchid, sedges, grasses, yellow-eyed grass (*Xyris* spp.), ladies' hatpins (*Eriocaulon* spp.), and many others.[25]

Savannas of the type included here are flat wet areas usually with some scattered slash pines, but occasionally with longleaf pine. Pondcypress may be present, but is generally confined to slightly lower areas within the site. The majority of the savannas included here are confined to the Pamlico Plain. As a result of frequent fires and abundant sunlight these savannas have a very rich herbaceous flora, including several species of pitcher plants, orchids, yellow-eyed grass, sedges such as *Rhynchospora*, *Dichromena*, and *Scleria*, and numerous grasses, including *Panicum*, *Andropogon*, and *Aristida*.

Notes

1. E. N. Lowe, "Plants of Mississippi," *Mississippi State Geological Bulletin* 17 (University, MS: Miss. State Geological Survey, 1921):49–55.

2. R. M. Harper, *Forests of Alabama*, Geological Survey Alabama Monograph, 10 (University, Ala.: Ala. Geological Survey, 1943), 188.

3. E. Lucy Braun, *Deciduous Forests of Eastern North America* (Philadelphia: Blakiston, 1950), 280–304.

4. E. Quarterman and C. Keever, "Southern Mixed Hardwood Forest: Climax in the Southeastern Coastal Plain," U.S.A. Ecological Monographs, 32 (1962) 183.

5. A. W. Kuchler, *Potential Natural Vegetation of the Conterminous United States*, American Geographical Society Special Publications, 36 (Washington, D.C.: American Geographical Society, 1964), 112 and map.

6. F. H. Eyde, ed., *Forest Cover Types of the United States and Canada* (Washington, D.C.: Society of American Foresters, 1980), unnumbered map.

7. Harper, "Forests of Alabama," 188–95.

8. R. M. Harper, "A Superficial Study of the Pine-Barren Vegetation of Mississippi," *Bulletin of the Torrey Botanical Club* 41 (1914):551.

9. Lowe, "Plants of Mississippi," 51–55.

10. J. C. McWhorter, *Climatic Patterns of Mississippi*, Mississippi State Agricultural Experiment Station Bulletin, 650 (State College, MS: Mississippi State Agricultural Experiment Station, 1962), 12-15.

11. W. Bartram, *The Travels of William Bartram*, ed. Francis Harper, Naturalist's ed. (New Haven: Yale University Press, 1958), 255.

12. J. F. H. Claiborne, "A Trip through the Piney Woods," *Publications of the Mississippi Historical Society* 9 (1906): 523, 524, 514.

13. E. W. Hilgard, *Report on the Geology and Agriculture of Mississippi* (Jackson, Miss.: E. Barksdale, 1860), 348, 349.

14. Ibid., 370.

15. E. Komarek, "Fire Ecology," *Proceedings of the First Tall Timbers Fire Ecology Conference* (Tallahassee: Tall Timbers Research Station, 1962), 98, 99.

16. E. Komarek, "Effects of Fire on Temperate Forests and Related Ecosystems: Southeastern United States," in *Fire and Ecosystems*, ed. T. T. Kozlowski and C. E. Ahlgren (New York: Academic Press, 1974), 252.

17. Harper, *Forests of Alabama*, 33; George W. Folkerts, "The Gulf Coast Pitcher Plant Bogs," *American Scientist* 70 (1982):266.

18. Harper, *Forests of Alabama*, 34.

19. C. J. Perkins, "Effects of Clearcutting and Site Preparation on the Vegetation and Wildlife in the Flatwoods of Kemper County, Mississippi" (Ph.D. diss., Mississippi State University, 1973), 6, 7.

20. Hilgard, *Report on Geology*, 349. A detailed discussion of the history and controversy of fire ecology is inappropriate here and has already been done by Harper (*Forests of Alabama*). See also Harper, "Historical Notes on the Relation of Fires to Forest. *Proceedings of the First Tall Timbers Fire Ecology Conference* (1968), 11-29. A more detailed review of the role of fire in ecology in the Southeast was given by K. H. Garren, "Effects of Fires on Vegetation of the Southeastern United States," *Botanical Review* 9 (1943):617-54. Although Lyell was apparently the first to comment on the significance of fire to longleaf pine, Hilgard (in *Report on Geology*) was the first to recommend the use of fire in the longleaf-pine region (Lyell, C., *A Second Visit to the United States*. London: John Murray, 1849, II, p. 80.). Unfortunately, Hilgard has been overlooked and has not received the credit he deserves.

21. Garren, "Effects of Fires," 645-48.

22. Folkerts, *American Scientist* 70 (1982), 265-66.

23. L. N. Eleuterius, "Floristics and Ecology of Coastal Bogs in Mississippi" (master's thesis, University of Southern Mississippi, 1968), 19-47.

24. D. R. Morgan, "A Floristic Study of Northeastern Jones County, Mississippi" (masters thesis, Mississippi State University, 1979), 15.

25. For further information on species composition, see L. N. Eleuterius and S. B. Jones, Jr., "A Floristic and Ecological Study of Pitcher Plant Bogs in South Mississippi," *Rhodora* 71 (1969):29-34.

Contributors

Thomas D. Clark is a professor emeritus of the history department at the University of Kentucky. He has written several books on the frontier and the South, the most recent of which, *The Greening of the South*, was published in 1984.

James C. Downey is administrative dean of William Carey College on the Mississippi Gulf Coast. Long a student of American Evangelical Music, he has written several articles on shaped-note hymnody, gospel hymnody, folk hymns, and Black church music.

Warren A. Flick is an associate professor of forestry at Auburn University. He has published extensively in the areas of regional analysis, forest taxation, investment analysis, and forest policy.

Nollie W. Hickman is the dean of Piney Woods Studies by virtue of his landmark study of lumbering in the Piney Woods, *Mississippi Harvest*. Retired from the history faculty of Northeastern Louisiana University, he is writing memoirs of his life in the Piney Woods.

W. Kenneth Holditch is a professor of English at the University of New Orleans. A scholar in American and southern literature, his particular specialty is the literature of New Orleans. He is writing a biography of Pearl Rivers.

Terry Jordan holds the Walter Prescott Webb Chair of History and Ideas in the department of geography at the University of Texas. A specialist in the cultural geography of Texas and the American South, he is particularly interested in the transferral of traditional European material culture to North America. He has written four books and numerous essays.

Sidney McDaniel is a professor in the department of biological sciences at Mississippi State University and director of the Institute for Botanical Exploration. He is an expert in the taxonomy and floristics of vascular plants and bryophytes in the Southeastern United States, and serves as the Principal Botanical Consultant to the Crosby Arboretum.

Thomas L. McHaney is a professor of English at Georgia State University. His two books and numerous articles on William Faulkner have established him as one of the leading Faulkner critics writing today, and he has published and lectured widely on other southern and American authors. He also writes fiction and drama.

Grady McWhiney is Lyndon Baines Johnson Professor of U.S. History at Texas Christian University. Author of nine books and dozens of articles, he has been active in exploring various aspects of southern history and culture.

John H. Napier III, Lt. Col., U.S. Air Force (ret.), is an adjunct member of the history faculty of Auburn University at Montgomery. A descendant of a long line of Pearl River Countians, he has just completed a history of Pearl River County, Mississippi, with a special emphasis on the importance of the lumbering industry to the region's development.

M. B. Newton, Jr. is chairman of the department of geography at Louisiana State University. A cultural geographer, he has special interests in cultural issues connected with the historical landscape. He is the author of *Cultural Preadaptation in the Upland South* and *Atlas of Louisiana*.

Noel Polk is a native of the Mississippi Piney Woods who has published widely on William Faulkner, Eudora Welty, and other Mississippi and American literary figures. He is a professor of English at the University of Southern Mississippi.

Harold K. Steen is the executive director of the Forest History Society. As an academic he has taught courses in conservation history and general forestry and has been active on history committees for the Society of American Foresters and the Sierra Club. He is the author of *The U.S. Forest Service: A History*.

William F. Winter is the distinguished past governor of the State of Mississippi. A lay historian, Governor Winter has published numerous essays on various aspects of Mississippi history.

Index

INDEX

Lowry, Col. Robert, 20
Luce, Gregory, 83
Lumberton, 21, 86

Macon, 97
Madison, James, 67
Marion County, 20, 43
McComb, 85
McCormick, George D., 93
McDonald, Forrest, 41, 44
McNeill, 17
McWhiney, Grady, 18
Miller, Hugh Barr, 138
Mingo Dabney (Street), 129
Mississippi (Keating), x
Mississippi Department of Economic
Development, x
Mississippi Guide, ix, 121, 122
Mississippi Harvest (Hickman), x, 145
Mississippi Land and Development
Association, 7-8
Mississippi Melodies (Coats), 98
Monticello, 21
Morgan, Justin, 92
Moss Point, 80, 81, 82
Musical Million, The, 95
"Myself" (Nicholson), 113

Napier, John Staples, 15
Napoleon, 87
National Park Service, 10
"Nature's Dumb Nobility" (Nicholson),
116
Naval Stores Industry, 79-91
Negroes, 79-91
New Orleans, La., 103-120 *passim*
New Orleans *Picayune*, 103-120 *passim*
New Sweden, 25-39 *passim*
Newton, Milton B., Jr., 43
Nicholson, Eliza Jane Poitevent,
103-120 *passim*
Nicholson, George, 107-120 *passim*
Noble Knights of Labor, 82f
Norwegian laborers, 86

Oak Grove, 96
Oh, Promised Land (Street), 110,
123-132 *passim*
"Old Home—Friday Morning"
(Nicholson), 114
Olmsted, Frederick Law, 18
"Only A Dog" (Nicholson), 115f
Owsley, Frank L., 73

Pascagoula River, 18, 59, 80, 81ff, 87
Pearl River, 13ff, 18, 20, 59, 87, 109ff
"Pearl River" (Nicholson), 113ff

Pearl River County, xi, 14, 17, 86, 137,
142, 180
Pearl River District, 14, 20
Pearlington, 21
Percy, Leroy, 136
Percy, Walker, x-xi
Perry County, 44, 80, 81ff, 142f
Picayune, xi, xii, 21, 96
Pierson, Hamilton W., 69, 71-72
Plain Folk of the Old South (Owsley), 73
Plato, 5
Poitevent, John, 110
Poitevent, William James, 110
Polk, Videt, 98
Poplarville, 21, 96
Practical Music Reader, The, 95
Pride of Possession (Street), 129
Purvis, Will, 142
Pyne, Stephen J., 13

Reconstruction, 80f, 160
Red Creek, 82
Roseberry, J. L., 97
Roseberry, Lloyd, 97
"Rough Riding Down South"
(Claiborne), 14
Rudiments of Music, 96
Ruebush-Kieffer Publishing Co., 95ff
Ruffin, Edmund, 60
Russ, Mary Amelia, 110

Sacred Harp (White), 92-102 *passim*
Saucier, John, 84
Scarbrough, Alexander, 80
Settlement of Piney Woods, 15ff
Sherman Antitrust Act, 8
Showalter, A. J., 95ff
Simpson, Joseph, 87
Smith, "Corn Club", 141
Smith County, 44, 142
Smith, William, 93
South in the New Nation, The
(Abernethy), 73
*Southern Harmony and Musical
Companion, The* (Walker), 92, 93
Southern Minstrel, The (Jones), 93ff
Spain, 13f
Sparks, W. H., 17
Springer, J. S., 61
Stamps-Baxter Music Printing Co., 96,
98f
Stamps, Virgil O., 98f
Standing Pine, 139
Star of Bethlehem, 96
Steam engine, 65ff
Stennis, John, 140
Stone County, 79

187